For John
Thank for your
"Buch" support

SPORES, PLAGUES AND HISTORY:
THE STORY OF ANTHRAX

SPORES, PLAGUES AND HISTORY:
THE STORY OF ANTHRAX

CHRIS HOLMES, M.D.

DURBAN HOUSE PUBLISHING

For information address:
Durban House Publishing Company, Inc.,
7502 Greenville Avenue, Suite 500, Dallas, Texas 75231

Library of Congress Cataloging-in-Publication Data
Holmes, Chris, 1941-

Spores, Plagues, History: The Story of Anthrax / by Chris Holmes

Library of Congress Catalog Card Number: 2003105052

p. cm.

ISBN 1-930754-45-0

First Edition

10 9 8 7 6 5 4 3 2

Visit our Web site at
http://www.durbanhouse.com

**For Marilyn
My best friend and biggest fan**

ACKNOWLEDGEMENTS

I'm especially grateful to Ted Robinson and Michele Ginsberg, both practicing epidemiologists, for their critical reviews of the manuscript. Thanks also to Bob Middlemiss, my editor at Durban House, for guiding me through the mysteries of editing, and to John Hamilton Lewis, my publisher, for his support and encouragement.

The dust jacket illustration depicting an ancient epidemic is from the National Library of Medicine. The red symbol on the central column is the international symbol for biohazard.

FOREWORD

S pores, Plagues and History: The Story of Anthrax is actually much more than the story of a microbe. It is a tale of history and prophecy woven into a fabric of what was, what might have been and what might yet be. We have come far in our understanding of nature, and yet the hazards we now face are perhaps as great as any in the past. In the 1950s and even into the 1960s mankind congratulated itself on the defeat of microbes as a threat. Those who studied infectious diseases saw fellowship and research money dry up as the War on Cancer and other chronic disease efforts came to the fore. Young physicians were advised not to pursue careers in infectious disease medicine or epidemiology, as infectious diseases would soon be eradicated. Penicillin and other more effective antibiotics were assumed to be the ultimate weapons against infections.

But this book illustrates how far the paradigm has changed. We have eradicated, officially, one disease: smallpox. In that same time we have found many others. The viral hemorrhagic fevers of Marburg, Ebola, and Lassa and the pneumonia of Legionnaire's Disease were among the first to be identified. A strange new syphilus-like organism called Lyme Disease emerged. And British livestock have been decimated by Mad Cow disease (bovine spongiform encephalopathy, or BSE). It is transmissible to humans and results in a severe and fatal Alzheimer's-like illness. Nature has truly rebelled against our presumed omniscience.

To compound the problem, we have discovered there are those amongst us who view these very microbes as weapons. The revelations of Dr. Ken Alibek—the Soviet bioscientist deserter — were truly astounding and not believed by many in the U.S. when he defected. The reason was simple: his story seemed unbelieveable. Viewing the history of infectious diseases, and equipped with the knowledge so elequently reviewed in this book of the horrors they inflict on mankind, it seemed incomprehensible that any rational society would intentionally unleash them. But it was true. Not only had the organisms been produced in mass quantities, they had been "engineered" to be more deadly and more contagious as well.

We have seen the effect of a few grams of anthrax delivered in letters. Suppose much larger quantities were aerosolized more efficiently. As Dr. Holmes points out, anthrax seems almost designed for terrorist use even without human manipulation. The tons of anthrax the Soviets produced would kill millions. If their seed cultures and expertise have escaped the efforts of the Defense Threat Reduction Agency's efforts to contain them, our next experience might not be confined to just a handful of cases.

As bad as anthrax is, it is not the most feared bioweapon. Dr. Holmes paints a vivid and accurate picture of the effects of an intentional release of smallpox upon an unvaccinated populace.

Books such as this one are an integral part of a generalized public education effort that will contribute to national security. What you are about to read is real; you are not in the Twilight Zone; adjusting your TV set will not change the picture. We are in a new world, and the paradigm has changed for the worse. However, it is not hopeless. And we are not helpless. The same technology that has been used to create horrible biological weapons can and will be used to protect us with better vaccines and treatments. Sometimes history does serve us well after all.

*Ted J. Robinson, M.D., M.P.H.
Medical Epidemiologist
Naval Hospital, Camp Pendleton, California

*The views expressed here are those of the author and are not to be construed as official or as reflecting those of the U.S. Navy Medical Department or the U.S. Department of Defense.

PREFACE

The history of a microbe seems like an oxymoron. History is usu ally about *big* things: wars, revolutions, great ideas, larger-than-life characters, momentous events. But the focus of this book is not on the *big*. It is on the *small*. The microscopic, in fact, something a little less than the size of a human red blood cell. *Bacillus anthracis*. Anthrax. There were only 24 cases of this disease during the bioterrorist attack of October-November, 2001, with five deaths. Why have so few cases been the focus of such great scrutiny? Is it because the word itself — anthrax — makes us tremble with visions of an ancient pestilence? Or is it the link to bioterrorism that gets the heart pounding? Maybe it's just the awful realization that America is no longer safe behind its two-ocean barricade. Like everyone else in the world, we are now vulnerable.

Just as a single drop of acid added to a beakerful of it can change the color of litmus paper from blue to red, the effects of those 24 cases have led to changes in U.S. society out of all proportion to their small number. These include greatly increased training for doctors and nurses on how to recognize and treat anthrax and other bioterrorist agents; a closer look at how poorly prepared our public health care system is to handle future outbreaks; the stockpiling of more antibiotics; and the development of new vaccines to counter genetically altered weapons of biological terrorism. That small bacterium has even affected how we handle our mail and with whom we shake hands.

The idea for this book grew out of research for my novel, *The Medusa Strain*, the story of an outbreak of a genetically-altered strain of anthrax. As I dug deeper, I was amazed at how often anthrax was not only a subject of history but a maker of it as well. From the time of Exodus to the present, it has made its presence known through its horrifying effects. And now seems like a good time to take an objective look at this frightening disease and place it in perspective.

I intend this work for the general, interested reader who wants to learn more about anthrax. Not in the sense of more of its microbiology. Rather more about its effects on society and, through it, on history. There are no new facts in this book, and I've omitted all footnotes. But I have appended a list of my principal sources and references. When I relied particularly heavily on one, I cited it in the text as well. Like any historian, I have used the publications of others to spin my own tale, come to my own interpretation of the historical record. But though I've stood on the shoulders of others, the responsibility for any errors is mine.

Some of my research led me to remarkable conclusions about the role played by anthrax through history. The chapters on the Plague of Athens, the death of Alexander the Great, and the European epidemic of 1346-1348 — known as the Black Death — may seem startling. But I trust I have grounded my argument on solid historical and medical evidence.

Where the historical record is complete, as it is for the modern era, I relied on it. For the medieval and ancient periods, where the record is sparse, I had to extrapolate from the history of medicine or from the general history of the time.

Finally, this is a work of history. And considerable recent history has been made since I wrote it, notably the run-up to and invasion of Iraq in March 2003. For the chapter on "Saddam" and others dealing with new events, I have used "addenda" in an effort to bring them up to date. I am confident, however, that even they will be overwhelmed by events before the published work is finally released.

Chris Holmes, M.D.
Escondido, California
April, 2003

TABLE OF CONTENTS

CHAPTER

AN ACT OF TERROR

First ask the patient, of what trade are you?

— **Bernardo Ramazzini** (1633-1714)
Father of Occupational Medicine

A nthrax is principally a *zoonosis*, a disease of animals which may be communicated to humans. The bacterium which causes it lives out its life in the soil and in the warm bodies of sheep, cattle, goats, mules and other grazing animals. Man is but an intruder, an accidental host, in this lifecycle, and human disease occurs mostly, therefore, in those who care for animals, work with animal hair, wool or hides, or handle infected blood, muscle or other tissues. Sheep and cattle ranchers, sheepshearers, goat farmers, tanners, wool sorters and textile workers of all kinds, as well as laboratory technicians and veterinarians, are the occupations at greatest risk. For these workers, anthrax is as much an occupational disease as carpal tunnel syndrome is for typists or black lung for coal miners.

In the 19th and early 20th centuries the inhalation form of anthrax was known as "woolsorters disease" in England and "ragpickers disease" in Germany and Austria. Before wool disinfection procedures were developed, many of these tradesmen, as well as others in the textile industry, died from the infection. But that was then. Now, human anthrax is rare and episodic, a chance disease of man. Unless, of course, man is not an accidental but a deliberate victim. A victim of biowarfare or bioterrorism.

The Index Case

The United States' most recent experience with bioterrorism began October 2, 2001, when a 63 year old man was taken to an emergency room in Boca Raton, Florida complaining of nausea, vomiting and worsening mental confusion. He would be the first U.S. case of inhalation anthrax in 25 years.

Bob Stevens was a British-born photo editor for *The Sun*, one of a handful of tabloids published by American Media, Inc. at its three-story office building in Boca Raton, a small, up-scale community about 60 miles north of Miami along the sun-swept Atlantic Coast. Other AMI publications — which leer at us from the check-out lines of our grocery stores — are: *The Star, The Globe, The National Enquirer* and *The National Examiner*.

By all accounts, Bob was an affable fellow and a thorough professional at work. He loved the out-of-doors and had been on an outing to North Carolina when his illness began. His medical history included high blood pressure, heart disease, and gout, all well-controlled with medications. Bob was in his usual state of good health until September 28, 2001, when he began to feel unwell. He complained to his wife of fever, weakness, sweating and a lack of appetite.

He thought it was just the flu. Symptoms like these are non-specific; all of us have had them many times. They usually improve after a few days. Sometimes we call them the "twenty-four hour flu," or the "forty-eight hour virus." Bob did what we all do when we have such sypmtoms: he waited it out, fully expecting to be better soon.

But his symptoms didn't get better. They got worse. Much worse. By the time he returned to Florida a few days later, he was very sick. His wife took him to a local Emergency Room for evaluation. Because of his stiff neck and mental findings, the doctors immediately suspected meningitis, an infection of the tissues covering the brain and spinal cord. A spinal tap was positive: there was pus and bacteria in the cerebrospinal fluid, both in large numbers. But the exact nature of the infection was still unclear. Many bacteria and a few viruses can cause meningitis. Most are much more common than anthrax. And Bob Stevens wasn't in any of the occupations usually associated with that disease. It had to be at the very bottom of the list of diagnoses.

But the suspicion that it was anthrax skyrocketed when the doctors looked at Bob's chest x-rays. First, they noticed a small amount of fluid in the chest, a pleural effusion. This finding, in itself, is not all that uncommon and is not specific for anthrax. But what really got their attention was the distance between the lungs on the x-ray. This usually narrow compartment of tissue running down the middle of the chest from the neck to the diaphragm is called the mediastinum. It contains the trachea, the esophagus, some large blood and lymph vessels and, on either side, the pulmonary lymph nodes. Bob's mediastinum was greatly widened (Figure 1). Very few diseases other than anthrax cause this effect.

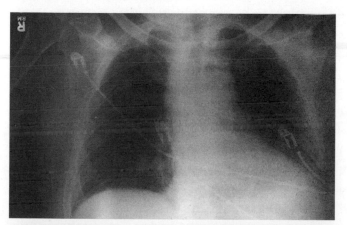

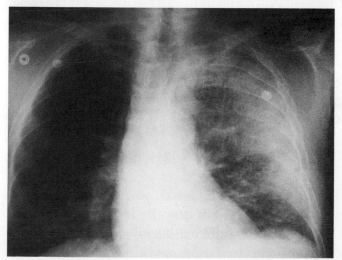

Figure 1.

Top: *Chest x-ray from initial case showing widened mediastinum.*

Bottom: *Chest x-ray from case 2 showing normal mediastinum but left-sided pneumonia.*

Source: CDC: ***Journal of Emerging Infectious Diseases***

Bob's chest x-rays and the positive results from his spinal tap alerted the doctors that they weren't dealing with a run-of-the-mill case. Although an old medical adage says, "if you hear hoofbeats in the night, think of a horse, not a zebra," Bob's doctors smelled a zebra. Within twenty-four hours, the spinal fluid and blood cultures grew *bacillus anthracis* on the blood agar plates. Bob Stevens had anthrax. Unbelieveable, but true.

The doctors were stunned. Like most U.S. physicians, none had ever seen a case of inhalation anthrax before. Hell, there had been only a handful of them in the U.S. during the entire past century. And all had been connected somehow to textile and wool workers or to animal handlers. In other words, all had been occupational diseases.

Bob was started on high doses of antibiotics intravenously. But it was already too late. Within hours of his admission to the hospital, he began to have seizures. A tube was put down his throat to protect his airway and assist his breathing. Anti-seizure medication was given, and more antibiotics were started.

Bob slipped inexorably into a coma. He developed toxic shock from the effects of the anthrax toxin on his heart and blood vessels. This led to kidney failure. He died October 5, 2001, three days after admission and eight days after first becoming ill. An autopsy showed the reason for the widened mediastinum on his chest x-ray: massive hemorrhage there, another effect of the anthrax toxin. *Bacillus anthracis* organisms were found in many of Bob's vital organs, carried there while his heart still pumped blood and his lymph fluid still flowed. Anthrax spores would later be found in high quantity on Bob's office computer.

Bob Stevens's inhalation anthrax was only the 19th U.S. case during all the 20th century. No one knew it at the time, but it was also the first U.S. case of bioterrorism.

The investigation into where Bob Stevens was exposed to an organism most people had never heard of now began in earnest. "Shoe leather" epidemiology it's called, tracking down contacts of the patient and tracing his whereabouts in minute detail. But nothing seemed to fit in Bob's case. He was not in any of the high risk occupational groups, nor did he have any risky hobbies, like weaving goat hair rugs. It was first thought he might have come in contact with anthrax spores during his recent outing to North Carolina, perhaps on a camping trip. But this turned out to be a dead end as well. Pubic Health officials tried to reassure a public more puzzled than worried that there was no cause for alarm. This disease was not now, nor ever has been, contagious. Bob Stevens' case was an isolated incident.

The next nine cases of inhalation anthrax occurred in rat-a-tat succession over a 30 day period. Eight were clustered around three work environments, their jobs all somehow connected to sorting or distributing mail. It began to dawn on government officials, as well as on the public, that Bob Stevens' case was only the tip of an iceberg. A shudder ran up the country's spine.

The second case was a colleague of Bob Stevens at AMI, a 73 year old mailroom clerk. One of his jobs was to deliver mail to other employees. His symptoms began the same day as Bob's, September 28: cough, fever, lethargy and sweating. He got sicker and was admitted to the hospital October 1. His nasal swab and chest fluid grew *bacillus anthracis*. Unlike Bob Stevens, he survived the disease and was discharged three weeks later on October 23.

No other cases turned up at AMI. But the consequences for the company did not stop there. The entire building was quarantined, the staff moved to temporary, cramped quarters. All 1100 employees were tested for anthrax. None was positive, but they were all started on 60 day courses of prophylactic antibiotics. Well into January, 2002, the AMI building was still ringed with yellow crime-scene tape. Visitors to the area regularly lined up to have their photographs taken in front of it.

More Clusters

The next cluster of cases was astonishing in its uniformity. And it convinced any doubters that the AMI occurrence was no freak accident. It was a deliberate bioterrorist attack.

Four men who worked at the United States Postal Service Brentwood Distribution Center outside Washington, D.C. all became ill on the very same day, October 16. Their symptoms were alarmingly similar but non-specific: fever, cough, fatigue, headache, sore throat and nausea. Two were seen by physicians prior to their hospital admissions. They were sent home with only symptomatic treatment and a diagnosis of "viral syndrome." Ultimately, all four were admitted to local hospitals between October 19 and 22. Anthrax was suspected in all of them due to heightened awareness from the previous cases, and *bacillus anthracis* was isolated from their blood cultures or from other body fluids and tissues. Despite aggressive antibiotic therapy and support measures, one of the men died on the day of his admission, another, a day later. The other two made full recovery and were discharged.

There was one more case epidemiologically linked to this Brentwood cluster, even though the victim didn't actually work there. He was a 59 year old contract worker at the U.S. State Department mail sorting facility in Washington, D.C., a facility which regularly receives mail from the Brentwood Center. This man's illness began October 22 with the usual flu-like symptoms. He visited a local emergency room two days later and was also diagnosed with a non-specific "viral syndrome." However, the physician was very suspicious, took blood cultures, and started the man on antibiotics anyway. The next day, October 25, the patient was asked to return to the ER because his cultures had grown *b. anthracis* and his initial chest x-ray showed definite widening of his mediastinum and a small pleural effusion on the left side. He was admitted, successfully treated, and discharged two weeks later on November 9.

The final cluster of cases also centered on a United States Postal Service mail facility, this one in Hamilton, New Jersey. These two cases, both women, appeared around the same time as the Brentwood Center cluster: October 14 for one, the next day for the other. The first woman went to an Emergency Room on October 19, was admitted to the hospital from there, and vigorously treated. Her blood culture was positive for anthrax. She responded to therapy and was discharged two weeks later, November 5.

The other woman's course was different in that she was seen by her primary care physician the day after her initial symptoms began and started on oral antibiotics. When she didn't improve, she went to an ER two days later and was admitted to the hospital. Because she was already on antibiotics, her blood cultures were negative for anthrax. However, fluid drained from her chest was positive for it. She also made a full recovery and was discharged October 26.

By now the country was well aware of the bioterrorist attack. Anxiety was mounting. The Postal Workers Union correctly saw the epidemic as an occupational illness of its members. It insisted the spore-infested postal facilities be closed immediately and the workers sent home. But CDC and the postal authorities vacillated, claiming the workers — now gloved and masked — were in no danger. Many knew better.

The growing public anxiety was not helped by statements from government health authorities. At a House Subcommittee hearing, the Secretary of Health and Human Services, the Head of CDC, and a top FBI official all looked like deer frozen in the headlights. Their answers to questions were baffling, their advice to the public head-scratching if not downright contradictory.

The Department of HHS made matters worse when, after finally admitting that a bioterrorist attack was underway, announced it had ordered millions of doses of ciprofloxacin, the expensive antibiotic recommended for anthrax infections. This inflamed public concern even more, as did a press release that HHS was going to purchase mega doses of smallpox vaccine, raising the spectre of that pestilence when there was no evidence for it.

The Executive Branch of government was not alone it its bungling of public relations. When spores began to turn up at a myriad of federal buildings, the House of Representatives abruptly closed its session and bolted out of town. The Senate, apparently made of sterner stuff, stayed in session throughout.

The epidemic had yet to find its Rudy Guiliani.

The above three clusters (nine cases) all had clear connections to the U.S. Postal Service, to mail rooms, to mail sorting facilities, or to mail delivery. The final two cases were not part of these clusters, nor did they have any apparent connection to the mail.

One was a 61 year old Asian woman who worked in the supply room of a New York City hospital. Her symptoms began October 25, around the time they started in all the others. She was admitted to the hospital three days later. Her blood cultures grew *b. anthracis*. Despite treatment, she died a week later. Though she had no obvious connection with mail sorting, she may have carried mail to other parts of the hospital as part of her regular duties.

The final case, case number 11, is the most baffling of all. On November 13, almost a month after the original clusters of cases, a 94 year old woman living in a remote area of Connecticut became ill. Her condition worsened and she was admitted to the hospital three days later. Blood cultures were positive for anthrax. Despite intensive treatment, she died a week later. Epidemiologic investigation has so far failed to find a source for her exposure to anthrax spores, though it has been conjectured she might have been exposed while tearing up contaminated junk mail. The genetic characteristics of her *b. anthracis* bacteria were similar to the other cases.

Summing Up

In summary, a bioterrorist attack on the U.S. occurred over the six week period from October 2 to November 16. There were 11 total cases of inhalation anthrax. Ten were work-related: nine had provable links to mail sorting, handling, or delivery, and the tenth may have delivered mail within her company. The final case remains a mystery. Her source of exposure to anthrax spores is still unproven.

The average *incubation period* (the interval between presumed exposure to the spores and the onset of symptoms) was 4 days during the outbreak, with a range of 3-6 days. This is right in line with published reports in the medical literature. Early in the outbreak the news media announced that the incubation period could be as long as 60 days. This is technically true. Animal research and a few human cases during a Russian outbreak twenty years ago did demonstrate such a prolonged period. What happens is that some spores are inhaled deeply into the lungs, where they can lie dormant for as long as two months. Many will decay over time. But, depending on the number inhaled, some may survive 60 days or longer. Then they germinate into bacteria and cause symptoms. But such cases are extremely rare. The vast majority of patients – including 10 of the known 11 U.S. cases (the date of exposure for the 11th case is still unknown) – will become ill within three days to a week after exposure. Because of the remote possibility of a long incubation period case, however, a 60-day course of prophylactic antibiotics is still recommended for anyone exposed to the spores.

The symptoms in the 11 U.S. cases were very similar to published reports. All had fever, chills and weakness at first; typical flu symptoms. Ten had nausea, vomiting and cough; nine had shortness of breath; seven had excessive sweating.

Chest x-ray findings were remarkably alike as well. Pleural fluid was detected in all 11 cases at some point during the hospital course, usually at the time of admission. Other positive x-ray findings included pneumonia in seven patients, mediastinal widening in seven, and enlarged pulmonary lymph nodes in seven.

Blood cultures were positive for anthrax in the eight patients in whom they were drawn before antibiotics were started. Other blood tests or tests on tissue from biopsies or autopsies confirmed the presence of anthrax in the remaining three patients.

The overall *survival rate* was 55%. Published reports quote rates of barely 20%. The only recent, well-documented comparable study was a 1979 outbreak in Siberia. There, the survival rate was 14%. The improved U.S. survival rate was undoubtedly due to earlier diagnosis and the use of multiple antibiotic regimens, as well as to better supportive hospital care. Still, despite the best that modern medicine has to offer, almost half the U.S. patients died in the recent attack. This is not good. Not good at all. Clearly, the best strategy is to avoid inhalation anthrax all together or get vaccinated against it.

Skin Cases

Although the 11 inhalation cases were the most serious, there were also 13 (eight confirmed, five suspected) cases of cutaneous anthrax. Eleven of these were in mail handlers and sorters or employees or visitors to one of several media companies. The twelfth was in a bookkeeper who worked in a New Jersey office near the postal center from where three of the anthrax-laced letters were known to be postmarked. And the unlucky 13th — reported on March 13, 2002 — was a lab technician who handled specimens from the other cases.

The skin lesions appeared mostly on exposed parts of the body, places which would have had direct contact with the spores: chest, neck, forearms and fingers. In general, the sores were painless, though some patients complained of tingling or itching sensations.

All eight confirmed cases were diagnosed through biopsy or culture of the lesions. All 13 patients got better with antibiotic therapy.

Cutaneous human anthrax is not nearly as rare as the inhalation form, nor as deadly. Its untreated mortality rate is about 20%, but this drops to less than 1% if appropriately treated. Cutaneous anthrax has been seen periodically in the U.S for years, usually associated with animal disease. Of the 236 U.S. cases reported between 1955 and 1999, all but a few were of the cutaneous type. The last case — before the recent 13 — occurred in North Dakota in August, 2000 when an *epizootic* (an epidemic in animals) broke out among 32 livestock farms. One hundred fifty-seven animals died. Sixty-two persons were involved with animal care during the outbreak, which included giving vaccinations, processing specimens, and dispossing of carcasses. There was one case of cutaneous anthrax: a 67 year old man who developed a lesion on his left cheek. He was treated with a 14 day course of ciprofloxacin — the currently recommended antibiotic for anthrax — and recovered without complications. The last U.S. cutaneous anthrax case before that was in 1992.

It Ends

Suddenly, it stopped. Almost as abruptly as it started, the bioterrorist attack was over. After just a few months and a handful of cases, there were no more. Spores continued to be found in unexpected places. And hoaxes were on the rise. But the outbreak was over. What happened?

Had the terrorist's anger finally been sated? Had he sufficiently proven to himself how clever and powerful he was? Did he think he had now made his point, whatever it was? Maybe the authorities were closing in, and he had to dismantle his homemade laboratory in haste and go underground.

Or was this attack merely a prelude? Is the terrorist even now producing and stockpiling spores for another, more massive assault on America?

CHAPTER

2

SPORES, HOAXES, AND THE HUNT FOR THE TERRORIST

Sometime in the long-ago past, when even microbes had to compete for survival, a few bacteria found an evolutionary edge. Anthrax was one of these. It developed a group of factors which enabled it to resist destruction by its host. Now, once it gained entrance, its continued existence inside the host was assured. But outside, in the cold world, it was still unprotected, fragile, easily destroyed by nature. What to do?

The answer was simple: develop a protective coating — armor plating, if you will — for those periods it had to spend in the wild. It could encase itself in this armor, lie patiently in the soil, in a pond, or on a leaf, until another host breathed or ingested it. Then it would discard the armor and resume its bacterial shape again, ready to infect its unsuspecting victim. We call this armor-coated form a *spore*. But unlike armor, this protective covering is not made of metal but of layers of tough protein, as tough as fingernails. Anthrax's ability to protect itself like this, by forming spores, is shared with only a few other organisms, most notably the ones responsible for tetanus, botulism, and a severe form of food poisoning. Deadly killers all.

The spore form of anthrax is remarkably hardy. It can lie dormant in the soil for decades, maybe centuries. It is immune to many disinfectants, and to boiling for up to an hour. Researchers have tried to burn them in fires, freeze them, even blow them up. The spores endured. They've been sprayed from nozzles and hoses and disseminated via explosions from missiles and bombs. They survived. Steam under pressure (autoclaving) and irradiation seem to be the best ways to kill the spores.

In nature, sporulation takes days or weeks to complete. A clever terrorist, however, can fool nature by spraying a mist of pure oxygen and dilute hydrochloric acid over anthrax colonies. This drives spore formation much faster. Within hours, new spores are formed in quantity. And it's easy to do, can even be done in a home made kitchen laboratory. It only takes 5,000 -8,000 spores inhaled or eaten to infect someone. Ten grams of anthrax powder (a pinch) would contain about a million spores.

For all these reasons — ease of production, hardiness, and ease of dispersal — anthrax spores are the perfect bioweapon.

Spores Everywhere

One of the blessed things about the recent anthrax-by-mail outbreak is the small number of actual cases: 24 total. Considering how far and wide mail-related spores were discovered, this final tally could have been much higher, could have logged many more deaths.

Except for a small amount of spores found in a non-public mail office, and those on Bob Stevens's computer at AMI, no more were found in Boca Raton. It was the federal buildings in Washington, D.C. which bore the brunt of the attack. The U.S. State Department, in particular, was heavily infested with them; spores were found in two different mailrooms at its D.C. headquarters, as well as in an off-site mailroom. One of the 11 inhalation patients worked there.

Spores were discovered as well in the mailrooms of the Department of Health and Human Services and in two sites at the U.S. Supreme Court: in the basement mailroom of the main building and at an off-site facility. The Voice of America did not escape the attack, nor did the Food and Drug Administration (FDA) mailroom. Spores were found at both locations, though no serious illness arose from either.

The Senate Office Building was attacked. Letters sent to Senate Majority Leader Tom Daschle and Senator Patrick Leahy were laced with spores. No one got sick, but 6,000 Capitol Hill employees were tested with nasal swabs (used principally to define the extent of bacterial spread). Thirty-one of these employees tested positive, including 23 members of Daschle's staff, five Capitol Hill police officers, and three employees from Senator Russ Feingold's office, all of whom were given 60-day courses of antibiotics. An interesting finding emerged from analysis of these spores. Silica had been added to them. Silica disperses the spores, allowing them to remain airborne much longer. This renders them more effective as biological weapons. This chilling discovery proved that the bioterrorist not only knew how to produce the spores, but how to weaponize them as well.

Other media centers were targeted in addition to AMI. ABC, CBS and NBC were all hit. The infant of a woman employed at the ABC building in Manhattan developed cutaneous anthrax. Apparently, the mother had taken the child to work with her on September 28, when the infant must have been exposed, though no specific source of the spores was ever found. The initial lesion — on the infant's upper arm — was originally thought to be a brown recluse spider bite with surrounding infection. The child was treated with antibiotics and recovered. Anthrax was diagnosed by Polymerase Chain Reaction (PCR) testing, a technique which produces large amounts of bacteria from a single cell.

At NBC, spores were found in a letter addressed to Tom Brokaw. One of his aides subsequently developed cutaneous anthrax. She was treated and recovered. And CBS anchor Dan Rather announced on CNN's *Larry King Live* that an assistant had been infected with the skin form of the disease.

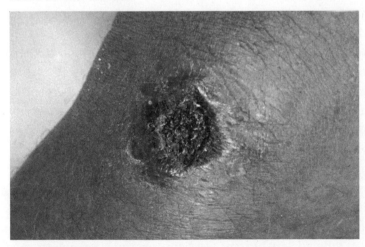

Figure 2.
Cutaneous anthrax in an adult.

Source: CDC — James H. Steele

In addition to these primary locations, spores were found at secondary sites far and wide. (Secondaries are locations where spores could be traced to known primaries.) In the continental U.S., they were found as far away as Indianapolis, Indiana and Kansas City, Missouri. But the long distance record was set by the U.S. embassy in Lima, Peru, where the spores were carried by diplomatic pouch from the State Department in Washington, D.C.

Hoaxes

Who knows how these things get started? Or why? Maybe someone just wants to play a practical joke on a fraternity brother, a friend, or a fellow employee. He spoons some flour, baking soda, or talcum powder into an envelope and slips it under the friend's door or into his mailbox. Or, to give it that official look, he puts a stamp on it and sends it through the mail. He might imagine his friend's face drained of color, his eyes wide with panic when he opens the envelope. Perhaps he even arranges to be on hand when the powder spills out, to witness the event firsthand.

This type of scenario, with multiple variations, has been played out ever since the Gulf War brought the threat of biological weapons into the headlights and raised public anxiety about them. An indicator of this rising level of worry is the steadily increasing number of *New York Times* articles related to "Biological and Chemical Weapons." From 27 in 1994, the number rose to 87 in 1996, then to 278 in 1998.

One catalyst for the dramatic increase in '98 was the appearance on national television in November 1997 of Defense Secretary William Cohen. He held up a five pound sack of sugar and claimed that an equivalent amount of anthrax spores could kill one quarter of the population of Washington, D.C. In that instant, Secretary Cohen made anthrax the number one subject for hoaxters. A December 1999 article in the *American Journal of Infection Control* documented the dramatic increase. From 22 incidents in 1997, the number of anthrax hoaxes shot up to 112 in 1998. Targets included abortion clinics, nightclubs, churches, schools, hospitals, post offices, stores of all kinds, and news media. Very few of the suspects were ever caught.

Some of the hoaxes have been diabolically imaginative. In April 1997, a petri dish labeled "anthrachs" and containing a red gelatinous substance was sent to the Washington, D.C. offices of B'nai B'rith. It was quickly determined there was no real danger. But the building was cordoned off and 100 or so employees were quarantined for up to 10 hours.

Between October 30 and December 23, 1998, seven anthrax threats were reported to the FBI. Some were letters alleged to contain the bacteria. Others were phone calls claiming anthrax had been dumped into the ventilation systems of health clinics in Indiana, Kentucky, Tennessee, and California. All told, about 1800 people had to be sent home. Some were required to disrobe and take showers before being released. Others were placed on antibiotics. A few were hospitalized for observation.

On Christmas Eve, 1998, in Palm Desert, California, a department store received a telephoned anthrax threat. Two hundred shoppers and employees were made to strip, shower, and scrub down in a make-shift outdoor facility. Several days later a similar threat was made to a nightclub in Pomona, California. Patrons and employees were quarantined for 4 hours. And in February 1999, perhaps an omen of what was to come, letters claiming to contain anthrax were sent to the *Washington Post,* NBC News in Atlanta, a Federal building in Washington, D.C., and a post office in Columbus, Georgia. Dozens of visitors and employees were quarantined, a few taken to local hospitals.

Though not real, these earlier threats were all taken seriously by authorities. But they attained a new urgency after the first actual anthrax cases were reported in October 2001. People were dying. Someone had made good on his threat.

Some of the recent hoaxes were very personal. A prosecutor assigned to an Illinois traffic court, perhaps bored with his hum-drum caseload, secretly placed an envelope full of sugar on the desk of a colleague. But his victim failed to see the humor in it. He reported the incident to his supervisor, and the traffic court prosecutor was forced to resign.

In Bethesda, Maryland, a white substance was sprinkled onto the dashboard of an unlocked car on Halloween night. Alarmed, the owner reported it to the police. They called in the FBI. After a careful and costly investigation, the Feds determined it was a hoax. The trick-or-treater was never caught.

In another case the jokester wasn't so lucky. He was an ex-con who planted a white substance on a bathroom counter at an Anderson, Indiana truck stop. He also taped a note to one of the stall doors.

It read, "Anthrax is here someplace." He was tracked down, arrested, and returned to prison for probation violation.

Incidents like these may have been sparked by playful, if mis-guided, motives. Others had more malicious intentions. They were designed to extort or terrorize.

In Los Angeles a man was arrested for mailing a letter containing a white substance to his ex-girlfriend. It turned out to be nothing more than baking powder. But the lady was frightened, and her ex-beau was identified, arrested and prosecuted.

Also in Los Angeles, an illegal immigrant who had quarrelled with another man sent him a letter threatening homicide by anthrax. He was arrested and deported.

Equally threatening were the hoaxes sent to some companies, in-stitutions and government officials. Senator Tom Daschle's office was impacted hard. First, an attack with the real thing in October. Then in January, a second letter addressed to him arrived at his Senate office. It too contained a white, powdery substance. Daschle and his staff had to go through it all over again: evacuation of the office and anxi-ety about this new threat. This time it turned out to be a hoax. Daschle wasn't amused.

Also in January, a Capitol police officer was accused of leaving a white powder at a police security station along with a threatening anonymous note. The building was closed and the FBI notified. It was another hoax.

Even the venerable Supreme Court Building was closed briefly af-ter the discovery of an envelope containing a white powder in the basement mailroom. It proved to be something other than anthrax. Something harmless. Maybe someone was still protesting the outcome of the Florida Presidential election?

Abortion clinics were favorite targets. Two hundred fifty letters containing white powder were sent to such clinics on the West Coast. They were intercepted before delivery. But another 200 got through.

Whatever their motives, the hoaxes were vicious. The psychologi-cal and social effects on the victims were, in some cases, devastating and lingered on and on. Some had to seek professional counseling. Others could not return to their worksites for months. Many refused to open their mail.

Mail continues to be looked at with great suspicion. Packages sent to news media offices are now routinely autoclaved before opening. For a brief period, even money was viewed as a possible source of spores. A joke making its way around New York City bars was that bartenders would only accept cash with two forms of identification!

The social effects of the hoaxes were almost as disruptive as exposure to real spores: forced out of one's home or office, required to remove one's clothes and shower, isolated from friends, loss of employment. Barriers to social intercourse were erected where none had existed before. The health care system was flooded with the worried well. Many were prescribed needless antibiotics.

There was also a substantial economic impact to the hoaxes, and not just to the victims themselves, but to the taxpayer as well. At last count, the FBI had received around 7,000 reports of anthrax threats, hoaxes, white powdery substances, or just funny looking letters. All had to be run down by trained agents. Many required environmental sampling and testing. Some victims had to be quarantined at government expense; others received antibiotics until their tests results proved negative. The final tally is not yet in but will probably be in the millions and millions of dollars. (Not all the economic effect was negative. Businesses which manufactured environmental anthrax detectors for the home and office, or produced face masks and respirators, began to do a thriving business, although both types of products proved to be of questionable value.)

In 2000, Congress finally passed legislation making an anthrax hoax a federal crime.

The Hunt for the Terrorist

Who could do such a thing, cause terror with bacterial spores? And why? What could be the motive? Clearly, this is someone very angry, someone with a grudge against the country in general and against the government in particular, as represented by Senators Daschle, Leahy and Feingold. And anger as well against other institutions which are seen as part of the "establishment," like the news media: AMI in Florida, NBC, CBS and ABC News in New York City, and the *New York Post*.

Experts have struggled to come up with a likely profile of the terrorist. Here's one from a biologist who works with the Federation of American Scientists (from *Time*, Nov. 19, 2001): The terrorist is a middle aged American male, a home grown product with no connection to Osama bin Laden, *al-Qaeda*, or any of the September 11 perpetrators. However, he may have used those events as cover for his own actions, and it may actually have worked; there was initial concern that one or more of the World Trade Center terrorists had taken flying lessons in a crop duster, maybe had even tried to rent one to spray the countryside with anthrax spores.

The terrorist is most likely a loner, a non-conformist seething with repressed anger. Perhaps he keeps a journal of what he considers governmental abuses, like the FBI raids at Ruby Ridge and Waco, which caused unnecessary loss of innocent lives. Probably, like the Unabomber, he lives alone, secluded, out of touch with family, friends or other moderating influences.

One thing seems certain. This man has a scientific background, especially in biological research methods. He knows his way around a laboratory. Although he could have made his anthrax spores in a home-made lab for as little as $2,500, he would have to know how to work with the cultures and fermenters required for such production, and how to protect himself from his own weapon. He's probably immunized against anthrax, perhaps from prior military service, or maybe from employment in a government or government-contract laboratory. And for extra protection, he's probably medicated himself with antibiotics.

Where would this man have gotten the hands-on experience necessary to make his bioweapon? Perhaps in a lab under contract to the CIA, or at a private company doing similar research? One thing stands out: he knows how to conceal forensic evidence. Although the FBI has generated a list of barely fifty or so people who fit this profile, they've been unable — as of this writing — to link any of them with hard evidence to the anthrax attacks.

Where would the terrorist have gotten his anthrax seed bacteria to start with? High on that list is the United States Army Medical Research Institute of Infectious Diseases — USAMRIID — at Fort Detrick, Maryland. This has been America's premier bioweapons research facility for over fifty years. During its Cold War heyday in the 1950s and '60s, huge amounts of anthrax, botulinum toxin, plague, tularemia and other bioweapons were produced and stored there.

But in 1969 President Richard Nixon disavowed the offensive use of biological weapons. Most of USAMRIID's stores were subsequently destroyed, the equipment dismantled, the technicians let go or reassigned. Now the Lab confines its research to defensive and peaceful uses of bioweapons: the development of new vaccines and better antibiotics against BW agents; more effective protective equipment for soldiers in the field; better ways to test environmental samples for suspected bioterrorist agents; and improved tests for diagnosing human disease. Could the bioterrorist be a former USAMRIID employee? Or even a current one?

The finger of suspicion has been pointed even more sharply at USAMRIID by a recent (February 4, 2002) report in *Time* magazine, which claims that security at the Lab during the '90s was poor. During an Army investigation in 1992, 27 samples of anthrax and other agents were found to be missing. (Twenty-three were subsequently found, but the security concerns linger.) Some employees claimed they were able to just walk out with classified records of how botulism toxin was produced.

In addition to these worries, *Time* reports that discipline at the Lab was poor, morale low. Alleged sexual and racial harassment charges have been filed against supervisors, and accusations of incompetence and research theft flowed back and forth as factions waged war for leadership positions. It was a "breeding ground for resentment and hateful high jinks," *Time* concluded. One Lab employee, Ayaad Assad, an Egyptian born U.S. citizen, was investigated by the FBI after it received an anonymous tip that he was preparing a biological attack. Assad was fired and is now suing for unlawful termination.

The current USAMRIID director disputes these charges. He maintains that employee behavior and morale have improved and that there was never any real risk of bioweapons theft. Furthermore, he notes — and he is correct on this point — the Lab has sent anthrax samples to at least five other military research facilities over the years, and to a half-dozen private ones. Any of them could be the home of the terrorist.

Another place FBI investigators are searching for the terrorist is in the Utah desert. The U.S. Army's Dugway Proving Grounds, a site as vast as the State of Rhode Island, produced and tested biological weapons starting shortly after World War II. The Army claims it stopped making weapons grade anthrax in recent years. "Weapons Grade" means the spores are in powdered form and the particles small enough — 1-5 microns — to be inhaled deeply into the lungs. This type of anthrax matches perfectly that found in letters sent to Senators Daschle, Leahy and Feingold.

The Army maintains that most Dugway experiments use anthrax simulants — harmless look-alikes — to test methods of decontamination and detection. However, certain tests, it concedes, need to be performed with live spores. But all such stock has been accounted for; none has gone missing, the Army asserts. Still, Dugway personnel who have had access to anthrax and have been vaccinated against it have been extensively questioned by the FBI, in some cases with polygraphs.

The genetic make-up of the anthrax bacteria used in the mail attacks has not been particularly helpful in narrowing the search for the terrorist. Its original source has been traced to a cow dead from the disease in a south Texas field in 1981. Samples of the animal's blood and tissue were sent first to the Texas Veterinary Medical Diagnostic Laboratory, then to the National Veterinary Services Laboratory in Ames, Iowa, a U.S. Department of Agriculture (USDA) facility. From there, numerous samples went to USAMRIID, which also receives samples from the Army's Dugway Proving Grounds in Utah. Because the return address on the USDA samples read "Ames, Iowa," this sample became known as the *Ames Strain*, implying that it originated there. This mislabelling caused vigorous protest from Iowa State University's College of Veterinary Medicine in Ames. They've had no research program with anthrax for 50 years.

In June 2002, the FBI startled the country by announcing it had radioactive carbon dated a sample of anthrax spores from the 2001 attack. The sample came from Senator Patrick Leahy's office, the only site with enough spores for this type of analysis. To their surprise, federal investigators found it was not the 21 year old *Ames Strain* they had assumed all along. Instead, it was fresh, made no more than two years before the attack, probably by someone sophisticated in bioweapons techniques.

The reward for information leading to the capture of the bioterrorist has risen steadily. As of 2003, it stands at $2.5 million. But there has been little progress in the investigation. U.S. Attorney General John Ashcroft has identified 25 "persons of interest," one of whom, Steven Hatfill, a former Army biologist, was recently singled out for intense FBI and media scrutiny. But despite hours and hours of interviews and polygraph testing by the Feds, the trail has grown cold.

James Woolsey, former Director of the CIA, has stated publicly that another terrorist attack against the U.S. is a virtual certainty. The only questions are when, where and with what weapons. Homeland Security Director Tom Ridge has echoed similar concerns. If the assault is of the bioterrorist variety, how can we better prepare for it? Government and private medical agencies have their roles. So does the citizenry, starting with becoming better informed about the agents of bioterrorism, including anthrax.

CHAPTER

3

THE VIEW FROM
THE PETRI DISH

Anthrax has existed throughout the world in both man and animals since the time of Moses, and probably before. It is still endemic, though rare, in the U.S. today, mostly in rural farm areas. In September 2000, for example, Del Rio, Texas reported an outbreak of anthrax in deer and livestock. An outbreak in cattle and horses was also reported from Minnesota that year. And Nebraska had animal anthrax cases as recently as January 2001. There were no human cases from any of these epizootics.

This paucity of U.S. cases is in sharp contrast to other parts of the world, where large epizootics, followed by human epidemics, occur regularly. In 1985, in East Nigeria, a study of 400 animals found that 5% of the cattle and 3.3% of sheep were infected with anthrax. An epidemic of cutaneous anthrax — called the "malignant pustule"— occurred in workers who butchered or skinned the animals, tanned the hides, or sold the meat.

In Serbia, from 1956-1987, 61 humans developed anthrax, most of it as the malignant pustule, all of it from animal contact. Three had signs of septic shock, and one died.

The largest documented human outbreak was in Zimbabwe between 1979 and 1985. More than 10,000 human cases were reported in association with anthrax disease in cattle. The majority of the human disease was of the cutaneous type.

Another large outbreak followed in Chad in 1988. Seven hundred sixteen human cases were reported, with 88 deaths, also following an epizootic in livestock.

Finally, in a dramatic report in a journal of tropical medicine in 1990, four of five persons who skinned and cut up a sheep carcass developed anthrax meningitis. One died. One also developed a malignant pustule.

Animal anthrax develops very much like human illness. It starts with the spores, formed when raw anthrax bacteria are deposited in the soil from decomposing animal carcasses, or from the bloody vomitus, diarrhea, nasal discharges and other fluids of diseased and dying animals. Once exposed to free oxygen, the sporulation process begins. It begins so quickly that in the laboratory *endospores* start to form during the bacteria's few minutes' exposure to oxygen during the staining process (see figure 3).

Spores are as hardy in nature as they've shown themselves to be in laboratory tests. They are resistant to heat, cold, freezing, and fire. The animal usually ingests the spores in its food or water. Feedlots used to be prime breeding grounds for the disease until modern hygiene procedures and animal vaccinations were introduced about 100 years ago.

If ingested, the spores initiate the gastrointestinal form of the disease, the most common one in livestock. In rare instances, the animal may breathe dust laden spores and trigger the inhalation form of the disease. Blowflies may transmit the bacteria directly into the blood stream; this has been observed in Africa. Should the animal get the spores or the naked bacteria into a break in its skin, it may develop the cutaneous form of the disease, just as humans do.

Figure 3:
Anthrax bacteria with endospores.

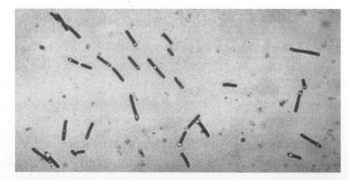

Source: CDC — Dr. William A. Clark

Once ingested or inhaled, the spores are engulfed by the body's scavenger cells — called macrophages — and taken to regional lymph nodes in the lungs or gastrointestinal tract. The spores themselves are not infectious. But in the lymph nodes they germinate back into the bacterial form and become infectious. Normally, the body's immune system of white blood cells, antibodies and other germ fighters immediately start to kill the invaders. But one of anthrax's most potent defense mechanisms is a capsule made of poly-D-glutamic acid. It effectively resists such destruction.

Symptoms begin shortly after the spores germinate, usually within a few days. The infection can kill in any one of several ways. Most deadly is a toxin the bacteria produces, a poison which persists in the body even after the bacteria themselves are dead, for example, if they've been killed by antibiotics. This toxin is composed of three parts. First, a protein called the Protective Antigen (PA) binds to a receptor site on the host cell wall. This exposes a secondary receptor site, which now becomes the target for the other two components of the toxin: the Edema Factor (EF), which further impairs the body's defenses; and the Lethal Factor (LF), which causes tissue death, hemorrhage, septic shock and vascular collapse. The human vaccine currently in use is directed against the Protective Antigen. The vaccine's effectiveness indicates how critical the PA antigen is for causing disease.

Like any other bacterial infection, anthrax can also kill by invading vital body organs and impairing their function. The infected organs swell and die, often with massive hemorrage. This leads to liver failure, renal shut-down, meningitis, and respiratory failure. Death is usually within a few days, preceded by high fevers, convulsions, bloody vomitus and diarrhea, muscle tremors, and respiratory distress. As the animal dies, it expels massive amounts of the anthrax bacteria into the soil in its bloody discharges. More bacteria are released as the carcass decomposes. New spores are formed. The cycle is repeated.

Except for continuing Third World epizootics and endemic disease in developed countries, animal anthrax has been all but wiped out by feedlot hygiene, proper disposal of carcasses and hides, and animal vaccinations. Animal vaccine is different from the human one. It is a live spore preparation known as the Sterne strain, which dates from 1937. It is good for one year. It is used only to innoculate animals when a case of anthrax breaks out in a herd. It is not used to maintain constant herd-wide immunity.

Human Disease

As in animals, the disease in humans may take any one of three forms. The <u>cutaneous</u> variety, which accounts for 95% of cases, begins when anthrax spores or bacteria gain access to a break in the skin. This may be from handling animal carcasses or hides, or from infected wool or hair. Rarely, human infection comes directly from the soil, though now we know it can come directly through the mail!

A red area appears first at the site of the infection, followed quickly by a raised red swelling known as a *papule*. Within a day or so, the papule turns into a fluid-filled blister, then into a *pustule* teeming with bacteria. The pustule breaks open and the skin becomes ulcerated. Regional lymph nodes in the area of infection, typically the groin, armpit, or neck, may become swollen and tender, mimicking the buboes of bubonic plague. At this point, healing may begin. But if the bacteria have invaded the blood stream, the patient gets much sicker very quickly. Many will die. Fortunately, this occurs in only about 20% of untreated cutaneous cases.

There is nothing about the look of cutaneous anthrax, especially in the early stages, which announces itself as that disease. It could as well be a brown recluse spider bite, a tropical ulcer, a streptococcal or staphylococcal skin infection, or even skin cancer. The key to making the diagnosis is for the physician to have a high level of suspicion in anyone with such a sore who is also in one of the high risk occupational groups. Or if the sore has developed during an epizootic of the disease and the person has handled animal caracsses, blood samples, cultures, tissue, hides or wool — or, recently, the U.S. mail.

Human <u>gastrointestinal</u> anthrax is very uncommon in developed countries, chiefly because livestock there are raised in clean environments free of the spores. In Third World countries this may not be the case, and the meat may be tainted with bacteria. If it is poorly cooked as well, gastrointestinal anthrax can occur.

The GI form of anthrax follows the same clinical course, and with nearly identical symptoms, in humans as it does in animals. From its source in the GI tract, the spores are carried to regional lymph nodes. There they germinate and release their toxin, or they invade the body directly through the blood stream. Bloody vomitus and diarrhea, internal hemorrhage, shock and vascular collapse quickly follow. Mortality rates are frightful in this form of the disease, close to 90%.

An even rarer variant of GI anthrax is the oral/pharyngeal form. Symptoms begin here with a sore throat. Ulcers on the tongue and in the mouth develop. The spores are carried to lymph nodes in the neck, where they germinate and release the toxin. Swelling of the neck can be so severe that it may cause respiratory distress. Death is the usual outcome.

The inhalation form of human anthrax comes from breathing the spores. It only accounts for 5% of naturally-acquired human disease, though in the recent terrorist cases it made up almost 50%. Its clinical course is nearly identical to the 11 recent U.S. cases, though there are some important differences. Mild flu symptoms begin first: malaise, fatigue, muscle pains, fever, mild chest pain and cough. These last 2-3 days. Then there is typically a brief period of improvement, a honeymoon, lasting a day or so. This remission phase was missing from the recent U.S. cases.

When the spores reach the pulmonary lymph nodes and regerminate into bacteria, they release their toxin. Sudden respiratory distress, air hunger, increased chest pains and sweating ensue, all caused by mediastinal hemorrhage, shock and vascular collapse. Meningitis has been reported in about 10% of cases, often accompanied by changes in mental status and seizures. The mortality rate has normally been over 80%. Improved antibacterial and supportive care reduced this rate in the U.S. cases to around 50%.

Diagnosis

Often, a simple blood stain reveals the organism. Cultures of blood, spinal fluid, other body fluids, organs, or tissues can confirm the disease within 24 hours. Under the microscope, the bacteria have very distinctive shapes, large, boxcar-like rods, usually in twos, threes or longer chains. Sometimes they have endospores as well. Differentiating anthrax from other common bacterial pathogens is normally not difficult, though there are two organisms of the bacillus type which can be confused with *b. anthracis*. *Bacillus thuringiensis* looks very similar to anthrax under the microscope; it may also have endospores. This bacteria is a pathogen of moths and caterpillars, not of humans. Figure 4 shows *b. cereus*, another close relative of anthrax. It is a normal inhabitant of the soil and has occasionally been implicated in outbreaks of food-borne illness in animals. Both *b. thuringiensis* and *b.*

cereus can be differentiated from *b. anthracis* by culture techniques and by tests for the presence of a capsule, which anthrax has and the other two don't.

Figure 4.
Bacillus cereus

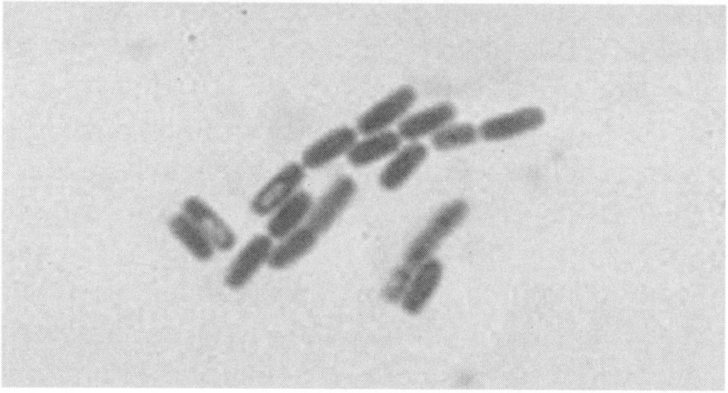

Source: CDC — Dr. William A. Clark

Another problem in diagnosis comes when the patient has been given antibiotics prior to collecting blood samples, which happened in one of the recent U.S. cases. The result is that the bacteria don't grow on culture media and may not be visible on stains. Yet they still inhabit the patient's lymph nodes and other tissues, are still capable of releasing toxin, are still lethal. Diagnosis must be made in other ways.

The polymerase chain reaction (PCR) is a new diagnostic tool. It takes a small amount of bacterial DNA and amplifies it greatly, allowing for proper recognition of the DNA sequence, identification of the organism, and differentiation of it from other look-alike pathogens. In nature, anthrax comes in only one strain. This means the bacteria found in a Kenyan cow should be identical to one found in a Washington D.C. post office. But if the organism has been genetically altered, as occurred during a 1979 Russian outbreak, the PCR technique can also be used to sort out these different strains.

Finally, there are a host of serologic tests for detecting the body's immune response to the organism, either against the bacteria itself or against the toxin. One of these is ELISA, enzyme-linked immunoabsorbant assay. It is a reliable test and rapidly done, but only in high-powered laboratories and medical centers. Another test, still under development, uses technetium-labeled monoclonal antibodies to image anthrax infection in its early stages.

Treatment

Many antibiotics are effective against *b. anthracis* on the culture plate: ciprofloxacin, doxycycline, clindamycin, rifampin, penicillin, and amoxicillin. But because of its frightful mortality rate in real patients, CDC recommends using multiple antibiotics for anyone sick with the disease. First line drugs are either cipro or doxy, usually given intravenously at first. One of the secondary drugs is then added. A regimen of cipro, rifampin, and clindomycin was used with success in some of the recent inhalation cases.

Prevention

Cipro or doxy should be offered to anyone who might have been exposed to anthrax bacteria or its spores. These would include veterinarians, laboratory technicians, sheepshearers, sheepfarmers, cattle ranchers, and slaughterhouse workers. Because of the slim but real possibility of a long incubation period, the antibiotics should be continued for a full 60 days. Shorter courses only delay the onset of the disease but don't prevent it outright. Even longer courses — 40 additional days, sometimes combined with the vaccine — have been offered for especially high risk patients.

But this long course of antibacterial prophylaxis comes with a cost, and not just an economic one. In a recent CDC study, 8424 postal workers were offered antibiotics. Of these, 3863 started taking them, 3428 (89%) on cipro, 435 (11%) on doxy or amoxicillin. Adverse events, especially in those who took cipro, were:

- nausea, vomiting, diarrhea or abdominal pain (19%);
- light headedness or dizziness (14%);
- heartburn or gastric acid reflux (7%);
- rashes, hives or itchy skin (6%).

Two percent of these workers had to seek medical care for their problems, though none was hospitalized. For 8% of those taking cipro, the adverse effects were so severe they discontinued the medication in mid-course.

Anthrax Vaccine

The standard human anthrax vaccine — which engenders immunity to the bacteria's toxin — is made from a cell-free filtrate (in other words, it contains no bacterial elements). Six injections are required at 0, 2, and 4 weeks, then at 6, 12, and 18 months. It is 92% effective when all six doses are given, but it takes at least two doses to be even minimally effective. This makes it impractical for large population post-exposure prophylaxis; by the time the first protective antibodies show up in the patient's blood, about two weeks after the first injection, many of those exposed would be long dead. The vaccine is primarily intended for persons in contact with imported meat, hides, furs and animal hair, for research workers, and for others who might be exposed to diseased persons or animals through their occupations. Troops going into harm's way have also been immunized, 150,000 during the Gulf War. The Department of Defense wants to increase this to 2 million, but production delays have kept this goal from being realized. Even more worrisome is that new, bioengineered strains of the organism may have been developed by terrorists or rogue states which will be unaffected by this vaccine.

In its natural environment, then, anthrax is a disease of both animals and humans. The symptoms and course of the human disease were probably little different during the recent cases than they were during all of past history, whenever man and animal shared common ground. How did the disease get from that ancient time to the present essentially unchanged? When was anthrax first recognized as a natural, as opposed to a divine, occurrence? When was its transmission from animal to man first recognized? And, more simply, how did it get its name?

CHAPTER 4

MOSES AND THE
TEN PLAGUES OF EGYPT

*But when the King despised the words of Moses, and had no regard
at all to them grievous plagues seized the Egyptians.*

— **Flavius Josephus** (37-100 A.D.)
Antiquities of the Jews

The word itself, anthrax, is of Greek derivation. But it evokes im-
ages of even more ancient disease; of divine anger; of thundering
biblical prophets; of widespread pestilence. It is precisely here, in the
Old Testament, that we find the earliest references to the disease, where
the veil of history is first lifted. Not surprisingly, it is in animals that
we get our first peek.

Almost 33 centuries ago, about 1250 B.C. in the biblical account,
the Prophet Moses was commanded by God to lead the Hebrew slaves
out of Egypt. Moses ordered Pharoah Ramses II to "let my people go."
But Pharoah's heart was hardened. Ten plagues, Exodus tells us, were
then visited upon Egypt, ten plagues before Pharoah relented and the
slaves were released from their bondage. (Today, the word "plague"
usually refers to bubonic plague. In ancient times it was a general term
for any widespread pestilence.)

The first evidence of God's anger was the plague of waters. The
Nile itself, Father of Waters to the Egyptian, turned to blood, and all

the fishes died and stank. This was followed by plagues of frogs, lice, flies, fleas, boils, fiery hail, locusts and a three-day period of darkness. Still Pharoah's heart was hardened. Only when the final plague appeared, the death of all first-born Egyptians, was he persuaded to free the slaves. Moses then led his people out of Egypt. After a generation of wandering, they came to the Promised Land.

For our subject, the most intriguing of these ten plagues were the 5th and 6th. The 5th affected primarily livestock: cattle, horses, asses, camels, and sheep. In a short time, all Egyptian animals were dead (Exodus 9:3). It must have been a catastrophic event to have caused such widespread loss, an epizootic of truly biblical proportions! Later writers refer to the disease as a "murrain," another archaic term for a pestilence of animals.

Many diseases can devastate livestock rapidly and in large numbers, maybe even an entire herd or flock. But there are few which can carry them off in the quantities and with the speed described in Exodus, and anthrax has to be at the top of any such list. While the Exodus author does not specifically mention that *people* were affected by this plague, the later Jewish historian Flavius Josephus does. Working from Talmudic sources, he refers to the disease as a "distemper" and clearly states that it affected man as well as beast. It is probable, then, that a destructive *epizootic* of anthrax in animals, followed by an *epidemic* of the same disease in humans, was the cause of the 5th Plague of Egypt.

The 6th Plague was one of boils. In modern medical terms, a boil is a skin infection around a hair follicle. Its technical name is *furuncle* or, if it invades the skin deeper, a *carbuncle*. In ancient times, any pustular infection of the skin was called a boil, including the malignant pustule of anthrax. The chief difference is that these other types of infections almost always remain localized to the skin. Anthrax does not. It can invade deeper and cause generalized illness.

The 6th Plague began, according to the Bible (Exodus 8:11), with ashes. These turned to dust and settled over the land, now dry and parched. The boils soon followed. They turned to sores in both men and beasts. Josephus calls them "blaines," an old name for skin inflammations. He also states that Egyptians who developed these boils were "inwardly corrupted," and many perished. That description of the 6th Plague fits the course of cutaneous anthrax perfectly. It began as a skin infection — a boil — then clawed its way deep into the skin, where it gained access to the blood stream. It was now *sepsis*, or blood poisoning, a generalized, fatal infection. The term *sepsis* is Greek. It translates into "corruption" or "decay within the body."

There is another piece of evidence pointing the finger of guilt at anthrax for the 5th and 6th Plagues of Egypt. Veterinarians will tell you that anthrax epizootics typically occur after both floods and droughts. In the former, sick animals are drowned, die, and release their anthrax bacteria into streams, lakes and ponds. The bacteria quickly turn into spores. As the standing water evaporates, the concentration of spores increases, also increasing the risk of an animal ingesting them when it drinks.

Conversely, during droughts like the one which accompanied the 6th Plague of Egypt, the grasses are stunted from lack of water. Animals have to forage closer to the ground, where they are more likely to pick up anthrax spores from the soil.

The Supernatural Explanation of Disease

It would be many centuries before disease was viewed as arising from natural causes. So what did these ancient peoples think caused the plagues which afflicted them? In a word, it was the divine, the gods, the supernatural. In the case of the Israelites it was *Yahweh*, their single deity; for the Egyptians it was one or more of the many gods in their pantheon. And for both peoples, only faith, prayer and sacrificial offerings could save them. When the Hebrews survived the 5th and 6th Plagues with both their livestock and themselves intact, they saw it as certain proof they were the chosen people of God.

The 13th century B.C., the time of the Exodus, was also the period of the Trojan War, memorably described in Homer's epic tale, the *Iliad*. Most of Homer's medical references are concerned with combat injuries. But he does describe a plague which descended upon the Greek camp in the form of arrows shot from the bow of the god Apollo. Homer provides no description of the symptoms, so we cannot presume to make a diagnosis of the infection. Its cause, however, was clear: punishment for the arrogant behavior of King Agamemnon, the leader of the Greeks. The epidemic only abated after proper sacrifices were made to Apollo.

A contemporary of Homer's, the writer Hesiod, also alludes to a plague in his *Works and Days*. He doesn't tell us where the epidemic broke out, but he is clear that it was sent by Zeus, and that "the men perish, the women are barren."

Though both Exodus and the *Iliad* describe events taking place during the 13th century B.C., neither writer was a contemporary of that period. Homer probably lived during the 8th century B.C., and Exodus was written around the same time, the 9th-7th centuries B.C. The descriptions of biblical and Trojan plagues, therefore, say more about the writers and their own times than they do about the times they were writing about. This means, on the one hand, that anthrax was recognized as a not uncommon disease during the 9th-7th centuries B.C., and on the other, that supernatural forces were viewed as causing these plagues during the same period.

The Cult of Aesclepius

Beginning around 750 B.C., the Cult of Aesclepius arose. It reached a peak in the 2nd half of the 5th century B.C., when it could count over 400 shrines and temples to the god (Figure 5). Though rooted in supernaturalist ideology, this cult provided a link to the later rationalist school of medicine founded by Hippocrates, who was one of its disciples.

Aesclepius (or Aesculapius) took the serpent as his symbol because the snake had been a sign of the healing power of the gods since even more ancient times. And Aesclepius' walking staff, the *Caduceus*, with its entwined serpents, has been the symbol of the healer ever since. Aesclepius is often protrayed in the company of his two daughters: Panacea, who had a cure for everything; and Hygiea, dedicated to hygiene and public health. To the priests and supplicants at his temples, Aesclepius was viewed more as a physician than a god.

The chief Aesclepiad Cult centers were at Athens and Epidaurus on the Greek mainland, and at Pergamum and Cos in Asia Minor. These large centers had baths, a small odeon or concert hall, a theatre, a stadium, a gymnasium and a library. The supplicants, depending on their ambulatory and social status, arrived on foot, in carts, or on horseback. They were usually accompanied by family members bearing gifts for the priests.

On arrival, the patient was bathed in the sacred springs, robed in a white chiton, and started on a purifying fast. He may have sacrificed

Figure 5. *Aesculapius*

Source: National Library of Medicine

to the god: anything from a small biscuit or cookie to an entire oxen. After this, he was helped to a couch where he prayed further and, aided to sleep by soporific potions, began his dream state. Sometimes the god appeared to him, talked with him, gave him medicines or even operated on him.

In the morning, the patient was ushered into a separate area for consultation. There, the priest interpreted the dreams and prescribed additonal therapy, typically more baths, herbal teas and soups, poultices, and dietary regimes.

Successful treatments — including the dreams — were inscribed on the walls of the temples. In one, a "man with a malignant ulcer on his toe" claims he was healed by the god who visited him in the form of a snake. (Could this have been cutaneous anthrax?) The walls of the shrine at Cos, where Hippocrates first began his medical career, contain many of these same therapeutic scratchings.

Hippocrates and the Beginning of Rational Medicine

By the onset of the 5th century B.C., new medical ideas were making themselves felt. More rational explanations for the causes of disease were being sought, along with more natural therapies. By the middle of the century, the physician would replace the gods as healer.

During this eight hundred year period — from the time of Moses to the birth of Hippocrates — there were many changes in medical thought and the general approach to disease. But the anthrax bacteria itself didn't change at all. It remained constant, cycling back and forth between its bacterial and spore forms. Farmers watched their flocks thinned by it, their own skin turn red, then ulcerous and black from it, their family members carried off by it. They prayed to their gods, consulted oracles, made sacrifices, drank herbal teas by the gallon, and applied smelly poultices. All to no avail.

Then, like a coiled serpent, the disease struck, and struck with a ferocity which almost destroyed the most famous city of the Golden Age of Greece: Athens.

CHAPTER
5

THE PLAGUE OF ATHENS, 430 B.C.

Life is short,
Art is long,
Opportunity fleeting,
Experience treacherous,
Judgement difficult.

— **Hippocrates**
   Aphorisms on Medicine

A Greek Drama in two Acts
Act I

Phillip the physician trudged heavy-hearted through the Athenian Agora, the city's chief market place. He mulled over his last group of patients; most had died. It was a hot summer day, dusty and crowded in the city. General Pericles had brought in all the farmers from the surrounding countryside to protect them and their livestock from the burning and pillaging Spartans. The city still controlled the Long Walls down to the port of Piraeus. And since the Spartans had no navy to mount a blockade, grain could still be imported from the Greek colonies around the Black Sea. But the livestock competed with the citizens for the grain, as well as for the limited water and sewage facilities. Many of the animals had become ill and died, their carcasses left to rot in the sun, along with the bodies of dead citizens. The city reeked of death.

Phillip glanced up toward the Acropolis on his left, crowned with

the just-completed Parthenon. This temple to Athena housed the won-
drous, colossal statue of the city's patron goddess. She held a spear in
one hand, in the other the *Aegis*, the shield of Zeus with its snake-
covered head of Medusa. The temple was doing an especially brisk
business these days. The number of supplicants offering sacrifices had
nearly doubled.

Phillip thought about his patients. Their illnesses had all started
the same way: first, a general malaise, a feeling of un-wellness, with
minor aches and pains and maybe vomiting and a low-grade fever.
Some even improved briefly after this. But that intermission did not
last long, and within a week at most, after complaining bitterly of
chest pains, difficulty breathing, and a dry cough, almost all of them
collapsed and died suddenly, almost as if they had been poisoned.
Nothing he had tried had halted their inexorable downward death
spirals. His colleagues had informed him they were having no better
success with their own patients.

Phillip continued on to his meeting atop the Pynx hill, where the
Assembly usually convened. He found about a hundred or so others
milling about when he got there. One man emerged from the crowd
and called for silence. He was Pericles, general of the army and ac-
knowledged leader of the Athenian state.

"Citizens," he began, his bearing disciplined, calm and military,
his speech clear and resonant, "I have called you here today in the
hopes of finding a way to stem the pestilence which is ravaging our
city." He pointed to Phillip. "First, I call upon the Macedonian, one of
our city's chief physicians, to give his report."

Phillip looked around the marble-columned hall, the fountain-
head of democracy. He recognized other physicians, selected members of the Assembly, judges, wealthy merchants, and military men
wearing helmets, armor and greaves. In short, all the city's leaders,
long-faced and grim.

"Sir," he said, addressing Pericles and bowing slightly, "I have recorded almost 100 deaths myself in the past three weeks. And I am
only one of many physicians treating this disease."

An Assembly member asked, "What is the cause of this Plague?"

Phillip had barely opened his mouth to answer when someone
abruptly interrupted him.

"We have angered the gods!" the other man shouted. "That is

what has led to our calamity. We have angered them, and this is our punishment."

It was Aristides, an old physician-priest. He elbowed his way to the front of the crowd to stand next to Phillip. Leaning on his walking stick, his back stooped with age, he shook a bony finger at the crowd and continued.

"Mark me well, Athenians. We have offended mighty Zeus and Apollo. Until we propitiate them, we will continue to labor under this burdensome pestilence. How else are we to explain this epidemic? It has always been so, for as long as I can remember. Illness, infirmity, disease. All are divine punishments visited upon us from Mount Olympus. And healing, likewise, will be at the gods' pleasure."

"What do you suggest, Aristides?" someone asked respectfully.

"More sacrifices, more prayers, more demonstrations of our fear and our love for the gods."

"But how?" Pericles asked. "Already the lines of animals waiting to be sacrificed grow longer outside our temples. The priests complain they get little rest even now."

"We must double, even triple our efforts, or all is lost." The old man was gasping for breath.

Pericles considered this, then turned to Phillip again. "What do you say, physician? Do you also say the plague is from the gods. . .?"

This conversation between Phillip, Pericles and the other Athenian leaders is speculation — fiction, if you prefer a stronger word. There is no record any such meeting took place. But it would be inconceiveable if one hadn't. A double calamity had hit the city. First, war with the Spartans had erupted the year before; they were now ravaging the countryside. And second was the devastating plague which had broken out during the summer. Under these trying conditions, it would be as natural for Pericles to meet with the city's physicians as it was for him to meet with its generals.

The Peloponnesian War

The root cause for this debilitating war between Athens and Sparta at the end of the 5th century B.C. must be sought in earlier times, the period known as the Archaic Age of Greece, roughly from 750-500 B.C. It was then that cities like Athens, Sparta, Thebes, Corinth and others grew into powerful city-states, nations unto themselves. But their paths of political development soon diverged. Sparta and a few others took a road leading to rule by the few, *oligarchy,* and to a society based on militaristic values, hardship, stern discipline and obedience to the state. No poet, artist, sculptor or philosopher of any merit ever came from Sparta. They were all warriors.

Athens' own political development went 180 degrees opposite Sparta's. After a brief flirtation with tyranny, she gave birth to the world's first democracy, for which she is justifiably famous. Under the guidance of her brilliant soldier-statesman Pericles, she sowed the seeds for all future western democracies.

But this was also a time of extreme danger for the Greeks. Athens and Sparta had buried their political differences to resist a Persian invasion force. First in 490 B.C. at Marathon, then again at Salamis and Platea ten years later, their combined armies threw the Persians back across the Hellespont.

For the next fifty years there was peace. Athens thrived. In drama, it was the time of that holy trinity: Aeschylus, Euripides and Sophocles, who gave full expression to complex political and psychological ideas. In sculpture, the stiff, stereotypic style of the Archaic period gave way to action, movement and expression. This was most gloriously expressed by Phidias in his statue of Athena, the city's patron goddess, and his Zeus Olympia, one of the Seven Wonders of the Ancient World. Architecture was epitomized by the soaring temples and shrines to the gods, the most wonderful of which was the Parthenon, begun in 447 B.C. at the instigation of Pericles himself.

New ideas about the cosmos were also emerging. Democratis argued that all matter is composed of tiny bits of invisible particles called "atoms." Anexagoras put forth the equally incredible idea that the sun, far from being a god, was nothing more than a lump of flaming rock!

Thucydides

By the second half of the 5th century B.C., relations between Athens and Sparta had begun to deteriorate. Athens had made herself *de facto* ruler of Greece through her control of the Delian League and its treasury. But power had corrupted her. She had grown arrogant. When a minor conflict developed in 433 B.C. over how to deal with each others' allies, Athens acted heavy-handed, imposed sanctions, and refused to negotiate. The Spartans, never very good at negotiations, saw no choice but to invade Attica, Athens' home turf. The Peloponnesian War had begun.

Fortunately for history, there was someone to tell the story: Thucydides the Athenian (460-404 B.C.), history's first professional historian. Whereas his predecessor Herodotus used his sources uncritically, repeated every tall tale he heard, and ascribed to the gods a divine influence on history, Thucydides did just the opposite. He refused to accept mere gossip, stories, or fables without verification. He gave the gods no role in the cause, course or outcome of the War. Furthermore, he was alive during the entire conflict and lived in Athens during a good part of it. He died just as hostilities came to an end in 404 B.C.

Thucydides' powers of observation and clarity of writing are no better witnessed than in his description of the Plague. It started, he tells us, in Ethiopia, then spread to Egypt and Persia, finally arriving in Athens in 430 B.C. It erupted first at the port of Piraeus, but soon spread along the Long Walls into the crowded city. Doctors were "incapable of treating the disease because of their ignorance of the right methods. In fact, mortality among doctors was highest of all." As for divine assistance, the historian is very clear on this point:

Equally useless were prayers made in temples, consultations of oracles, and so forth.

Death for the victims usually came on the 7th or 8th day. They often remained unburied, their bodies heaped on top of one another, rotting in the streets and temples or finally burned on pyres whose smoke covered the city like a shroud. Survivors were sometimes left with partial paralysis, amnesia and blindness.

Animals also died in great numbers, especialy those who fed on the bodies of the dead: birds of prey, jackals and domestic dogs. Lawlessness stalked the city, for the "catastrophe was so overwhelming that men. . .became indifferent to every rule of religion or law." Thucydides noted that the infection conferred immunity on its survivors; few caught it twice.

As much as one-third of the population perished, including 4,000 of the city's hoplite infantry, the very backbone of its military and political power.

Act II

Phillip the physician began slowly, after considering at length his response to Pericles' question. "You asked me whether the Plague was from the gods or not. Sir, I come from the green hills of Macedonia, the son of a physician. My father held the same beliefs as many of the other physicians here today, that epidemics are the work of the gods. He practiced the craft of healing in the same way they do, by offering sacrifices to propitiate the gods. But when I determined to study medicine, I traveled to the island of Cos to learn from the cult of Aesclepius and especially from a teacher there named Hippocrates."

A ripple of excitement ran through the crowd.

"I have heard of this Hippocrates," Aristides said accusingly. "Full of ideas about disease and health and medicine. . . revolutionary ideas. Those of us who practice in the old ways. . ."

Pericles held up his hand for silence. "Let us hear what Phillip has to say." He nodded to the Macedonian. "Speak. Tell us what you think."

Phillip took a deep breath and started again. "We — that is, the disciples of Hippocrates — do not accept the idea that disease is caused by divine anger. Rather, if you observe your patients closely, examine them thoroughly, and watch them carefully as their disease progresses, you will conclude, as we do, that disease is a natural condition which runs its course within a set period of time, independent of the will of the gods."

"Sacrilege! Sacrilege!" Aristides spluttered. "You have condemned us to further suffering!" Others joined in the chorus of accusation.

Phillip struggled to continue. "I mean no disrespect to the gods," he said quickly. "I too believe they influence our lives in many ways, and I pray and sacrifice to them regularly. But in this matter I feel they play no direct role."

"How do you treat your patients, then," Pericles asked, "if not by consulting the oracles and propitiating the gods?"

"In the natural ways my teacher taught me. With proper diet and refreshing drinks. With cool baths if they feel hot. With teas and soups made from herbs. With poultices applied to feverish brows."

Pericles considered this. "And what does your school of Hippocrates say is the cause of a Plague such as ours, if not a visitation from the gods?"

Phillip answered honestly. "I am not certain about this. I can only report my own observations and what truths I've drawn from them, which is what my teacher taught me to do."

"Well," Pericles demanded, "what have you learned?"

"Our patients all have nearly identical physical signs, and their conditions run similar courses. The cause of this disease, therefore, must be attributed to something which is common to all."

"And what might that be?"

Phillip hesitated, then gathered his courage and continued quickly, all in one breath. "The air, which we all breathe. The disease is caused by a corruption of the air." He paused and swept his hand around the city stretched out below. "Look for yourselves. See the clouds of dust and smoke. Can you not smell the stench of dead bodies, the excretions of man and beast, the offal of animal carcasses? The air is polluted. That is the cause of the epidemic."

Pericles and the others said nothing. They continued to gaze down at their beloved city. Several coughed.

Finally, Pericles asked, "What do you call this disease? Have you put a name to it? Is there some way it is commonly known to you healers?"

Phillip nodded. "Some of the victims developed sores on their bodies. . ."

"Yes, yes." The general was impatient. "What is the name?"

"We call it 'anthraka.'"

"'Anthraka'? You mean 'coal'? Anthraka means coal in our language. Is that what you mean?"

"Yes. We have named the disease after the coal-black ulcers which form over the sores. They remind us of a type of coal we call 'anthrakitis.'"

Hippocrates

Little is known about the life of the man who would be called the "Father of Medicine" (figure 6). He was born on the island of Cos in the eastern Aegean, probably around 460 B.C., and died in 370 B.C., about the time Aristotle and Plato were leisurely strolling the vine-covered walks of their Academy. Most of what we know about

Hippocrates comes from his writings, the *Corpus Hippocraticum*, a collection of treatises on almost every aspect of medicine. What is most remarkable about them is their complete absence of magic, the occult, and superstition. Medicine, with one stroke, had entered a rational, an empirical — a naturalist — stage.

Hippocrates was clearly influenced by the Cult of Aesclepius, to which he paid tribute in his famous oath (which I myself recited on graduation from medical school):

> *I swear by Apollo the healer, by Aesclepius,*
> *by health and all the powers of healing. . .*
> *that I will use my power to help the sick to*
> *the best of my ability and judgement.*

Hippocrates also must have learned dietary and herbal treatments at the Aesclepium at Cos. But though he owed this debt to the past, by the time of his death he had lit a revolution in medicine which was to last until the modern age.

Figure 6.
Hippocrates of Cos

Source: National
Library of Medicine

Hippocrates' philosophy was based on several principles. First, as Phillip the fictional Macedonian physician articulated, was the belief that all disease had a natural cause and ran a natural course. By listening to, examining, and otherwise observing his patient, the physician could discover the cause of the disease.

The second principle expanded on the first: man was but a

microcosm of the macrocosm, the universe. And the universe was composed of only four elements: fire, air, earth, water. Man, correspondingly, was composed of four fluids or *humors*: yellow bile, blood, phlegm, black bile. These humors arose from, respectively, the liver, heart, brain and spleen. Disease was an imbalance of these four humors, just as natural catastrophies were imbalances of the four elements. Hippocrates' treatment aimed to restore this imbalance in the body through natural therapies: diet, herbal teas and soups, baths, emetics and cathartics. [The role of the four humors also extended to personality traits, and we still speak of someone as being phlegmatic (phlegm), sanguine (blood), melancholic (black bile) or choleric (yellow bile)].

The humoral theory, refined and continued under Aristotle, remained the dominant medical explanation of disease for over 1,300 years. Ever more violent remedies would be used to restore the supposed disequilibrium of the humors: bleeding, cupping, purging, blistering. It was not until the germ theory of disease emerged under Robert Koch and Louis Pasteur in the mid-19th century that this concept was finally extinguished.

Hippocrates' treatise on *Epidemics* may be the most startling of all the works in the *Corpus Hippocraticum*. Phillip, our imaginary physician, enunciated the basic principle in his meeting with General Pericles:

Whenever many are contemporaneously affected by a single disease, the cause must be attributed to that which is most common and which we all use most.

And what is the thing we "all use most"? It is air, of course. Epidemics must arise from corrupted air, the very air "we all inspire to live." This idea of polluted air as a cause of disease persists in our environmental health laws and in the word "malaria," which means *mal* = bad, *aria* = air: bad air.

What was the Cause of the Plague of Athens?

Can we *retro*-diagnose the past and identify a likely agent for this ancient epidemic? Thucydides would not attempt such a feat, leaving it to "other writers with or without medical experience." But his vivid description of the symptoms points to anthrax as a possible or even likely cause. In fact, all three forms of the disease can be inferred from his description.

The symptoms began with headache, red eyes and sore throat. These were soon followed by sneezing and hoarseness. As the infection descended into the chest, pain and coughing ensued. Stomach aches with vomiting and diarrhea followed. Some patients developed a rash, which was "reddened and livid, breaking out into small pustules and ulcers." High fever and thirst were present. Gangrene of the extremities may have set in. Confusion and loss of memory were common.

The initial flu-like symptoms noted by Thucydides are nearly identical to the ones recorded in the recent U.S. inhalation cases (see Table 1). These symptoms were followed by sudden collapse and death for Athenian patients, just as they were for 5 of the 11 anthrax-by-mail cases in 2001. The gangrene of the extremities described by Thucydides was probably a secondary effect, the result of toxic shock on the body's coagulation system. And the mental confusion, loss of memory, and blindness may have been symptoms of meningitis.

Table 1. *Symptoms in recent U.S. cases and in the Plague of Athens.*

Symptoms	U.S. cases (n=10)	Plague of Athens
Fever, Chills	10	+
Sweats	7	?
Fatigue, lethargy	10	+
Cough	9	+
Nausea/Vomiting	9	+
Shortness of Breath	8	+
Chest Pain	7	+
Muscle Aches	6	+
Headache	5	+
Confusion	4	+
Abdominal Pain	3	+
Sore Throat	2	+
Runny Nose	1	?
Red Eyes	?	+
Sneezing/Hoarseness	?	+

Sweating and runny nose were present in the U.S. cases but not specifically mentioned by Thucydides. Red eyes, sneezing and hoarseness were the only symptoms described by Thucydides not apparent in the 10 U.S. cases.

This course of illness described by Thucydides sounds so similar to the 11 recent cases that one must suspect that anthrax caused the Plague of Athens. The kicked-up dust and smoke from the funeral pyres disseminated the anthrax spores throughout the crowded city. But where did the spores come from in the first place? Where was the epizootic in animals which usually accompanies naturally-occurring anthrax outbreaks and is the source of the bacteria and spores for human epidemics? Thucydides states that animals did die, but they were mostly carrion eaters and birds of prey, not livestock. So where did the spores originate if not from dead and dying animals?

The answer is that the human dead were the source of the spores. Without proper burial outside the city, large numbers of victims rotted in the street. Their decomposing bodies released anthrax bacteria, which quickly turned to spores in the dirt. Even the still-living contributed to the spore load through their bodily discharges. Animals who ate this flesh became ill with the gastrointestinal form of the disease. They then made their own deposits to the growing spore population in their discharges and decomposing flesh.

Finally, the rash described by Thucydides — red with small pustules and ulcers — is a good description of the stages of cutaneous anthrax. Most of the victims with the skin form of the disease probably survived. But others, up to 20%, would have perished when the infection entered the blood stream.

Students of the History of Medicine have argued a number of other candidates for the Plague of Athens. Scarlet fever was a front runner for a time. But the rash in that disease (which I have personally seen many times) looks nothing like Thucydides' description. Furthermore, while large populations can get sick from scarlet fever, very few die from it.

Bubonic plague has also been considered as a cause of the Athenian epidemic. But where are the dead rats? Bubonic plague is primarily a disease of rats and small rodents, whose infection-bearing fleas jump to humans only when they die. There should have been piles of dead rats in the houses and temples of Athens. Thucydides is silent on this. And he's equally silent on the presence of "buboes," the massively swollen and blackened lymph nodes in the groin and armpit from which the disease takes its name. It's not likely Thucydides would have overlooked these findings if they had been present.

An epidemic of influenza has also been suggested as a cause for the Athenian outbreak, one similar in virulence to the world wide pandemic of 1918. But influenza is usually a disease of late fall and winter, not the dead of summer. And while many become ill with influenza, few die, certainly nothing like the 30% or more overall mortality rate suggested by Thucydides for the Plague of Athens. To get past these inconsistencies, proponents of the influenza theory speculate that a *second* epidemic of staphylococcal skin infection took place at the same time as the influenza one. And it was this second epidemic which caused the toxic shock and high mortality rate. But requiring two epidemics of two separate diseases to occur at exactly the same time in order to explain the Plague of Athens strains credulity.

Finally, Ebola virus, a recently recognized killer from central Africa, has been put forth as the cause of the Athenian calamity. This virus is readily disseminated, causes many of the symptoms Thucydides describes, and is very often fatal. But how would such a disease get from central Africa — tropical Africa — to Athens? In every other case where Ebola has jumped continents, there has been a history of a human bite from an infected animal, typically a monkey, which ignites the epidemic. There is no evidence for such a scenario in Athens of 5th century B.C. Furthermore, if it were Ebola, there would have been many more deaths than estimated by Thucydides.

When all these competing theories are judged in the balance of Thucydides' description, then laid against the ruler of known cases of anthrax, *b. anthracis* emerges as a highly probable cause of the Plague of Athens.

The Athenian epidemic smoldered on for another three years. Thousands of sacrifices were made to the gods. Nothing helped. Pericles himself fell victim to the disease in 429 B.C. The Peloponnesian War continued as well, neither side able to gain the decisive edge. Other powers, especially one in the north, waited patiently to step in and fill the political vacuum.

CHAPTER

THE DEATH OF
ALEXANDER THE GREAT, 323 B.C.

Events surrounding the death of this world conquerer are as shrouded in mystery as was his birth. On the night of his nativity, July 23, 356 B.C., the great temple of Artemis at Ephesus, one of the Seven Wonders of the Ancient World, burned to the ground. Legend has it that the goddess was so busy tending to Alexander's birthing that she neglected her own shrine. His death 33 years later spawned two millenia of romantic fiction, debate and speculation.

Alexander ascended the throne of Macedonia at the age of 20 years, following the assassination of his father, King Phillip. In the dozen or so years of life remaining to him, he became *de facto* ruler of Greece, Pharoah of Egypt, Lord of the Persian Empire, and Master of the Indian Punjab. Even as he lay dying, he was planning a grand maritime expedition to Arabia. Like the candle which burns twice as bright but only half as long, he, like his hero and mythical ancestor Achilles, lived fewer years but twice as meteoric ones.

His first task on mounting the Macedonian throne was to put down local rebellions. This was quickly done. Once his supply line and rear echelons were secure, he crossed the Hellespont and invaded Asia in 334 B.C. He was the first one off the leading ship, threw his spear into the beach, and claimed the Empire of Persia his by right of conquest. In two great battles at the Granicus and Issus Rivers, he overwhelmed the forces of King Darius III. Then he marched on to tame Egypt, where he was proclaimed Pharoah in 332 B.C. One final battle remained for control of Persia. On the plains of Gaugamela, not far from the ruins of ancient Nineveh, he destroyed the rest of the Persian army on October 1, 331 B.C. and put Darius to flight.

He next led his men over the Hindu Kush and down into Afghanistan, founding a city there called Ghandara. Today it's known as Kandahar, the second largest Afghan city and southern base for U.S. forces during the Afghan War on Terrorism. He then pushed into Transoxiana, capturing the cities of Samarkand and Bukara, later to become oases on the silk route from China. He finally ended his eastward campaign in the Punjab, where he defeated a force augmented with several hundred war elephants.

All Alexander's battles were so classic in their strategy, so bold in their tactics, that they are still taught at many of the world's leading military academies. Though he sustained many injuries — some life threatening — none, he was proud to say, were to his back. And he often pointed out to his men that he had never lost one of them to a wound sustained while fleeing from the enemy.

Some of his injuries included a head wound when part of his helmet was sheared off at the Granicus; a thigh wound at Issus from a sword thrust; an arrow wound to his leg on the Jaxartes; another head wound from a thrown rock in Sogdiana; and a missile injury to his shoulder in Bactria. His most serious battle injury was a chest wound from an arrow. He coughed up blood and air leaked from the wound. His life was in great peril for many days, but he finally recovered. In addition to his injuries, he suffered several bouts of fever — one with convulsions — sweating sicknesses, and dysentery.

Alexander was versed in the medical arts. His boyhood teacher, the great Aristotle, had learned these from his own father and passed them on to his young student. On campaign, Alexander was often seen tending to his soldiers' wounds, prescribing treatments, and giving advice to the doctors.

What could have taken the life of this incredibly tough, hale and knowledgeable man in the flower of his youth?

Alexander's Last Days

The facts surrounding Alexander's death are few. The most reliable account comes from Flavius Arrianus (90-175 A.D.), a Roman general and governor. He retired from Imperial Service in 138 A.D. and spent his remaining years in Athens as a writer. In addition to his works on Alexander, he wrote a history of Parthia, a history of Bithynia (where he governed), and other books on military matters. Arrian relied heavily on the works of Ptolemy, Alexander's boyhood friend and comrade-in-arms, and Aristobolus, Alexander's chief engineer. None of the campaign descriptions by writers who accompanied Alexander have survived.

Alexander had settled into garrison life in Babylon in the spring of 323 B.C. Though most of King Nebuchadnezzar's ancient splendors were in ruins, the city was still Queen of Asia. Surrounded by massive double walls of brick and bitumen, Alexander had first entered it eight years earlier, marching his troops through the blue-tiled and turreted Ishtar Gate, then parading them down the Processional Way. He had taken Nebuchadnezzar's old palace for his own. It was still resplendent with remnants of the famous Hanging Gardens, which were in fact high-standing artificial terraces planted so thick with trees and shrubs they seemed to hang in the air.

Figure 7. *Alexander and his physician, Phillip*

Source: National Library of Medicine

An omen of Alexander's impending death occurred in early May. He was standing on a dais on the parade ground, shuffling new troops into their assigned regiments. He stepped down briefly to get a drink. At that moment an escaped prisoner mounted the throne and put on the King's royal cloak and diadem. Alexander's aides were thunderstuck. When they regained their wits, they immediately suspected treason. But even under torture the poor man revealed himself to be simply deranged, claiming divine voices had ordered him to commit his prank.

Alexander's final illness began a few weeks later, May 29, with a slight fever, vomiting and abdominal pain. It did not cause much concern either to him or to his doctors. He expected this illness to be over in a few days, just like all the others. And he did seem to improve at first, enough to attend festive banquets the next two nights, where he drank heavily. During the days, he was well enough to meet with his advisors and generals to plan the forthcoming Arabian expedition.

But his condition worsened. From June 2-7 the fevers increased, accompanied by chills and sweats. He remained strong enough to play dice with some of his Companions, however. Later, he was rowed to a park on the far side of the Euphrates, probably the site of Nebuchadnezzar's summer palace. The temperate climate there and frequent cool baths refreshed him.

On June 8, he took a turn for the worse. His fever spiked higher. He was carried back to the main palace. By the next day, he had lost the power of speech. The cause of this new and alarming symptom is uncertain. But it was not due to coma; he remained conscious, still able to make eye contact with his officers and signal his responses to their questions with his hands. He was coughing more now, bringing up bloody sputum. His breathing was raspy and labored. He had lost all color from his face. The end was near.

On the 9th of June, his troops rioted. They had not seen him for 10 days and were concerned he was dead and that it was being kept from them. They were allowed to file past his bed. Though now near death, he was still able to lift his head and gesture to them with his eyes.

The next day, June 10, he died. When Perdicas, his second in command, asked to whom his empire should go, Alexander's last whispered words were, *"hoti to kratisto* — to the strongest."* He left two pregnant wives but no legitimate living heirs. His successors tore his empire apart.

Diagnosing The Final Illness

Alexander The Great may very well have died of inhalation anthrax, a disease little different at that time from the one which would take the life of Bob Stevens in Boca Raton, Florida almost 2300 years later. The King of Macedonia had the same symptoms at the beginning — fever, weakness, chills, sweats — as Bob Stevens and 80% of the other 2001 U.S. cases. And Alexander's abdominal pain and vomiting were shared by 30% and 80% respectively of those recent cases as well.

For two days, from May 30-June 1, Alexander may have been in the honeymoon phase of the disease, the brief interlude between the prodromal symptoms and the start of the final plunge into toxic shock. This feature was not well demonstrated in the 2001 U.S. outbreak, but it has been consistently noted in the reports of many other published cases.

Finally, there was Alexander's loss of speech — known as *aphasia* — two days before his death. This may have been due to profound weakness, or perhaps from a flare-up of the old chest wound which made speech too painful to attempt. It was not because he had slipped into a coma; he remained able to signal his officers through eye and hand movements. This *aphasia* could have been a symptom of anthrax meningitis, which had impaired his motor speech function. Four of the 11 recent U.S. cases, including Bob Stevens, developed confusion and worsening mental changes — some from anthrax meningitis — just like Alexander.

On his last day of life, Alexander developed a cough with bloody or blood-tinged sputum and labored respirations. These soon led to respiratory failure and, along with skin pallor, were harbingers of the final phase of shock. He finally lost consciousness and died in the early morning hours of June 10, 323 B.C.

Competing Theories

The *Royal Diaries* of Alexander, written by his secretary, purport to give a detailed account of the King's last days. They focus on his drinking bouts with friends on May 29 and 30 and speculate that, drunkard that he was, Alexander simply drank himself to death. But in fact he drank no more than usual on those days, certainly no more than his Macedonian companions. And neither acute alcohol poisoning nor the effects of chronic alcoholism fit Arrian's description of his last days.

A modern medical theory has added a new twist to this death-from-drinking scenario. It claims the cause of death was acute pancreatitis, a well-known complication of alcoholism. The theory cites Alexander's behavior during the drinking bout on May 29, when the King drank deeply from a cup, then suddenly "shouted with pain as if he had been struck through the liver by an arrow" (Plutarch says it was a spear). This was supposedly the pain of pancreatitis and an accompanying perforated gastric ulcer. The problem with this theory is that there is no mention of such a pain at any other time during the next 10 days. And with the onset of peritonitis (infection of the lining of the abdominal cavity), which would have been inevitable, the pain would have become excruciating. It would not have been overlooked.

A second myth, promulgated by the *Romance of Alexander*, a popular but mostly fictitious pamphlet published 500 years after his death, claims that Cassander, an ambitious member of the Macedonian Royal Family, had smuggled poison into Babylon concealed in a mule's hoof. He secreted the poison to his brother Iollas, one of the King's cupbearers, who then slipped it into the Royal Wine Cup. While the art of poisoning was well known and well practiced in Alexander's time, the usual ones, hemlock and belladonna, kill quickly, within minutes to a day or two at most. Even strychnine, which can be administered slowly and cause a lingering death — and whose bitter taste is easily camoflauged in wine — doesn't cause a febrile type of illness.

A stronger candidate for Alexander's death, widely held by historians of medicine, is malaria, which he may have picked up during a recent boating trip through some of the swamps around Babylon a few days before his final illness began. The disease worsened, so goes this version of events, and developed one of its most feared complications, *cerebral malaria*. It was this which finally took the King's life. This scenario is a highly attractive alternate explanation to anthrax and deserves to be seriously considered.

Malaria was well known to the ancient Greeks and Persians. In his *Aphorisms*, Hippocrates lists the regular paroxysms of fever so characteristic of the disease. The fevers in modern malaria cases caused by *P. vivax* and *P. ovale* still recur in those same, regular, 2-day cycles (tertian), that of *P. malariae* every three days (quartan). But Alexander's fever never regularized, which would be more typical of malaria's fourth cause, *P. falciparum*.

All four causes of malaria are characterized by many of the symptoms from which Alexander suffered: weakness, lethargy, fever, chills, loss of appetite, even vague abdominal pain. *Vivax, ovale*, and *malariae* forms also cause profound sweating and teeth-chattering chills, sometimes lasting 1-2 hours. These were *not* mentioned in Alexander's case, but such rigors are usually missing from *falciparum* disease, which is another point in its favor.

But the hallmark of cerebral malaria, almost a *sine qua non,* is coma. This usually develops 3-4 days after the onset of initial symptoms and lasts 2-3 days, when death intervenes. This symptom was completely missing from Alexander's clinical course. In fact, right up to his last hours he was alert enough to gesture to his companions and troops. Finally, cerebral malaria is almost always accompanied by seizures, either focal (typically an arm or a leg) or generalized. There is no discription of seizure activity during Alexander's entire course of illness. It could hardly have been missed.

How Might Alexander have been exposed to Anthrax?

If Alexander died of inhalation anthrax, how was he exposed to the spores? He may have inhaled them purely by accident. He was by nature restless and inquisitive and looked after every aspect of his army's well being. On an inspection tour, for example, his horse might simply have stirred up some spore-laden dust in a field where a cow or sheep had died of the disease. But a serendipitous encounter like this with the spores seems unlikely. And except for sacrificial duties, he had little or no contact with animal care or slaughter, with their shearing or skinning, with food preparation, or with the production of wool or hair products.

He also may have been *deliberately* exposed to the disease. Murder by spores. Regicide by anthrax. This presumes, of course, that there was contemporary knowledge that anthrax *can* be transmitted from animals to man. But that's not too big a stretch either.

The first unequivocal description of the spread of anthrax between beasts and man can be found in the writings of Virgil (70-19 B.C.), the Roman poet, writer and scientist. Virgil is most famous for his epic poem, *The Aeneid*, a tale of the wanderings of Aeneas after the fall of Troy. But he also wrote poetry about the countryside (*Bucolics*) and treatises on agriculture (*Georgics*). In his 3rd Georgic, penned about 25 B.C., he writes in great detail about a plague in the Roman Alpine district of Noricum. From his careful description of the symptoms in sheep, cattle, oxen, horses and swine, it is clear this was a large epizootic of anthrax. In horses, for example, he records that in the later stages of the disease their breathing was "labored and groaning and. . .a dark bloody discharge appeared at their nostrils." And in the ox near the end, "blood mixed with froth issued from his mouth as he groaned his last."

Virgil also noted that the risk of illness to humans in contact with pelts or hair from these sick animals was great:

> *The pelts of diseased animals were useless, and neither water nor fire could cleanse the taint from their flesh. The sheepmen could not shear the fleece, which was riddled with disease and corruption, nor did they dare even to touch the rotting strands.*

> *If anyone wore a garment made from tainted wool, his limbs were soon attacked by inflamed blisters and a foul exudate, and if he delayed too long to remove the material, a violent inflammation consumed the parts it had touched.*

This is as perfect a description of how animal anthrax spreads to man as can be found anywhere in the scientific literature until Robert Koch identified the bacterial cause of the disease over 1900 years later.

But Virgil's description of the Plague of Noricum wasn't recorded until 200 years *after* Alexander's death. Was knowledge of the transmission of anthrax known *before* this time, knowledge one of Alexander's contemporaries might use to kill the King? It is possible. Scientifically-proveable knowledge always lags well behind folk knowledge. Housewives knew that certain plants and molds were therapeutically helpful in febrile illnesses long before Fleming discovered penicillin. And it was common knowledge that water from certain sources was poisonous well before the germ theory of disease was developed in the 19th century. Alexander and his physicians knew that boiling such water rendered it potable. The Kings of Persia had always drunk boiled water and Alexander was no exception.

Finally, farmers in Alexander's time must have know about the spread of anthrax to humans from the hides, pelts and hair of diseased animals. They would know this because they would have observed it centuries before Virgil wrote it down. They would have known it from *empirical* knowledge, from trial and error, from personal observation.

What was the motive for killing Alexander?

All killers must have a weapon, an opportunity, and a motive for their homocides. Who would have the greatest motive to kill Alexander, knowledge of how to use anthrax to do it, and the opportunity to get close enought to the King to carry it out? The list is not long. Court intrigues and assassinations were as much a part of the Macedonian Royal Court as was warfare. Alexander had detected and foiled several plots already. But these treasons would have been carried out with cold steel, not through such a devious means as anthrax. Still, the lust for power is a powerful motive for regicide.

But there is an even stronger motive: love. It is no secret that passion can motivate murder. It was no different for Alexander. And one who loved him more than most, one who was passionately *in love* with him, was Bagoas, the Persian Boy.

Admired for his beauty and castrated soon after his father's murder by King Darius III, Bagoas's early life had been the wretched existence of a sexual slave. Taken as a lover by Darius, he accompanied the Royal Household on campaign against the Macedonian invaders. Then disaster struck, the crushing Persian defeat at Guagamela, Darius' craven flight, and his subsequent murder by his own nobles. Trembling, Bagoas was brought before Alexander as a spoil of war. His looks, gentleness, and skill as a dancer got him admitted first to the Royal Table, then to the Royal Bed. But as he found his way into Alexander's heart, his own was conquered by an intimacy he had withheld from all others.

Never far from Alexander's side during seven years of adventure and campaigning, Bagoas brought some of the gentling Persian refinements to the rough Macedonian Court: trousers, for one, which Alexander's grizzled veterans thought sissified; the wearing of the tiara by the King for another; and the practice of *proskynesis* — kowtowing — before Alexander for a third.

Bagoas had seen rivals for Alexander's affection come and go. Barsine, the wild concubine taken after the Battle of Issus and impregnated by Alexander with a bastard son, had been left to wither in the harem. A more serious competitor was Roxane, daughter of a Sogdian baron Alexander had married from passion and for political ends as well. Though dismissed from the Royal Bed shortly after the honeymoon, she remained a dangerous and veteran schemer. Worse, she was pregnant.

But Bagoas's greatest rival had always been Hephaestion, Alexander's boyhood friend, constant companion, and lover. Hephaestion had first endured Bagoas with difficulty, then had come to a silent detente with him. When Hephaestion died the previous summer, Bagoas thought he would have clear sailing. He was wrong.

Alexander was more profoundly affected by Hephaestion's death than Bagoas could have imagined. Even after days and days of grieving, the King remained inconsolate, rejecting Bagoas's tenderness, bereft of his usual lusty libido. When he finally did come to his senses, he turned not to his Persian lover but to the therapy of frenetic activity, consuming himself with plans for the new Arabian adventure. He had no time for Bagoas, whose duties in the Bath and Bedchamber — his exclusive domain until now — were taken over by pages and other eunuchs. This hole in Bagoas's heart initially caused depression and despair. But when Stateira, Darius's daughter and Alexander's new wife, showed up pregnant as well, his despair turned to jealous rage. If he could not have Alexander, no one would! He waited until the time was ripe, then acted. "Each man kills the thing he loves," Oscar Wilde wrote. Though not a complete man, it was probably no different for a eunuch.

From his years in the Persian court, Bagoas would have been familiar with the Black Arts. It would have been easy to obtain a sheepskin cloak or rug from an animal known to have died of anthrax and whose shearers and weavers had also succumbed to it. Feigning ill health, Bagoas could have had one of the Royal Pages innocently deliver the object to Alexander, who paid little attention to his personal attire or furnishings. Even washed and clean-appearing wool and sheepskin pelts can be deadly, loaded with thousands of invisible anthrax spores adherent to their fibers. All Bagoas had to do was wait until the disease ran its course. It didn't take long.

After Alexander's death, Bagoas, never suspected in the murder, is lost to history, though he may have found refuge at the court of Ptolemy of Egypt, one of the Successors. (For a fuller, if fictional, account of this intriguing character, see Mary Renault's *The Persian Boy).*

Alexander's generals, obedient to him in life, were true to his orders in death. They fought with one another over his empire for years. No one of them emerged victorious, but several became great kings and founders of dynasties in the conquered lands. Ptolemy, one of the seven Royal Bodyguards, ruled in Egypt and was followed by an unbroken line of successors until the last of them, Queen Cleopatra, was defeated by Octavian Caesar at the battle of Actium in 30 B.C.

Seleucus, Commander of the Shield Bearers, seized the remains of the old Persian empire. Antigonus the One Eyed, one of Alexander's 23 governors, extended his power from his province of Phrygia into all of Asia Minor. And Antipater, Alexander's Viceroy in Macedonia, was succeeded by his son, the cruel and rapacious Cassander, in 319 B.C. He ruled Greece for another twenty years.

Alexander's death gave birth to the Hellenistic age, a 300-year period known for its extension to the ancient East of Greek art and architecture, Greek ideas and culture, and, above all, the Greek love of learning. Only the tramp of Roman boots would crush this lamp of enlightenment, supplanting it with those more practical adjuncts of power, law, engineering, and medicine.

C H A P T E R 7

THE BLACK DEATH, 1346–1350

In London, the children in the square danced round and round singing their new nursery rhyme:

Ring around a rosie
A Pocket full of posies
Ashes, ashes,
All fall down!

In Florence, the writer Giovanni Boccaccio and his ten wealthy young friends hurried across the piazza of the Cathedral of Santa Maria del Fiore, renamed the "Piazza del Duomo" when Brunelleschi completed the Cathedral's mighty dome a century later. The piazza was a fearsome place this day. Many Florentines, too ill themselves to give their deceased family members proper burials, simply dragged the corpses into the street and left them there to be picked up later. Carts bearing these dead souls creaked back and forth over the cobblestones day and night. Citizens, herbal "posies" pressed to their faces, gave them wide berths.

But garlic amulets could not keep out the stench from the diseased bodies, some still warm, their steaming vapors mixing with the early morning sun and the mist from the river in a kaleidoscopic miasma. Not even the pink glow of sunrise on Giotto's newly-completed Campanille, nor the Romanesque facade of the octagonal-shaped Babtistry — later immortalized with Ghiberti's bronze doors — could lift the city's spirits today.

For the year was 1347, and the Black Death — bubonic plague — had come to Florence.

"We must hasten," Boccaccio urged his friends. "There is no time to lose. It may already be too late for us."

"What of our families?" asked Catherine, a teenage beauty, through her tears. "How can we just abandon them?"

"They are already dead," Boccaccio's cousin Pietro hissed, "or soon will be. And so shall we be if we remain in the city any longer."

Their belongings and supplies loaded onto rough carts, the little troop made its way down the Via dei Calzaiuoli. As they passed the Via degli Speziali, new smells greeted them, wafting over from the Piazza della Republica, site of the old marketplace. There, butchers slaughtered pigs, sheep, goats and cattle and piled the meat high on wooden planks, dumping the offal into the gutters next to the remnants of the bloody animal hides thrown out from the nearby tanneries.

The little band paused at the Piazza della Signoria, the city's governmental center and site of the city hall. One day this would become the most famous square in Florence, where the monk Savonarola would hurl his worldly possessions into a "bonfire of the vanities," then be hanged and burned by the mob himself. Today, the piazza was deserted. Even the windows and doors of the Palazzo Vecchio, where the city's guild leaders regularly met, were closed and shuttered tight.

It was now but a short walk to the Ponte Vecchio, the new bridge over the River Arno. The group picked its way past more butcher shops on the bridge and then was finally across, climbing up to their villa in the green Tuscan hills. The fresh air and scent of spring flowers cleansed their senses of the sights and smells of death.

"We may be here for many months," Pietro warned. "We have few books and will have no music for our entertainment. How shall we amuse ourselves?"

"We will tell stories to each other," Boccaccio said.

"What kinds of stories?"

"Stories of adventure. Stories of love and romance."

"Stories of chastity undone," Catherine said, blushing scarlet.

"Exactly. Stories to raise our spirits. They will take our minds off the pestilence." He considered his next request. "I want ten stories from each of you, one per night. And I will write them all down."

"What will you call it, Giovanni?" someone asked.

"What else? *The Decameron*."

That night, Boccaccio began his new work. *The Decameron* would mark him as one of three giants of the Italian Literary Renaissance (the others were Petrarch and Dante). In telling his 100 profane tales, Boccaccio helped wrest literature away from the exclusive domain of the Church, where it had languished for almost a thousand years.

In the introduction to the *Decameron*, Boccaccio penned a vivid description of the plague as he had witnessed it. There is none better. He noted first the "tumors" in the groin or armpit, some of which grew as large as apples. These must have been the "buboes," infected lymph nodes from which the disease took one of its names, "bubonic". ("Bubo" derives from a Greek word for groin.) Boccacio also noted other characteristic signs of the disease: "the black spots, or livid. . .on the arms, thighs or elsewhere, now few and large, now minute and numerous." This rash, red in the center with a ring of blisters, was the 'ring around a rosie' of the children's nursery rhyme.

Boccaccio had also witnessed firsthand some of the plague's other signs and symptoms: raging fevers, bloody vomitus, bloody diarrhea. The raspy wet cough which led to respiratory failure. The collapse into shock from septicemia, often with meningitis. And finally, quickly, death.

What Boccaccio couldn't have known was that all this death and misery was caused by a tiny, unseen bacterium. It would be named, centuries later, *yersinia pestis,* after a colleague of Louis Pasteur's (Alexandre Yersin, 1863-1943) who discovered it. Although the name itself, the Black Death, was thought by later writers to refer to the infected lymph nodes which turned black and gangrenous, the word may not have referred to either color or symptom. Rather the term "black" may have been used in the sense of awful, dreadful, calamitous.

Yersinia Pestis

There are only two bacteria capable of causing the massive number of cases of fever, cough, septic shock, a fulminant course and the high mortality rate that occurred during the Black Death (one-third of the population of Europe perished from it). One is anthrax. The other is bubonic plague. The two bacteria share other characteristics. Both are primarily diseases of animals, zoonoses, where man is only a serendipitous victim. Both organisms cause skin lesions which, in their end stages, look somewhat alike. And both can kill by blood stream spread: sepsis.

But there are so many differences between the two organisms and the two diseases that it is now relatively easy to differentiate them clinically as well as in the laboratory. It was not so in the past.

Yersinia pestis is a small gram-negative bacillus. This means it stains red, not blue, like anthrax. Also unlike anthrax, it has no spore form. It cannot survive for long outside a living host. When the host dies, it must find another one quickly or it too will perish. It relies on its vector — the rat flea — to make this transition for it. Also unlike anthrax, plague lacks a powerful killing toxin. It kills instead by over-whelming the patient by spreading through the body.

Plague is primarily an infection of small mammals. In cities, its principal reservoir is the black rat, *rattus rattus.* In the countryside, other animals serve as reservoirs: ground squirrels, gerbils, mice, guinea pigs and even prairie dogs, badgers and foxes. When there is human over-crowding, plague may spread to domesticated animals such as cats and dogs and maybe to an occasional pig or sheep. But plague is *not* a disease of livestock in the field.

When its animal host dies, the blood-sucking flea carries the plague to a new one. It bites it to obtain a blood meal, then deposits the plague bacteria at the bite site. Symptoms begin within a couple of days, or sooner, with small fluid-filled blisters which teem with plague organisms. The infection then spreads into the lymph system, typi-cally with red streaks flaring away from the bite site (Figure 8). This is called *lymphangitis.* Sometimes the blisters break and healing begins at this point, leading to the formation of a leathery scab. These cases are the lucky few. In most patients, a ring of vesicles forms around the inflamed bite site. These coalesce, then invade deeper into the skin to form a carbuncle. From this point, three distinct clinical outcomes are possible.

<u>Bubonic Plague.</u> Within a few hours from the time the carbuncle develops, or even at the same time, the infection is carried to lymph nodes nearest the flea bite site, typically in the groin, the armpit or the neck. Massive swelling, often egg-sized, occurs as the lymph nodes are overtaken by infection and become boggy with pus, hemorrhage and plague bacteria (Figure 9). The skin overlying the lymph nodes becomes black and gangrenous. The pain is intense, and depending

on which lymph nodes are involved, the patient's gait or posture may be affected: if in the groin, there is a marked limp; if in the armpit, the person involuntarily splints that limb; if in the neck, the head is held to the opposite side. If the infection remains localized to the lymph nodes, healing may occur at this point. But it usually does not (less than 10% of the time). It most often proceedes to the next phase.

Septicemic Plague. Here, the bacteria gain access to the blood stream, which carries them to all parts of the body. When the blood vessels are effected, shock intervenes, septic shock. This signals the beginning of the end, usually within a few days. The mortality rate for this form of the disease is appallingly high, 80-90% if untreated.

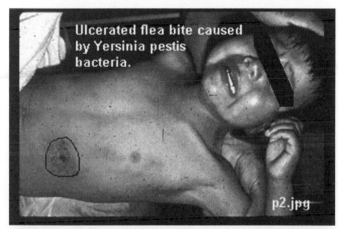

Figure 8.
Early bubonic plague

Source: CDC

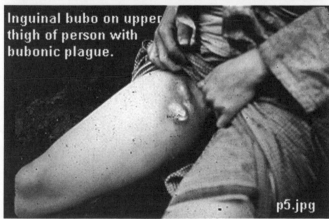

Figure 9.
Plague bubo

Source: CDC

Pneumonic Plague. This is the most feared form. During the septic phase, bacteria are carried to the lungs. There they cause pneumonia, with all its typical symptoms: high fever, chills, sweats, sneezing and coughing productive of bloody mucous. While the other forms of plague are not communicable from person to person, the pneumonic form is, through airborne droplet spread, or from sputum-contaminated clothing, towels, bed linen, etc. But this contagious spread only occurs if there is very close contact between people, i.e. among household or family members, or between other intimate contacts. This would not have been much of a requirement in the over-crowded conditions of most medieval cities. And a famine which spread through Europe from 1345-1350 might have further lowered the population's resistance to the infection. It is this contagious form of the disease — the "pneumonic" — which is thought to have caused the majority of deaths and the rapid spread of the disease during the middle ages.

Though an ancient and medieval disease, plague still occurs in large outbreaks even today. India had 10 million deaths from it early in the 20th century. In the 1960s and 1970s, Vietnam became the leading source of the disease, with 10,000 cases reported annually. More recently, the World Health Organization reported 18,739 cases in 20 countries between 1980-1994. Plague is even reported in the United States, about 13 cases per year from 1979-1998, with a high of 40 cases in 1983. U.S. cases occur most frequently in American Indians and in other rural dwellers. This is because urban plague has been wiped out by rat control, whereas the sylvatic rodent population maintains the infection in the countryside.

European Epidemics before the Black Death

Between the anthrax-caused Plague of Noricum described by Virgil in 25 B.C. and the Black Death 13 centuries later, Europe suffered through several other epidemics. All occurred in what was then the Roman Empire and may have contributed to its ultimate decline and fall.

The first of these great outbreaks took place in 79 A.D., shortly after the destruction of Pompeii by Mt. Vesuvius. An estimated 10,000 persons died in the Campagna area alone, accompanied by large scale destruction of livestock. This plague, like the Plague of Noricum, was most likely caused by anthrax.

The next epidemic was the Plague of Antoninus during the years

164-189 A.D. It is also known as the Plague of Galen because of that physician's vivid description of the symptoms: high fever, sore throat, raging thirst, and diarrhea. The skin lesions were unlike those of either bubonic plague or anthrax. Galen described them as small, red, sometimes dry, sometimes pustular. In many cases, the patient died even before the rash appeared. This epidemic defies diagnosis, though smallpox is a leading candidate. The epidemic soon spread to the Eastern provinces, where the legions guarding the frontier were affected. It took the life of the Philosopher-Emperor Marcus Aurelius.

Seventy-five years later, in the year 250 A.D., the Plague of Cyprian broke out. Cyprian was Archbishop of Carthage, and he made an effort to list the symptoms: diarrhea, vomiting, sore throat, fever, and gangrene of the hands and feet. There was no rash, nor did he report any increased livestock deaths. It's unlikely this epidemic was either bubonic plague or anthrax. Scarlet fever and toxic shock syndrome are two of the diagnoses put forth for it, but it's probably best to leave this one undiagnosed also.

In 542 A.D. the Great Plague of Justinian started in the Eastern Roman Empire (the Western branch had long since collapsed). This epidemic lasted only four months, but there were an estimated 10,000 deaths per day during the period. Of great importance to historians, this is the first large-scale outbreak which can be diagnosed with some certainty: because of the clear description of "buboes" associated with it, it is thought to have been bubonic in origin.

For the next 800 years Europe remained free of plague. Until the Black Death in 1346. After that, there were recurrent lesser outbreaks in the 14th and 15th centuries, and one massive one, the Plague of London in 1665-6. This was most likely bubonic plague. No further European outbreaks are recorded after that. Why they suddenly ceased has been a continuing source of mystery to historians. One biologist, Hans Zinsser, in his famous book, *Rats, Lice and History,* thinks the plague outbreaks stopped simply because there was a change in the relationship between the rat, the flea, and man. Perhaps, due to climate, humidity, increased flooding, fewer fires — or whatever — the rats became fewer, the fleas less active, or the humans more resistant. Whatever the cause, it must have changed both the clinical and epidemiological manifestations of the disease, resulting in the sharp drop in outbreaks.

Cause and Treatment

Most medieval writers viewed the Black Death as a corruption of the air, the old Hippocratic notion of a "miasma". This corruption, presumably originating from the diseased and decaying bodies of the sick, was then breathed in by those still well. And the nose lent credence to this theory; the stench from rotting corpses and their excretions must have been staggering. No amount of herbs, flowers or sweet-smelling ointments could prevent this corrupted air from gaining access to the body. Once inside, the infection unbalanced the equilibrium of the four humors, the other old Greek medical idea which had persisted into medieval times.

Diagnosis was based on examination of the patient's blood, urine, stool and sputum. This told the physician which of the four humors was out of balance. Bleeding, purging, emetics, leeches, cupping and blistering were then used to restore the equilibrium. Blood letting was usually done by barber-surgeons. The barber's symbol, a red and white spiral-striped pole, is a hold-over from those sanguinous times.

The Black Death was also blamed on a medical idea even more ancient than the theory of the four humors: divine anger. Punishment from God for mortal sin. But instead of sacrificing animals like the Greeks, some medieval citizens whipped themselves into a frenzy of self-flagellation. This was intended to expiate their sins and free the world of the pestilence. Roving bands of ragged, bleeding Flagellants wandered the roads of Europe. Initially, the Church approved of their religious zeal. But the movement turned revolutionary, went out of control, and directed its energy against wealthy landowners and the Church itself. A Papal Bull against self-flagellation was published in 1349. The movement was brutally suppressed thereafter.

Another target for blame were those perennial scapegoats and outcasts, Jews, lepers and gypsies. Jews were accused of poisoning city water supplies and were harshly treated. At Basle and Freiberg, all Jews that could be identified were hunted down and killed, some by stoning, others burned alive. In Strassbourg, 2,000 were hanged.

Two positive health care developments emerged from the horrors of the Black Death. The first was the rise of city hospitals. Prior to this time, medical treatment centers — like everything else — were controlled by the Church. But starting in the 13th century, city governments built and operated their own facilities. The most famous of these, the Hotel-Dicu in Paris, treated thousands of patients during the Black Death.

The second development was in the area of prevention. It began in Venice in 1374. Instead of simply closing the city's gates to *all* travelers during plague years, which seriously restricted trade, the Venetians appointed officials to inspect and sequester any visitor from a town or region known to have the infection. These officials were also empowered to bar infected ships from Venetian ports. The term of confinement was set at forty days, *quaranti giorni* in Italian. From this early beginning comes the modern pubic health technique — and the word — "quarantine."

Where did the Black Death Originate?

Gabriel de Mussis, a contemporary Italian notary, claimed it started in the Genoese port of Kaffa in the Crimea (modern Feodisiya), though his credibility is compromised by the fact that he never left the comfort of his villa in Piazenza, Italy. In 1334 Genoa had developed this port into a major trading center. It soon became a serious Asian rival to Constantinople, and it was not long before its wealth and creature comforts were hungrily coveted by Mongols of the Golden Horde. In 1346, led by Khan Yanibeg, they besieged the walled city. But the defenses held, and a plague broke out among Yanibeg's troops.

Enraged by his failure to take the city, the Khan abandoned his efforts, but not before catapulting his dead soldiers over the walls in retribution. This may have been history's first documented case of attempted biological warfare.

Though the defenders hastily disposed of the Mongol bodies by dumping them into the sea, plague broke out in the city nonetheless. The Genoese quickly took to their ships. *Rattus rattus,* and presumably its plague-infected fleas, went along for the ride, perhaps comfortably ensconced in a bag of grain or a bale of cotton goods. The ships' first port of call was Constantinople, which reported the presence of plague in 1347. Then by sea again, it spread to Egypt and Italy, where it made appearances in 1347-1348. It exploded across Europe in 1348 also, finally leaping the English Channel and showing up in Britain in 1349, where it continued into the following year.

This is the standard theory for the origin and spread of the Black Death. It's been held as sacred as an icon by historians. But like mosquitoes buzzing around on a hot summer evening, there's a swarm of questions surrounding it.

The first is how the Genoese actually got the plague from the dead Mongol troopers. The rat flea, *Xenopsylla cheopis*, doesn't stay long on a dead host; it seeks a new, warmer one almost immediately, one able to provide it with another blood meal. It was demonstrated in a classic experiment over 100 years ago that people are only at risk of infection by contact with living or *recently-dead* rats; they are safe if the rat has been dead for more than a day. The same is probably true for dead people. In short, a human cadaver, like a dead rat, poses little risk for anyone else. *Yersinia pestis* dies very soon after its host does. Even if the Mongol soldiers had died of bubonic plague, their only risk to the Genoese would have been the fleas they carried. And while those fleas might have bitten a city dweller, it's more than likely they would have left the Mongol corpse even before it was catapulted over the walls or soon after. Now, if Yanibeg had sent over flea-infected living *rats*, not dead men, that would have been another matter.

In summary, it's unlikely the Khan deserves credit as history's first biological warrior. The plague in Kaffa, if it was bubonic, was probably started the old-fashioned way: flea-infested rats carried the disease into the city themselves.

But that begs the question: how did the disease then spread from Kaffa to the rest of Europe? Some infected fleas might have traveled in merchandise with the Genoese as they fled, then infected the person who unpacked the goods. But that would only cause, at most, a few sporadic cases. Unless those fleas quickly found a new rat population — their favorite hosts — in which to start an epizootic, it's difficult to see how the disease would spread much further.

A distinguished historian, David Herlihy, and an eminent zoologist, Graham Twigg, have raised other questions about the standard theory for the origin of the Black Death. In his book *The Black Death and the Transformation of the West*, Herlihy contends that since plague-bearing fleas will not leave the rat until it dies, the human epidemic should have been preceded by an epizootic in rats. Dead rats should have been piled high in every doorway, gutter and privy. They were not, whereas in more recent and better-studied epidemics in China and India, human plague was *always* preceded by large numbers of rat deaths. An old Indian saying goes, "when the rats begin to fall, it is time for people to leave their houses." In other words, when the rats start dying, get out! The plague is coming.

Furthermore, Herlihy argues, if rats were the spreaders of the plague, there should have been massive rat migrations observed all across Europe. But there were no reports of such migrations. Therefore, how did the epidemic spread faster among the human population than it can spread among the rats themselves? For even if rat colonies were contiguous all across Europe — border to border — the disease would have had to spread as much as 2 to 5 miles per day among the rats, an incredible rate since rats are not known travelers to begin with.

Another unanswered question is how the disease continued to spread through the winter months. Medieval travel by both man and rat was considerably restricted during that season, even in normal times. Could humans have spread the disease to others from their own fleas? Not likely. Studies of modern plague epidemics have shown that the human flea seldom if ever spreads the disease from person to person.

Proponents of the standard theory contend that none of these questions is germane because you don't need rats or their fleas for the Black Death to spread like wildfire. Just a few to get the epidemic started. After that, it can be transmitted from person to person through its pneumonic form, through airborne droplets. No rats or fleas, just a lot of infected coughers and sneezers. But this argument falls apart from within. While such contagious spread might occur within a family or a village, where the close contacts required might be expected, it's a big stretch to imagine infected persons traveling all through Europe in the space of a few years, coughing, sneezing and spreading the disease as they dragged themselves along. Twigg, in his book *The Black Death: A Biological Reappraisal*, admits that pneumonic cases may have initiated a fresh epidemic by droplet spread. But this means of transmission is rare and only occurs under exceptional conditions of temperature and humidity, none of which was present during the middle ages.

If the Black Death wasn't caused by bubonic plague, what did cause it? Twigg, who studied the biology of plague vectors extensively, offers up the startling opinion that it was . . .anthrax! This view has been largely dismissed by historians. But Twigg makes a fair case for it by focusing particularly on the skin lesions of the disease. The rash described by Boccaccio and others could as easily have been the cutaneous form of anthrax as of plague. And a carbuncle is a carbuncle is a carbuncle, whether it's caused by staph, plague or anthrax bacteria. Even the word "bubo," the *sine qua non* for the Black Death, had a different meaning in medieval times than it does today. In the 14th century, the term was more likely to denote pustules or boils, perhaps even the malignant pustule of anthrax. Even the red rash — "livid," Boccaccio described it — and the "ring around the rosie," may have been a freckle-like spotted rash rather than the vesicles of plague.

Twigg also contends there was an epizootic of anthrax in sheep, cattle and other livestock during the years of the Black Death. Such an animal outbreak has invariably accompanied or preceded other human anthrax epidemics. Twigg cites many reports of "murrains" in cattle and sheep during the Black Death. For example, Henry Knighton, a Canon of the Church at Leicester, England in 1349, noted that

> *a murrain of sheep occurred throughout the realm. . .*
> *5,000 sheep died in a single pasture. . .*
> *no animal or bird would touch them. . .*

An account from a German monastery reported that wolves feared to feed on the flesh of dead livestock, presumably because they sensed the presence of infection. Again, the monks of a Cathedral priory at Christchurch, England, claimed to have lost 275 oxen, 511 cows, and 4585 sheep to the great pestilence of 1350. Reports from Denmark and Germany also noted plague in both men and animals during the years 1348-1350. It was probably anthrax.

No less a distinguished historian than Norman F. Cantor, one of the preeminent medievalists, has also accepted Twigg's hypothesis that the Black Death was caused, at least in large measure, by anthrax rather than bubonic plague. In his book, *In The Wake of The Plague,* Perennial

Press, 2001, Cantor says of Twigg's work:

This is the most important book, by a British Zoologist, ever published on the biomedical history of the Black Death. I cannot see how anyone who has read this book carefully can persist in believing that the Black Death was exclusively bubonic plague. How much it was anthrax, as Twigg believed, is moot, but it is likely that anthrax or some similar murrain (cattle disease) was involved (p. 228).

Cantor also buttresses the anthrax argument with some evidence of his own. He cites a paper read by Edward I. Thompson about an archaelogical dig near Edinburgh in 1989. A mass grave for Black Death victims was unearthed near a medieval hospital. Anthrax spores were found in the hospital's cesspool, into which human waste must have been dumped. Thompson also noted the large number of monasteries which reported diseased cattle herds at this time, which is consistent with a murrain of anthrax.

Cantor further notes, from another communication he received, that the island of Iceland was also affected by the Black Death in the 14th century. But this was 300 years before rats first appeared on the island. The disease was probably anthrax instead.

Finally, the spread of anthrax from livestock to humans was doubtless facilitated by the fact that in medieval times animals frequently shared a dwelling with people. In one extreme example from Britain, 12 adults and 3 children shared three rooms with 4 buffaloes, 6 bulls, 1 goat, 1 cat, 1 dog, and 3 chickens!

Summary

Can we conclude that the Black Death of 1346-1350 was or was not caused exclusively by bubonic plague? Or that it was started by history's first episode of biological warfare, Yanibeg's catapulted troopers? Has history gotten it wrong all these years? Was it really *yersinia pestis* which devastated medieval Europe, or was it *bacillus anthracis?* These questions must remain unanswered. One alternative explanation for the epidemic has been offered: anthrax. And it deserves due consideration.

Whatever its bacterial cause, the Black Death led to both short-lived and long-term economic and social consequences. Boccaccio would have noticed some of them immediately when he returned to

Florence later that year, beginning with a general break down in law and order characterized by increased numbers of bandits roaming the countryside. He might even have had trouble getting into his own city, so xenophobic and fearful had the Florentines become.

Once inside, the most immediate change he would have noticed would have been the absence of so many of his friends, family and neighbors: fully one-third to one-half the population had died. The loss of the neighborhood butcher, grocer, mason, constable or priest would have been quickly felt, as would the loss of the services they provided.

The poet Petrarch (1304-74) wrote letters and made woodcuts about the epidemic. He lost Laura, the love of his life and the inspiration for much of his poetry, to the disease in 1348. He despaired that future generations would not believe how much the Black Death had disrupted his society. These generations would not see the abandoned houses, the empty towns and villages, the fields littered with dead. They would not feel the frustration and impotence of doctors unable to treat the sick or halt the spread of the pestilence.

Economically, there was complete paralysis during the years of the Black Death. Trade came to a halt. Farms were left unworked, stores untended by merchants. Prices plummeted; there was no one left to buy the finished goods. Labor costs increased due to the shortage of manpower. This decrement of so much of the work force kept food scarce — and costly — for years. And feudal lords who expected the same services for the same pay after the plague as they had gotten before it, were met only with spiraling wage demands or smoldering resentment. These led, in turn, to riots like the Peasants Revolt in Britain in 1381.

Some historians speculate that the continuing manpower shortage from the Black Death triggered the development of labor-saving devices like the steam engine centuries later. This new technology would ultimately power the Industrial Revolution and usher in the modern era. It would also usher in a new version of anthrax: Woolsorter's Disease.

C H A P T E R

THE INDUSTRIAL REVOLUTION, PUBLIC HEALTH, AND WOOLSORTER'S DISEASE: PART I

The end of the 18th century and the beginning of the 19th witnessed great changes in the economic and political make-up of Europe and the New World. The rights of the common man *vis-a-vis* the state, spawned in England by the *Magna Carta* six centuries earlier, now matured to full bloom in the French and American Revolutions. Britain was the nursery for another revolution as well. Less bloody, less dramatic, it was no less important for the future: the Industrial Revolution, the period when hand tools gave way to powered machines.

The name itself — "Industrial Revolution" — was coined by the Frenchman Jerome Blanqui in 1837. In addition to its marvelous inventions and big new machines, it also sired a new economic idea: capitalism. This doctrine was then used to justify the process of industrialization. It was a time of excesses: of great wealth and grinding poverty; of corpulence and starvation. These excesses and ill-gotten gains led to political reaction in the form of liberalism and socialism. Public Health emerged, diseases of workers were studied, and the discipline of epidemiology was born.

One of the illnesses spawned by industrialization was Woolsorter's Disease. It has the distinction of being history's first well studied and effectively controlled epidemic of occupational illness. It is caused by anthrax. Woolsorter's Disease proved to be a triumph for epidemiology and public health. But this achievement couldn't have taken place without corresponding improvements in medicine in general and in occupational medicine in particular.

The Wealth of Nations

The Industrial Revolution was born and grew to maturity in Britain. The reasons for this are as many and as varied as those which gave birth to democracy in Athens or to the Renaissance in Florence. First, the defeat of Napolean in 1815 allowed Britain to shift from a war-footing to one of trade and industry. And technological innovations which had been quietly going on for almost a century, especially in the textile industry, had now finally begun to return profits on their investments. In 1733, for example, a new "flying shuttle" was invented which required only one person instead of two to operate a loom. Then, in 1760, the Spinning Jenny came into use, a mechanized spinning wheel on which several threads could be spun at once, markedly improving efficiency and reducing labor costs. By 1780, Mr. James Watt's steam engine was being manufactured in quantity and adapted to a variety of industrial applications. One of these was steam-driven spinning. In 1800, the complete power loom was developed. It replaced hand labor altogether. It was faster, never tired, and never got sick.

Britain's Industrial Revolution extended well beyond the factory door. Improved methods were required to haul raw materials to the factory and take finished products to market. The country's entire transportation system had to be expanded and modernized. And it was. By 1850 there were over 20,000 miles of good roads and 5,000 miles of river-canal routes. And during the one decade from 1840-1850, 6,000 miles of railroad track were opened as well, almost half the mileage of all of Europe combined, and nearly as much as the United States opened during the same decade.

Beyond her own borders, Britain pursued the development of new markets with the rifle and the sword, and with the support of a government which was composed of men favorably disposed toward industrialism. Expansion of trade was often accompanied by territorial conquest and colonization. The British Empire, given the green light under Queen Victoria, roared into being like a lion rampant. British soldiers were used to protect the new markets and develop others. All that was needed now was an economic philosophy to justify the industrial expansion. A Scotsman would provide one.

Adam Smith (1723-1790)

In 1776, this scholarly writer from just north of Edinburgh published a treatise on economics which would influence governmental policies around the world well into the present era. Only the *Communist Manifesto*, published 75 years later in 1848, would have anything like the same effect. Smith titled his work *The Wealth of Nations*, and he maintained that such wealth could best be achieved by eliminating all restrictions on trade and all regulations on industry. Keep the government out of business — *laissez faire* economics, we call it today. Allow men of vision to pursue their own self-serving goals, and the general wealth of the country would inexorably increase. Capitalism, Smith called this idea, and it was just the holy water needed to sanctify the new industrialism. Economic freedom was now good, and good for the country as well.

These men of vision quickly saw that mass production would not only produce more goods, it would also create — by making them affordable — its own markets, a vast number of new customers eager to buy its products. In America, Henry Ford's genius was not just in inventing the Model-T Ford. It was making it cheaply enough and in large enough quantities to create its own customers. Everybody could now have one.

Public Squalor and Public Health

One consequence of the Industrial Revolution was a shift of the population from the farm to the city. Urbanization was the mate of industrialization. In 1750 there were only 2 cities in Britain with a population of 50,000 or more, London and Edinburgh. By 1801 that number had risen to 8, and by 1851 to 29. Unfortunately, the basic city services needed to support the increasing urban concentration — services such as clean water, lighting, heating, sewage and refuse disposal, and adequately-maintained streets — couldn't keep up. Even space was extremely limited; entire families lived in a single room of a tenement house, with a bucket for the communal toilet.

City life became squalid, full of soot from the factories, the air barely breathable. Tuberculosis, that scourge of poverty and malnutrition, stalked the streets along with prostitutes, thieves and beggars. Epidemics of smallpox, cholera and typhoid fever raged through the towns. The working poor, who often labored 14 hours a day (including little children), were so depleted of resistance they were easy victims for disease.

But finally, enough was enough. A liberal philosophy, which held that the state had an obligation to step in and check the excesses of unrestrained industry, slowly made its way through the government. Slavery was the first to go, abolished in 1832, 31 years before Abraham Lincoln signed the Emancipation Proclamation in America. The following year those other slaves — the children — were emancipated by the Factory Act of 1833. It forbade children under the age of nine to work in the textile mills. Finally, in 1847, the Ten Hour Act was passed. It limited to ten hours the time women and children could work in the factories.

Reforms in sanitation, hygiene, public health, and preventive medicine paralleled those in the workplace. In 1796 Edward Jenner began the field of immunology by demonstrating that cowpox vaccination could prevent smallpox. In 1837 the first preventive health agency came into effect, a National Vaccination Board, which set up smallpox innoculation stations around the city of London.

But the real impetus for change came five years later with the publication of Edwin Chadwick's report on *The Sanitary condition of the Labouring Population of Great Britain.* The following year a Board of Health was established for London. It was soon imitated in other cities. Other reforms followed quickly. Legislation was passed to improve child welfare, care for the elderly and the mentally ill, and for improvements in sanitation and hygiene.

In other medical areas discoveries came fast as well. A new day was dawning for the health care practitioner, and it included new equipment for detecting disease. Rene Laennec (1781-1826) watched a boy listening with his ear against a nail at one end of a wooden beam while a friend tapped out a signal through a nail at the other end. Laennec took this idea into his clinic, stuck a roll of paper to a patient's chest, and heard the heart sounds more clearly than he could have with his naked ear. He fashioned a wooden cylinder to replace the paper roll. This improved the hearing tremendously. He displayed it to the world in 1819. He called it his "stethoscope."

The ophthalmoscope was invented to examine the eye in 1853. That same year the hypodermic syringe came into use. And William

Withering made his contribution to pharmacology in 1786 when he showed that a broth made from the purple foxglove plant cured dropsy, the ankle swelling symptomatic of heart failure. Purple foxglove is a source of digitalis, which is still used to treat heart failure today.

The scientific study of pathological anatomy was begun by Giovanni Morgagni (1682-1771), professor of anatomy at the University of Padua. That was the same institution where a century and a half earlier the great Andreas Vesalius first laid out the normal anatomy of the human body. Morgagni's work, *On the Site and Cause of Disease*, linked the symptoms of disease to detectable anatomical abnormalities. Specifically, Morgagni studied and described the pathological changes in angina pectoris, blood clots, pulmonary tuberculosis, tumors of the small intestine, and strokes.

In surgery, several paths converged. Morgagni's description of diseased organs and the symptoms they presented with helped surgeons choose more carefully which organs needed to be removed. Nitrous oxide anesthesia was introduced in 1800, ether in 1846, chloroform in 1847. Finally, Joseph Lister (1827-1912) described in an 1867 article in the British medical journal *Lancet* how carbolic acid could prevent the wound infections which usually followed even the most "successful" surgeries and ended up killing the patient. Thus was antisepsis born.

The stage was now set for a major attack on epidemic diseases. Enter Dr. John Snow.

Snow and the Cholera

Cholera is a gastrointestinal infection characterized by voluminous but painless diarrhea. It has none of the abdominal cramps and fever typical of GI infections from other bacteria such as staphylococcus, salmonella and typhoid. The diarrhea in cholera can be so profuse it can cause rapid dehydration, leading to shock within a few hours. Coma, convulsions and death are the end stages of the disease.

Cholera still causes epidemics as well as sporadic cases around the world, especially when man-made disasters (wars, civil unrest) or naturally-occurring ones (earthquakes, fires) disrupt the water supply, which is the usual mode of infection. Sometimes undercooked food, such as shellfish eaten raw, causes a cluster of food-borne cholera cases. The infection also can be spread by the fecal-oral route from unwashed hands. Boiling water or chlorinating it easily kills the organism. The treatment for a patient with cholera is to replace fluid losses and eliminate the bacteria from the GI tract with antibiotics.

In 1884 Robert Koch discovered the organism responsible for cholera, *vibrio cholerae*. He also showed that its mode of transmission was by water and that water filtration could prevent epidemics of the disease.

John Snow (1813-1858, Figure 10) had none of Koch's experimental discoveries available to him; they would come only after he was long dead. And proof that specific diseases were caused by specific organisms — the germ theory of disease — was still 30 years into the future. But in 1832 Snow was sent to Newcastle to help with the first English epidemic of cholera. Though trained as an anesthetist, he would make cholera his calling, and the Newcastle outbreak started him down that road.

The disease hit London in 1848. Snow studied the pattern and distribution of the epidemic and published a pamphlet on his conclusions, *On the Mode of Communication of Cholera*. He was convinced it was a water-borne disease. But his critics maintained it was passed through the air.

Figure 10. *Dr. John Snow*

Source: National Library of Medicine

Snow had a chance to test his theory five years later in 1854, when a severe outbreak struck the Soho district of London. Almost 600 people died within the first 10 days. Using "shoe-leather epidemiology", Snow went door to door, counting the number of cholera cases and the number of deaths from it. He plotted these numbers on a map then converted them into rates per 10,000 houses. In this way he had a basis for comparing the effects of the disease in different areas of London and how prevalent it was in different water supplies. He also determined where each house got its water and plotted this data on a map of the city's water distribution system (see Figure 11).

In Snow's London, most residents got their water from hand-operated pumps scattered about the city. Snow soon saw that the greatest concentration of cholera cases occurred in those houses which drew their water from the pump on Broad Street. His recommendation to the authorities — the Parish Board of Guardians — was simple and direct: remove the pump's handle. They did, and the number of new cases declined dramatically. (Ironically, the Board didn't believe the results.)

But Snow wasn't finished. He discovered that two water companies served the Soho district: the Southwark and Vauxhall Company, which drew its water from the Thames River below where the city dumped its sewage, and the Lambeth Company, which got its water upstream from the polluted flow. Snow tabulated the number of cholera deaths for each company:

Southwark and Vauxhall Co.	*1263 deaths*	*315 deaths/10,000 houses*
Lambeth Co.	*98 "*	*38 " " "*

Most of the deaths were linked to the pump in Broad Street. Even though many people *lived* closer to another water source, they drank from the Broad Street pump because that's where they *worked*.

The data were clear. Snow had made his case that cholera was a water-borne disease. Not bad for a guy who knew nothing about germs but had to base his conclusions on simple observations. For his efforts, Snow earned the title, "Father of Epidemiology".

There is still a Broad Street Pump. It is a London pub by that name, located on the exact spot where its infamous 1854 namesake had stood. It serves 15 kinds of beer, or just clean water if you prefer.

The Rise of Occupational Diseases

The growth of Occupational Medicine during the Industrial Revolution was in response to an expanding list of workplace diseases. It paralleled Public Health's efforts to contain communicable diseases like cholera in the public sector. Both Occupational Medicine and Public

Health are examples of "denominator" medicine. Unlike "numerator" medicine, which treats one patient at a time, these other disciplines care for populations: whole cities, entire countries, or groups of workers. The two preventive specialties share another trait; they are especially concerned with preventing diseases, not just in treating them. Eliminating or reducing noxious exposures at the worksite is akin to eliminating water or food-borne diseases in the public arena.

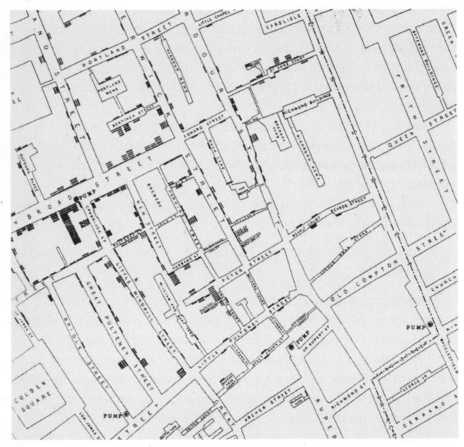

Figure 11. *Map of Cholera Deaths and Locations of London Water Pumps*

Source: National Center for Geographic Information Analysis, UCSB

Bernardo Ramazzini (1633-1714), an Italian physician, is known as the Father of Occupational Medicine, and for good reason. In 1700 he published his monumental work, *On the Diseases of Workers,* in which he not only described the illnesses of 42 work groups (expanded by 12 more in a later edition), but also recommended ways to prevent them. Some of the groups he studied were miners, apothecaries, midwives, printers, bakers, potters and many other tradesmen and artisans. Ramazzini's famous dictum,

First ask the patient, of what trade are you?

is as applicable to the recent anthrax-by-mail cases in U.S. postal workers as it was in other work groups 300 years ago.

By the end of the 18th century other occupational disorders were being described and their causes identified. Scurvy — the Black Death of the Sea — became epidemic during the Age of Exploration, the 16th through 18th centuries. British sailors in particular suffered its ravages during long sea voyages. James Lind (1716-1794) made the connection between scurvy and a diet low in citrus fruits. In 1795 the British Admiralty ordered all its men-o'-war to carry a supply of lemons and limes. Scurvy was elminated, and to this day British sailors are still known as "limeys".

The first occupational disease linked to an external agent was described in 1775 by the British doctor Sir Percival Potts. Potts discovered the high rate of scrotum cancer in chimney sweeps. He also noted the soot which collected in the scrotal folds and assumed it was the cause of the cancers. He was right.

The Industrial Revolution exposed countless groups of new workers to occupational illnesses. Using the principles of epidemiology laid down by John Snow during his work on cholera, workers' diseases began to be studied more rigorously. Some of them included:

- the health of sewer workers
- lead poisoning
- occupational groups with high risk for tuberculosis
- other industrial poisons
- the disease of match factory workers known as "phossy jaw," a disease of the jaw caused by phosphorus
- dust diseases of workers' lungs

But the most dramatic of these occupational illnesses was

Woolsorter's Disease. Having set the stage for it, we can now examine it in detail.

C H A P T E R

9

WOOLSORTER'S DISEASE: PART II

There seemed to be in the anthrax bacteria something almost oc-cult. . . extraordinary that a disease which caused only sixty or sev-enty cases per year in factories, of which about fifteen were fatal, should cause so much anxiety, and should in Bradford be consid-ered as a scourge.

— **Dr. T. M. Legge**, 1913
   On Woolsorter's Disease

As recently as 1971, the mechanism of action and the pathology of inhalation anthrax in humans was still unclear. There had been episodic reports of human cases or small clusters collected over months and years. And in 1955, the anthrax toxin was identified. But it was not until 1979 that a large epidemic of the disease broke out in Sibe-rian Russia. Because of Cold War geopolitics, it could not be investi-gated for another 13 years.

To fill this vacuum of knowledge about how the pulmonary form of anthrax caused its havoc on the body — its *pathophysiology*, the actual changes in the tissues — three researchers in 1971 decided to use an experimental model to study the process. They knew the story of Woolsorter's Disease, how anthrax spores had infected wool indus-try workers in the past. So they hit upon the idea of using this same type of exposure, but in a controlled setting. If they could produce the disease in this way, it could be carefully studied.

They chose monkeys as the experimental animals. Ninety-one of them were exposed over a month's time to dusty air from a mill processing imported goat hair known to contain anthrax spores. Twenty-three of the animals developed the typical symptoms of the disease: mediastinal widening, enlarged pulmonary lymph nodes, pleural effusion, septicemia, toxic shock, circulatory failure and death. Nine of the monkeys developed meningitis as well. Twenty of the 23 animals died. *B. anthracis* was cultured from the blood, other body fluids, and the organs of all 23 infected animals.

The investigators were able to study the way in which anthrax actually killed the animals. They concluded that the principal effect was a vascular injury from the toxin. This toxin caused the cells lining the blood vessel walls to swell, leak fluid and lose their tone, resulting in poor perfusion of the vital organs and a plummeting of the blood pressure. The end result was cardiopulmonary collapse and death.

These investigators had perfectly re-created in monkeys the disease which was prevalent in the woolen textile industry of Britain during the latter two-thirds of the 19th century. It was called Woolsorter's Disease.

Bradford, England

During the American Industrial Revolution, cotton was king. This was true in Britain as well. The principal fiber for English textile mills was imported cotton, which was turned into cheap, durable work clothes and other day wear. But for better clothing, for warmer wear, for tougher uniforms, wool was still the fiber of choice. In Scotland, the wool industry thrived in Glasgow, where it had the benefit of readily available Highland wool and cheap labor from clansmen who had moved into the city seeking employment.

In England, the city of Leeds and the nearby town of Bradford, both just north-east of Manchester, were the centers of the wool industry. In Leeds, shorter, coarser wool, mostly domestic in origin, was turned into felt products. But in Bradford, beginning about 1837, home grown wool was supplemented more and more with imported wool and hair, especially goat hair (mohair) from Pakistan and Turkey, wool from Persia, camel hair from Russia and alpaca from South America.

Prior to 1837 no specific disease was associated with wool workers. Sporadic cases of anthrax had occurred in both Scotland and England among sheep shearers, slaughterhouse workers, shepherds, tanners, sheep farmers and other centuries-old high risk occupational groups. These cases were mostly of malignant pustules, the skin form of anthrax. But during the period 1837-1847 a growing number of wool workers, most of whom were from Bradford, developed a rapidly fatal disease characterized by fever, cough, chest pain and sepsis. This was also the time of a tremendous increase in the import of foreign wools and hairs into the Bradford factories. A new occupational disease had been detected. It began to be called Woolsorter's Disease, even though its cause was still unknown. It was also known as "Bradford disease," since most of the cases came from there.

But Bradford wasn't the only place to see the new sickness. In 1878, a number of cases occurred in a Glasgow factory processing horsehair (used for furniture and pillow stuffing). And during the 1890's, 119 cases were reported in London. They were thought to be from imported goat hair. Also during that period, 60 cases — 9 pulmonary, 51 cutaneous — were reported in prisoners sorting mohair and other foreign wools.

The Factory Walk-Through

The best way to investigate a workplace illness is to visit the worksite personally; walk through the factory and watch how raw materials are turned into finished products; observe what specific tasks each worker does along the production line. In this way, the risks of each job become clear, and the workers at highest risk can be identified.

We cannot do a walk-through of a nineteenth century wool textile factory. But we have descriptions of the process by several contemporary physicians, notably John Bell and F.W. Eurich.

The raw fleeces arrived at the Bradford plant in large bales, compressed and bound with iron hoops. The first step was to break the hoops. This typically released a cloud of dust into the air, even after it was carried out on a table fitted with a funnel-shaped receptacle to which a fan was attached to collect and extract the dust. This primitive fan collection device could not hope to capture the smaller, airborne, anthrax-laden dust particles.

Next, the fleece was placed on an "opening board." This was nothing more than a wire mesh also fitted with a receptacle and extraction fan. Here the bales were unrolled and the fleeces taken out one by one and thrown into large baskets.

Sorters then separated the various qualities of wool and hair and picked out obvious foreign material from it, such as locks of hair, bits of rag and string, and rocks or clumps of dirt. Some of the sorted wool was taken directly to the wash basins. Wool which was especially knotted or clumped was first put through a machine called a "willey." It shook and roughly tore the fibers to get out the course clumps of sand and dirt. This was a very dusty operation. Once completed, these fleeces joined the others at the wash basins.

The wool remained in the wash baths (water at 130 degrees F. with a mild alkalai) for 10-20 minutes. Such soaking would not kill anthrax spores adherent to the fibers, though it might wash away some of the loose ones. The wool was then dried and made ready for carding.

The carding machine contained a series of rollers with teeth. As the wool passed through it, the teeth opened up the fibers and arranged them in parallel bundles. They emerged from the machine in a loose rope-like form called a "silver," which was then rolled into a ball. The carding machine was supposed to have a cover and an extraction fan to carry away any dust and spores which survived the washing process. This was not always the case.

The wool was then combed. Here the fibers were straightened and the shorter ones separated from the longer. After combing, the wool was ready to be spun into yarn, then sent to the mills to be made into textiles.

In all the above procedures except the washing, some dust and anthrax spores invariably became airborne hazards for the workers.

John Henry Bell

Medical science usually progresses incrementally, new discoveries slowly building on top of prior ones, sometimes going off into dead ends: two creaky steps forward, one step back. But occasionally there are individuals who stand out like beacons in the darkness and drive the process by the clarity of their observations and the force of their personalities. Hippocrates, who brough rationalism to medicine, was one. Andreas Vesailus, who defied the church and proved that the best way for a doctor to learn human anatomy was through a hands-on approach, was another. And John Snow, who single-handedly brought epidemiology into being, was a third. Woolsorter's Disease had two such heroes: John Henry Bell and Frederick William Eurich.

When the first cases of the new disease began to appear in Bradford, they were not initially noticed. The symptoms were so vague and common, and the patients died so quickly — usually at home within a short time after the symptoms started — that they made little impact. On death certificates, the cause of death was typically listed as pneumonia, pulmonary embolism, aneurysm or some other. But by the 1870's, the deaths were becoming so frequent that people knew something terribly wrong was going on in the mills.

John Bell was a Bradford native son, born there in 1832 to Scots parents. He received his medical training at St. Andrews University in Scotland and quickly became concerned about the spate of sudden deaths of healthy young men in the wool trades. He personally inspected the wool sorting rooms of all his patients and observed that often several men in the same room would get sick and die suddenly. He noticed that all the wools and hair in the Bradford factories were "dusty, dry and filthy from contamination with decomposing animal matter. . . and 'fallen fleeces' from diseased animals." He did an epidemiologic investigation of the problem. It showed that whereas lung disease in Bradford for the years 1856-1860 accounted for only 17.4% of all adult deaths, in the years 1872-1876 it accounted for 62.2%, a whopping three-fold increase. He was convinced he was dealing with a new occupational disease of wool workers.

When a colleague who had recently visited Robert Koch's laboratory in Germany suggested the symptoms were similar to those of inhalation anthrax, Bell began his own bacteriological investigations. He innoculated blood from a fatal case of Woolsorter's Disease into mice and rabbits. They all died, and he found bacteria "identical to Koch's anthrax in their blood specimens." That was in 1879, two years after Koch had identified the anthrax bacillus as the cause of the disease in sheep and cattle. Bell also injected animals with material from a malignant pustule on a wool worker. These animals died as well, and he also found anthrax in their blood. He was certain he had found the cause of Woolsorter's Disease.

But few of Bell's colleagues supported him. They prefered not to believe that the association between the anthrax bacterium and Woolsorter's Disease was a causal one. At that time, the theory of "spontaneous generation" was still in favor, the notion that bacteria could be spontaneously generated by disease. Although Louis Pasteur and Robert Koch had driven a stake through the heart of this old notion, many still clung to it. Bell's bacterium, they said, was not the *cause* of anthrax but was itself *generated* by the disease.

Frustrated, Bell took a dramatic step in 1880. He had a patient named Samuel Firth who was a woolsorter and who had died of the disease. He certified Mr. Firth's death as due to anthrax and then added to the death certificate that it was "from his employer's neglect in not having the mohair he was sorting disinfected beforehand." A coroner's inquest was convened and public concern was aroused. The inquest confirmed Bell's findings and a coroner's jury made a list of recommendations to prevent the problem. They were agreed to by the manufacturers and implemented industry-wide. They were known as the Bradford Rules.

The Bradford Rules

- the bales of wool should be steeped in salt water for at least twelve hours before being opened;
- the bales should then be washed twice in water at a temperature of at least 120 degrees Fahrenheit;
- the wool and hair should be sorted while still damp;
- the sorting rooms should be well ventilated;
- the floors of the rooms should be swept daily;
- workers in the sorting rooms should have access to a washroom outside the sorting area.

In 1884 additional rules were added:

- dangerous wools (alpaca, mohair, Persian wool, etc,) should be opened in a separate room;
- all sorting should be done on tables fitted with fans which directed the dust down and away from the workers.

The Bradford Rules caused a drop in woolsorter's cases almost immediately. But the improvement was confined to those who handled the raw material *before* it was washed. Workers further down the production line — for example, those engaged in carding and combing the wools — continued to get sick and die.

In 1887, the Bradford Rules were enacted into law. But because cases continued to occur, an Anthrax Investigation Board was established in Bradford. Clearly, there was still a source of anthrax spores at the worksite which had not been eliminated.

F. W. Eurich

Eurich grew up in Bradford but got his medical training at the University of Edinburgh. He returned to Bradford and began a medical practice in 1896. He became friends with John Bell and showed an immediate interest in the problem of Woolsorter's Disease. He was appointed the official bacteriologist for the city of Bradford in 1900, and in 1905 he was made a member of the Anthrax Investigation Board. He would study the problem for the next 30 years.

Eurich first noted that for the period 1902-1912 there was a total of 133 cases of anthrax in the wool workers of the Bradford district. This represented 13% of the work force, or an "attack rate" of 13%. Eurich kept meticulous records of 110 of these cases. Nineteen were of the pulmonary variety; all these men died. Ninety-one were cases of malignant pustules; 13 of these men died as well. When Eurich tabulated the number of cases for each specific job type, he discovered that 66 of the 110 were in workers who had contact with the wool *after* it had been washed. Why, he asked himself, if it was just dust-laden spores from the soil which got into the wool, should there be so many cases after the wool had been thoroughly washed and the dust and spores presumably removed?

Eurich approached the problem with the discipline of a bacteriologist. First, he discovered a way to culture anthrax directly from the raw wool and hair. This had never been done before. He then carefully examined over 200,000 specimens of alpaca, mohair and wool, taking more than 1400 cultures. (It's amazing he never became ill himself!) He finally found the problem: contamination of the fleeces with infected blood. Even though the alkalai in the wash bowl denatured the hemoglobin in the blood — which meant the red taint was no longer visible — the albumin (a blood protein) in the serum acted like a glue to stick the spores to the wool or hair fibers. There they remained, bound fast, through the wash cycle. This explained why workers other than sorters got infected; even apparently clean, washed wool could yield almost pure cultures of anthrax bacteria. The worst offenders were East Indian goat hair and Egyptian wool. Prohibiting fleeces grossly contaminated with blood was one step in reducing workplace exposures.

But Eurich further discovered that even fleeces *without* obvious blood contamination yielded positive cultures. He thought this was probably due to their all being washed together in the country of export before they were shipped. The spores, he guessed, must have been washed out of the dust of contaminated fleeces and made their way through the water to fleeces previously clear. If old blood was present, the spores became bonded fast to the fibers.

Since even clean, untainted wool might contain anthrax spores held tightly to the fibers, the best solution was a disinfection procedure which treated *all* high risk wool and hair *before* workers were exposed to it. The problem was how to accomplish this without damaging the wool and rendering it commercially worthless.

Disinfection

Eurich and other members of the Anthrax Investigation Board experimented with various disinfection processes. Further heating of the wool turned out not to be the answer. High enough temperataures to kill the spores irretrievably damaged the wool and goat hair. Eurich tried various solutions of plain water, dilute formic acid and dilute hydrochloric acid. None met the requirement to kill the spores without damaging the wool.

Steam sterilization — especially steam under pressure — did the job in 15 minutes. But it adversely affected the fibers. The lustre of mohair, in particular, was sharply diminished. It turned yellow, lost much of its elasticity, and became rough to the touch.

Eurich finally tried formaldehyde. He used different concentrations at different temperatures for varying lengths of time. He finally concluded that the best of these was a 2% solution kept at a temperature of 100 degrees Fahrenheit. This killed the spores in 30 minutes. Eurich's discovery was adapted to the wool industry in a series of steps:

- first, the bales were opened in a bath of warm, soapy water with a mild alkalai;
- next, they were immersed in a bath of soapy water alone;
- then they went into the 2% formaldehyde bath, which was enclosed in a special chamber to protect the workers from the vapors;

- the wool then went through a series of rollers to break up any remaining clots of hair and blood;
- the product was then dried in a chamber for 2-3 days, during which time the formaldehyde vapors continued to work on the wool and kill the spores;
- after this, the wool was ready to be sorted, carded and combed.

Elmhirst Duckering

Duckering was an engineer and a wool factory inspector. When the question of how to make Eurich's disinfection process more compatible with industrial operations was referred to a subcommittee of the Anthrax Investigation Board, Duckering teamed up with Eurich to consider the problem. During WWI, the two men worked together to find a solution. They discovered that a stronger alkalai in the wash solution turned the old blood clots into a jelly, which allowed the washing process to flush out more of the spores. Duckering also verified a fundamental finding of Eurich's, that the formaldehyde vapors continued to kill the anthrax spores long after the wool was dried.

In 1919, the Anthrax Protection Act was passed by Parliament. No mohair, raw wool or alpaca was allowed into Britain unless it had first been decontaminated. On July 4, 1921, a Government Disinfection Station was opened in Liverpool. It was capable of treating 10-12 million tons of imported wool and hair per year. Eurich continued to sample the wool before and after disinfection. He proved that the process worked. Those fleeces and hairs which were positive for anthrax initially failed to yield the spores after going through the procedure.

Cases of inhalation anthrax in the wool industry diminished sharply after this. The last case in Britain was reported in 1939. Dr. Eurich finally retired from his duties in 1937. He received acclaim from his colleagues, honors from the wool industry, and thanks from countless wool workers in the community. But neither he nor John Bell ever received any recognition from their country for what they had accomplished.

Today, some countries test their raw wool for anthrax, and, if positive, irradiate it prior to export. This kills the spores without damaging the fleeces. But very high doses of radiation are required, and few nations have this capability. Most follow the World Health Organization's recommendations, which are a modification of Elmhirst

Duckering's process. It is a five-step procedure, each stage 10 minutes long. All bath waters are kept at a temperature of at least 40.5 degrees centigrade:

    i. immersion in 0.25-.30% alkalai;
    ii. immersion in soapy water;
    iii. immersion in 2% formaldehyde;
    iv. a second immersion in 2% formaldehyde;
    v. immersion in rinse water.

After these five steps, the wool may be dried and baled for export.

Woolsorter's Disease never became a problem in the United States for the simple reason that there was never much of a wool industry here. Cotton remained the principal industrial fiber all through the American Industrial Revolution. U.S. cases of inhalation anthrax associated with wool or hair occurred very sporadically. Though 5 cases occurred in New Hampshire wool workers during the 1950s, others were almost always in hobbyists who used imported Middle Eastern mohair or wool for their crafts. The last such case — from Pakistani goat hair — occurred in 1976.

    Though the eradication of Woolsorter's Disease was a microbiological and technological triumph in Britain, Europe continued to suffer disastrous epizootics of anthrax in its livestock, along with corresponding human cases. Robert Koch's effort to nail down the bacterial cause of the disease opened the door for Louis Pasteur to develop a vaccine to prevent it in animals. This all happened in the last 25 years of the 19th century.

C H A P T E R

10

KOCH

Nunquam otiosus — never idle

— Motto of **Robert Koch**

If you look in any textbook of bacteriology, under any of three different bacteria, you will see Robert Koch's name listed as the discoverer: anthrax, tuberculosis, and cholera. Every microbiologist dreams of having even one such listing. But three! In addition to these discoveries, Koch (Figure 12) demonstrated the bacterial cause of wound infections, later proven to be from the staphylococcus and streptococcus organisms.

You may also see in the same textbook a list of Koch's other accomplishments. They may seem less dramatic than his discoveries. But they were arguably more enduring and had a greater impact on medicine and public health. He was the first to obtain photomicrographs of bacteria, the first to use a plate method to obtain pure bacterial cultures, and the first to recommend sanitary engineering and water filtration to prevent cholera. But perhaps his greatest legacy wasn't even these successes, as dramatic as they are. Rather it was the rigorous scientific approach he used and advocated, in which he laid down the prerequisites for identifying the causal organism of *any* infectious disease. Known as "Koch's Postulates," they are still studied by medical and bacteriology students today.

Figure 12. *Dr. Robert Koch*

Source: National Library of Medicine

Biographical Sketch

Robert Koch was born on December 11, 1843 in the small town of Claustral in Lower Saxony, the third child of a family of 13. This was a mining community, and Robert's father was an administrator of mines. The boy's early education was a traditional one: elementary school followed by the local gymnasium (high school). At age 19 he entered the University of Gottingen to study medicine, which he completed with a doctorate four years later in 1866. For the next few years he sought work as a practicing physician in various communitites, including a stint as the doctor at an institute for retarded children. His need to become self-supporting became more urgent when, in 1867, he married; within a year, he had an infant daughter.

The outbreak of the Franco-Prussian War in 1870 interrupted his plans. He volunteered for the Army and served in a battlefield hospital near Neufchateau. This combat experience gave him an up-close look at battle injuries. Wound infections were common, and he never forgot what he saw. Later, he would seriously investigate them and identify the principal organisms responsible.

In 1872 Koch got his first big break; he was appointed the District Medical Officer for the Wollstein District. For the next eight years he toiled away in this sleepy German backwater. He supplemented his government income with private medical practice, which was well-received by the local population. In his spare time he began his work on microscopy, photomicrophotography and anthrax.

Working essentially alone in his spare time, and with limited equipment, Koch identified and linked the anthrax bacterium to the disease it caused. Then he photographed it and its spore form.

The work on anthrax catapulted him into national prominence. He was offered a position on the staff of the Imperial Health Office in Berlin in 1880, which he immediately accepted. In addition to larger and better equipped laboratory facilities, Koch no longer had to work alone. He now had a staff of colleagues and assistants to help him and to discuss new ideas with. He worked on the technique for developing pure cultures of bacteria, a process known as the "Koch Plate Technique."

Within a year after his move to Berlin, he started work on tuberculosis. Six months later he had found the answer. He was able to stain and culture the bacteria, notoriously hard to do even today. His efforts were widely acclaimed. The only bad taste to all this success was his growing disagreement — bordering on outright hostility — with the eminent French scientist Louis Pasteur.

Three years after his tuberculosis triumph, Koch took on the problem of cholera. He lead a team first to Egypt, then to Calcutta in 1883. He finally isolated the organism and became convinced, like John Snow before him, that the disease was waterborne.

The next year the Koch Institute for Infectious Diseases opened. While Koch spent less and less time personally in the laboratory, and more time in administration, the Institute recruited and supported many of the men who would make up the second generation of bacteriological discoveries. A short list of these included:

- Wasserman, who developed the test for syphilis which bears his name;
- Behring, who discovered the diphtheria toxin and later teamed with Ehrlich to demonstrate an antitoxin for this dreaded disease;
- Loeffler, who discovered the causal agent of diphtheria (*corynebacterium diphtheriae*);
- Ehrlich, who discovered the acid properties of the tubercle bacillus, worked with Behring on diphtheria antitoxin, and invented Salvarsan, an arsenic derivative for treating syphilis.

Two years later, in 1893, Koch and his wife Emmy divorced. He had become infatuated with a young 20 year-old, whom he soon married. The next ten years involved research on tropical medicine in Africa, plague in India, malaria in Italy, typhoid fever in Trier, and rinderpest — a viral disease of cattle — in Rhodesia. In 1904 he retired officially from government work and returned to Africa for more research on malaria, sleeping sickness, and amoebic dysentery.

In 1905 Koch was awarded the Nobel Prize for Medicine. He continued to travel, including a trip to the United States and Japan in 1908. He died of a sudden, overwhelming heart attack on May 27, 1910, at the age of 67. His cremated remains were placed in a mausoleum at the Institute which bears his name.

The Art of Microscopy and Microphotography

If he was going to study the world of microbes, Koch knew early on that he would have to improve his skill as a microscopist. That meant getting good equipment and learning how to use it. It also meant learning how to culture and stain his specimens and how to take pictures of them.

The first human to look into a "microscope" was probably Galileo, when he adapted the lens of his telescope to focus on small objects. But the first genuine microscopist was the Dutchman Anton Van Leeuwenhoek (1632-1723). By trade a draper, Leeuwenhoek became fascinated with the science of optics and the craft of lens grinding. He modified Galileo's instrument, taught himself basic microscopic technique, and was the first to observe microorganisms moving about under his 'scope, probably one-celled creatures like amoeba, paramecium and other protozoa. Leeuwenhoek called them "animalicules."

But Leeuwenhoek was an amateur, an enthusiastic hobbyist, ill trained to use his new tool scientifically. That would come later with the Italian, Marcello Malpighi (1628-1694). In 1661 Malpighi observed blood in the capillaries of animals, adding further proof to Harvey's theory of the circulation of blood. He was also the first to see human red blood cells, the papillae of the tongue, and the pulmonary alveoli (the lung sacs). In other studies he described the histology of the spleen and kidney.

Robert Koch wanted to do more than just look at bacteria under his microscope. He wanted to photograph them. Without a photograph, the only way to communicate to the scientific world what he saw was through hand drawings. While he was a good artist, he knew that the subtleties of form and size which differentiated one bacterium from another could never be captured by the naked eye with pen and paper. A photograph was called for.

He approached this problem in the same systematic way he did all his work. First, he would have to get a better microscope. Then he would have to discover stains for the bacteria which would make them stand out better under the microscope and on photographs. Finally, he would have to adapt a camera to his microscope and experiment with various photographic techniques. All this occupied him, on and off, for the next six years.

Koch bought the best microscope he could afford. But he soon discovered that the glass slides and cover glasses he used for his specimens diffracted the light so much that much of it never made its way up the microscope tube. This meant the object he wanted to view or photograph was so poorly illuminated, its detail so obscured, it might even be missed altogether. Fortunately, an optical physicist named Ernst Abbe had developed a condenser which gathered the diffracted light and combined it with direct light to produce a full cone at the eyepiece. With this apparatus, Koch announced that he could now see "bacteria in the blood of septicemic animals." His use of and praise for the Abbe Condenser brought it to the attention of the scientific world.

Koch's next task was to prepare his specimens for photography. He experimented with staining techniques using various aniline dyes, notably methyl violet, fuchsin, eosin and methyl green. When he found what he wanted, he took up the problem of photography itself. He had to learn how to prepare the sample, make ready the photographic plate, take the exposure, then develop it. It took him an average of four hours to complete one exposure, that is if the sunlight didn't fail him! But by 1877 he had his technique perfected to the point where he could publish the first-ever photomicrographs of bacteria. His methods became the standard technique well into the next century.

Within a couple of years, Koch would overcome another microscopy problem: how to resolve the intimate details of the organisms he wished to study. Magnification with more powerful lenses only made them bigger, not more clear. He needed a way to get more resolving power. He began using another invention of Ernst Abbe, the oil immersion lens. This increased the resolving power of the microscope many times. Combined with the Abbe Condenser, he could now differentiate and photograph many different forms of bacteria within infected tissues.

By 1877, Koch had refined the microscopic, photographic, culture and staining skills needed to take on the big problem which was now presented to him: anthrax.

Bacillus anthracis

Koch began his work on anthrax in 1873 when the disease broke out in the sheep of his district. Humans, too, were becoming infected. He was the District Health Officer and accepted the responsibility for doing something about it.

Others had worked on the problem of anthrax before Koch. Rayer, in 1850, reported he had found "rod-like" bodies in the blood of animals with the disease. Pollender confirmed this finding five years later. And Brauell, in 1857, discovered these same bacteria in the blood of a man and was then able to transmit the infection to a sheep by innoculation. Casimier Davaine, a French scientist, claimed in 1863 that a single drop of blood from an infected animal contained millions of these bacteria and that he could infect other animals through injections. He also found the same bacteria in human malignant pustules, the cutaneous form of anthrax.

By the middle 1860s, it was clear that the anthrax bacillus was somehow connected to the disease suffered by both man and beast. But there were still serious objections to accepting it as the *cause* of the disease rather than merely being *associated* with it. No one had yet been able to grow it outside the body, then inject it into an animal and produce the disease. That would be real proof of causation.

Another objection was the common knowledge that animals could get the disease either directly from another infected animal or from the soil. If only one bacteria was the cause of the disease, how could there be two such disparate sources for it?

A chance to answer these questions came in 1875 when Koch was given the hide of an animal which had died of anthrax. Its blood teemed with the bacteria. He experimented with various culture techniques and discovered he could grow it exuberantly in the aqueous humor of a rabbit's eye; he had found a way to culture the bacteria outside the body. He purchased a supply of cows' eyes from a nearby slaughterhouse and grew it in quantity, pure cultures of anthrax. He gave it a new name; *bacillus anthracis*.

By the following year, Koch had crafted a primitive incubation chamber. Anthrax grew better at warm temperatures and with exposure to the air, so he built a small glass culture chamber which exposed the bacteria to air but did not dry them out. One day, while he was observing some glass culture slides, he saw long filaments of anthrax bacteria with spheres inside them. They refracted the light of his microscope. Spores! He had observed the spore form of anthrax. He instantly knew that the problem of two sources for the infection was now moot. In his own words:

> *When these spores have once formed in the soil of a region, there is good reason to believe that anthrax will remain in this region for many years. . . A single cadaver, handled improperly, can furnish almost innumerable spores. . .*

Koch had now worked out the complete lifecycle of anthrax. From a diseased animal, spores formed in the soil when it died. These converted back to the bacterial form if a new animal ingested or inhaled them, which then caused a new infection in that animal. He also reported that spores did not form inside a living host. He never found even one in all the animals he studied; he only found them outside the body, in the soil or in his laboratory.

But there was one more step to go. He had to demonstrate that this bacteria — and only this one — *caused* the disease. He began by injecting mice at the base of their tails with anthrax from his pure cultures. When they died, he took blood from their spleens and found the same bacteria he had injected. He then injected this blood into another mouse and got the same results. He repeated the process 20 times, with exactly the same outcome each time. He had now proven that the bacteria had reproduced themselves inside the mice, the same bacteria he had injected initially from his pure culture. He took pictures of them with his new microphotographic equipment.

As a final control measure, Koch obtained a sample of a culture of *bacillus subtilis*, a relatively harmless cousin of anthrax and a spore former as well. When he injected these bacteria into healthy animals, they remained healthy. Only *bacillus anthracis* caused the disease known as anthrax. This was the first time a specific disease was proven to have been caused by a specific microorganism. The Germ Theory of disease, initially advocated by Pasteur, had now received strong support from his archenemy Koch.

For his work on anthrax, Koch received glowing praise from his colleagues in the scientific world and, in April 1880, the offer of a job in Berlin at the Imperial Health Office. Within three months he had closed his private practice in Wollstein, arranged his financial affairs, and made the move to Berlin. Never idle!

The Koch Plate Technique

The first task Koch assigned himself at his new laboratory was to improve his culture techniques. He had learned with anthrax the value of pure cultures for identifying organisms. But using aqueous humor from the eye of a cow was impractical for large scale research. Besides, this medium had the same problems as all the other media then in use: they were all liquids. When they turned cloudy, it indicated the presence of bacterial growth. A small amount of the liquid was then used to innoculate another culture. This was repeated again and again. It was assumed that a relatively pure culture of one organism would be the end result of this multiple transfer process.

The problems with liquid culture media were many. First, the process of serial transfers was very time consuming, and there was no guarantee a truly pure culture would result at the end of it. There was also no way to count the number of colonies in the broth to determine the bacterial load in the sample. Finally, samples of some body fluids, for example, stool, vomitus or sputum — or environmental ones from water, food or soil — contained many organisms, most non-pathogenic. It was virtually impossible to separate these using liquid media.

In 1882, Koch hit on the idea of using *solid* culture media. But instead of developing a spectrum of such media, one for each organism, he selected the best *liquid* nutrient and then *solidified* it by adding gelatin. This worked for a time. But there was no refrigeration in his day, so the gelatin turned back to liquid during the warmer months of the year. Then Koch discovered agar, a complex sugar derived from seaweed. It kept its solid shape even when it was warm outside.

Koch's culture apparatus consisted of a glass slide layered with his solid culture media. When the specimen had been spread onto the slide, it was placed under a bell jar to incubate. Later, a colleague named Richard Petri (1852-1921) invented the dish which bears his name. In the Petri dish, the media is poured directly in and allowed to dry. Then the specimen is streaked onto it and incubated. This is still the process used in most microbiology labs today.

Koch's "Plate Technique" became world famous, the standard procedure for culturing specimens described in every textbook of bacteriology. It is hard to underestimate its value to science. With this technique microorganisms streaked onto the solid media grew into individual, readily *visible* colonies, even if they had started out as a single cell. The colonies could be counted if quantitation was a goal (as it was in food, water, or soil analysis), or each colony could be re-cultured separately, stained, examined under the microscope and photographed. The separation and identification of multiple organisms in a single specimen became routine.

Koch's paper describing his plate technique was one of the first publications from the Imperial Health Office. Koch himself said simply, "the pure culture is the foundation of all research on infectious disease." His biographer was more effusive in his praise:

> *Perhaps Koch's greatest contribution to the development of bacteriology and microbiology as independent sciences was his introduction of a pure culture technique using solid or semi-solid media — soon known throughout the world as* Koch's plate technique.
> (**Thomas Brock**, *Robert Koch: A Life in Medicine and Bacteriology*.)

Tuberculosis

Tuberculosis was the "Captain of the Men of Death" in Koch's time. It accounted for almost 15% of all human deaths. Crowded city slum dwellers were especially susceptible to its ravages, but not even the nobility were immune. The English romanticized the pulmonary form of TB with the name "consumption." It aptly described the body's wasting away, slowly consumed by the disease. In Europe it was known by the barely pronounceable name, "phthisis."

By the time Koch started his own work on TB, its communicability had been well demonstrated, first in 1865, then later by Koch's friend Klebbs. But no one had actually seen the causative organism, either in diseased tissue or on cultures. This was not surprising. Unlike anthrax, a huge organism which grows quickly on culture media, the tubercle bacillus (*mycobacterium tuberculosis*) is barely one-tenth the size of anthrax. Very tiny. Very hard to see. Furthermore, it grows painfully slowly compared to other organisms, sometimes taking up to two weeks to become apparent on culture. It is also hard to stain. But it was at this part of the problem — the stain — that Koch took direct aim.

He began his research in the fall of 1881. By spring of the following year he had succeeded. Experimenting with various stains, and using an alkalai pH, he quickly demonstrated the tubercle bacillus in specimens from diseased animal tissue. That was Step one. The next step, culturing the organism, proved more difficult. But he kept at it, for he knew that to *prove* the organism caused the disease, he had to grow it as a pure culture.

Fortunately, he had perfected his plate culture technique by this time and used it to good effect. He chose coagulated blood as the solid nutrient media. He innoculated slanted tubes of it with organisms he got from diseased tissue. Then he waited. One week: no growth. Ten days: still no growth. Finally, after two weeks, tiny colonies appeared on the slants. He stained and photographed them; they were the same organism he had observed in the diseased tissue. Step two.

But there was one more step to go. He innoculated the bacteria from his cultures into guinea pigs. Then he waited some more. The animals finally got sick. When he examined their organs, he found the same bacteria he had injected. Step three. He had proved that the tubercle bacillus was the cause of tuberculosis. Another point in favor of the Germ Theory of Disease. Another dagger to the heart of spontaneous generation.

Koch's paper on the discovery of the tubercle bacillus was published in April 1882. His fame spread around the world. He was now a *bona fide* superstar. A colleague of his, Paul Ehrlich, refined and further developed Koch's TB stain. Ehrlich discovered the acid-fast property of the bacillus, its ability to remain stained after an acid wash had decolorized all surrounding tissue and other organisms. This acid-fast stain is still used today. The bacteria stand out as "little red bandits" in a sea of decolorized fluid or tissue. It is axiomatic to physicians: if you spot even one of them under the microscope, you've made the diagnosis.

Koch's early work on TB was brilliant and the acclaim for it was well-justified. But later, he misstepped. In August, 1890, he announced he had found an extract from the tubercle bacillus — he called it "tuberculin" — which could cure the disease. But, as time and further testing proved, he had not found a cure at all. Instead, he had stumbled on what is known as delayed hypersensitivity, a component of cellular immunity. And while tuberculin wasn't a cure, it eventually proved valuable for diagnosing the disease. A version of it, PPD — Purified Protein Derivative — is the standard skin test used for TB today. It does not diagnose the disease but detects the presence of infection from prior exposure. This allows treatment to be started to prevent actual clinical disease.

Koch's Postulates

From his research on tuberculosis Koch had discovered something else, a more fundamental truth. The three steps he had followed to identify the tubercle bacillus could be generalized into an approach for all infectious diseases. He enunciated this in 1883 as his famous postulates. These were essentially the requirements necessary to prove that a particular organism *caused* a specific infectious disease. Simply put, they were as follows:

1. The organism must be present in the tissues or organs when the disease was present and absent when there was no disease;
2. The organism must be grown in pure culture;
3. The cultured organism must cause the same disease when injected into a healthy animal and then isolated again from that animal.

The Search for Cholera

To crack the problem of cholera, Koch had to use not only his microbiologic skills, but his epidemiologic ones as well.

In 1883, cholera came to Egypt. Koch was asked to lead a team to investigate. He brought with him a portable version of his Berlin laboratory: culture plates, cover slips, media, sterilization equipment, microscopes, glass slides, stains of all kinds — in short, everything necessary to examine and process specimens.

His first efforts to isolate the cholera organism from the blood, spleen and other tissues of patients who had died from it were unsuccessful. Nor could he transfer the infection to animals, though he tried all kinds: monkeys, dogs, cats, chickens, mice. Koch was puzzled and frustrated. This process had worked before with both anthrax and tuberculosis. Why would it not work now with cholera?

What Koch didn't know was that cholera is an infection confined to the human species. Animals don't get it, so it cannot be transferred to them. Furthermore, cholera is a localized infection of the small intestine. It does not become septic or bloodborne. Naturally, Koch could not have found it in the spleen, liver, lungs or blood of any patient. He did note, however, that he had found a "comma-shaped" organism in the small intestines of every patient who had died of the disease. He thought this might be the causative organism. But when he tried to culture it from the intestine, he failed again. A French team, which had come to Egypt at the same time and was led by Pasteur, had no better luck.

The epidemic in Egypt subsided. Without further cases to study, Koch was about to return home. But an outbreak of the disease was reported from India. Koch immediately packed up his equipment and headed for Calcutta with his team. He arrived there just as the epidemic was building. This meant he had access to very fresh specimens. And that made all the difference.

Within days of his arrival, he obtained fresh specimens from a 22 year-old man who had died from cholera just three hours earlier. Using these, he was finally able to grow the organism — that funny comma-shaped one he had seen in Egypt — on pure culture. He realized his previous failure had been due to the absence of fresh specimens: the longer the bowel sat after death, the more it became contaminated with other bacteria; whereas fresh material still teemed with almost pure cholera organisms. Though he had been able to isolate the bacteria, which he named *vibrio cholerae*, he could never transfer it to experimental animals from the cultures.

Koch also did some studies on the water distribution system of Calcutta. He was suspicious that water was the route through which the disease was spread. (History had forgotten about John Snow.) But he didn't get a chance to prove his point until almost a decade later.

In 1892, cholera hit close to home: Hamburg, Germany. There were 17,000 cases, with 8,000 deaths reported in just a few weeks. Koch was now presented — like Snow had been 40 years earlier — with an experiment of nature. Altona, a city downstream from Hamburg, had poor quality water; it got all the industrial and organic waste from its big-city upstream neighbor. But Altona filtered its water through sand filters. Koch showed that it had no cholera cases, whereas Hamburg had an epidemic of them. Koch's epidemiologic proof was as solid as John Snow's had been. Not only had Koch shown that cholera was waterborne, he had also demonstrated that it could be prevented by the simple sand filtration of drinking water.

Not everyone was willing to accept Koch's proof that he had found the causative organism of cholera. In fact, he was hoisted on his own pitard by critics who pointed out that he had failed to fulfill the 3rd of his own Postulates; he had not transferred the disease to an animal from a pure culture. It would be years before the truth was finally realized, that cholera is a disease only of humankind. In fact, an adequate animal model has never been found for the organism, so there was no way Koch's 3rd Postulate could have been met. But science is sometimes ironic. A student at Koch's Institute accidentally swallowed some cholera organisms from a pure culture and got the disease from it. The 3rd Postulate was finally fulfilled.

The Koch-Pasteur Controversy

It was probably inevitable that the two greatest bacteriologists of the 19th century should get into a tiff sooner or later. Both were strong willed men of genius, vying for some of the biggest prizes in science. Koch, especially, drove himself hard (never idle!), was autocratic toward his assistants, and expected the highest level of achievement from both them and himself. He was the most argumentative in the exchanges with Pasteur.

The personality cults which grew up around both men also contributed to the rivalry, taking their mentor's position at every turn and accusing the other side of poor work or equivocal results. (We saw this same thing happen a dozen or so years ago between the French and American teams over who had first discovered the AIDS virus.)

The Franco-Prussian War was an additional source of friction between the two men. The French had been decisively beaten. Paris had been occupied by the Germans for months. Bitter residual feelings ran high. And it didn't help that Koch read French poorly and spoke it even worse, and that Pasteur was completely illiterate in German.

There had been times of direct competition between the two men, which exacerbated the ill feelings. During the Egyptian cholera outbreak both teams struggled to find the organism. Both failed. And later, when Pasteur speculated that earthworms may be responsible for distributing anthrax spores through the soil, churning them up from buried carcasses and exposing them to new animals, Koch would have none of this idea and said so harshly. (Pasteur may have been right.)

Koch also faulted Pasteur for his heat attenuation method of producing an anthrax vaccine. Pasteur was clearly right here; the vaccine worked. Finally, Koch's premature announcement about his "tuberculin's" curative effects gave his opponents more bullets to shoot at him.

But beyond these few areas of controversy, which seem petty in the context of all their other great work, it's hard to see any real basis for the intense Koch-Pasteur rivalry. If anything, it appears more related to their different approaches to research rather than to any substantive disagreement. Koch was the laboratory perfectionist, primarily interested in finding the organisms responsible for a disease and then discovering a way to prevent it through public health or sanitation methods.

Pasteur did not have the pure plate culture technique of Koch. But that was all right. His genius lay elsewhere, in the new science of immunology. His discovery of the vaccines for anthrax and rabies alone guaranteed him a place in the pantheon of great scientists. And he accomplished so much more besides.

C H A P T E R

PASTEUR

Chance favors only the prepared mind.

— Motto of **Louis Pasteur**

By identifying the organism which caused anthrax, Robert Koch offered strong evidence for the germ theory of disease. Louis Pasteur then added to it by showing that he could *attenuate* — weaken — that very anthrax germ and make a vaccine which would prevent the disease. Both men's efforts contributed a blow to the idea of spontaneous generation, the notion that organic material could breed microorganisms by itself.

But many diehards wanted more proof, more *direct* evidence. After all, spontaneous generation was an idea that went back 2500 years. The Egyptian scarab or dung beetle was believed to have emerged newly created from a manure pile: it was revered by the Egyptians as a symbol of spontaneous regeneration. And everyone could see with his own eyes maggots and flies arising from decaying organic matter.

Louis Pasteur (Figure 13) took on the problem of spontaneous generation in 1859-60 and kept at it for 20 years. To show that organisms were not engendered by organic matter, despite what one's senses suggested, he devised a classic experiment. First, he added nutrient broth to a flask then boiled it to sterilize it. When the flask was sealed, no bacteria grew. Then he dropped a piece of cotton through which air had been filtered into the broth; microorganisms promptly colonized the liquid. Clearly, they had not spontaneously generated in the broth but had been in the air and become trapped in the cotton filter.

Figure 13. *Dr. Louis Pasteur*

Source: National Library of Medicine

He carried the experiment one
step further. He crafted a swan-necked
flask with a long s-curve in the neck.
Dust would be trapped in this curve,
but air could still flow in and out.
When no growth appeared in the ster-
ile broth, it was apparent that air
alone could not cause colonization.
But when he tipped the flask to allow the dust in the curve to drop into
the liquid, bacterial colonies promptly grew again. He had demonstrated that the organisms were not spontaneously generated by the
organic broth. It was colonized by something in the air which had
contaminated it.

The Man

Louis Pasteur was a harsh teacher, a martinet of an administrator
and a fervent defender of his ideas and accomplishments. He was not
above *ad hominum* attacks on his critics nor claiming for himself discoveries actually made by his assistants. The kindly, bespectacled professor seen in photographs, paintings and movies is a gross distortion
of the man himself. But, like his great rival Koch, he was venerated as
a saint, the protector of French wine, milk, sheep and the world's children. Like most saints, his warts were overlooked.

Pasteur's beginnings were, like Koch's, humble. He was born December 27, 1822, the only son of a poor tanner from Dole, a village in
eastern France close by the Swiss border. His early education was
through the local schools. From 1843-1847 he studied chemistry at
the Ecole Normale Superieure in Paris, from which he received his
doctorate. His first post-doctoral assignment was the study of crystals
and their ability to refract light. These studies brought him to the
attention of an influential physics professor who secured an appoint-
ment for him at the University of Strassbourg in 1849.

He must have felt himself financially secure by this time, for he
courted and wed a 22 year old woman named Marie Laurent (he was

26). She remained at his side for the rest of his life, bearing him five children. Three of them died while both parents were still alive, each death a heartache.

Pasteur spent a brief period as Professor of Chemistry and Dean of the School of Sciences at the University of Lille in northern France. But in 1857 he returned to where he had begun, the Ecole Normale Superieure, this time as a full professor. He remained in Paris — later as Professor of Chemistry at the Sorbonne — until his death from a stroke at age 72.

Pasteur was not a physician and had no formal training in the healing arts. Though he developed vaccines for one human and three animal diseases, he was not a microbiologist either. He was a chemist and was not even allowed to give injections of his own vaccines. He had to rely on physicians and veterinarians for this.

In Vino Veritas

Pasteur began his microbiological career not by discovering the bacterial cause of a human disease, nor even the cause of an animal one. His beginnings were much more down to earth: the process of fermentation. Brewers and vintners couldn't understand why different batches of their products contained vastly different amounts of alcohol, some of it turning vinegary. Or why beer might lose its taste altogether. Or why vinegar, when it *was* wanted, did not form at all. The producers knew they had no hope of controlling the quality of their products unless they understood the basic principles of how the various sugars in these beverages fermented.

It was the belief among French scientists at that time that the process of fermentation was a simple chemical one: complex sugars decomposed and formed alcohol, carbon dioxide and water. But chemistry didn't explain the wildly different results the manufacturers might get from two or more identical batches of grapes. Pasteur worked out the principles of fermentation. In so doing, he saved his countrymen millions of dollars previously lost in the export of beer and wine.

Pasteur discovered, over about two decades of work, that each type of fermentation (grapes into wine; grapes into vinegar; the spoilage of milk or butter) was caused by a different microorganism. In the case of wine, yeast exposed to air (oxygen) produced little alcohol. This was known as "aerobic" fermentation. When deprived of oxygen, however, the yeast shifted its cycle to "anaerobic" fermentation (a term coined by Pasteur) and produced alcohol in abundance. As Pasteur himself put it:

"Fermentation is the consequence of life without air."

When wine spoiled or turned into unwanted vinegar (acetic acid), it was due to a separate microbe altogether. And another bacteria caused milk to sour (lactic acid) and butter to turn rancid.

Pasteur did more than just discover the cause of all this spoilage. He found that by heating wine to 60 degrees centigrade for an hour he could retard the growth of harmful bacteria without affecting the yeast which produced the alcohol. He recommended similar heating to preserve the quality of beer and dairy products. This process soon became universally known as "pasteurization" and is still used today to prevent spoilage in the dairy industry.

Silkworms and Chickens

Later in life, after he had successfully developed vaccines for both human and animal diseases, Pasteur was often heard to preach,

"One disease, one germ, one vaccine."

But he did not arrive at this basic truth of immunology through some blinding flash of insight. Rather he groped and probed towards it for years. The first infectious disease he cut his teeth on was not human at all, and barely animal: the lowly silkworm.

In 1865, twelve years before Koch's discovery of the anthrax bacillus, Pasteur was asked to investigate an epidemic destroying the French silkworm industry. Originally imported from China along with the mulberry trees whose leaves were their principal source of food, the French silkworms (really caterpillars) produced 26,000 tons of silk annually, over 10% of the world's total. When the epidemic hit, this amount dropped by more than 80%. The silk breeders faced ruin unless something could be done to stop the disease.

Pasteur discovered that sick silkworms were covered with black spots. He thought these contained the microorganism responsible for their illness. Though he was never able to isolate a specific germ, he devised a relatively fool-proof means of combating the disease. He instructed the breeders to examine the worms under a microscope and use only the eggs from those free of the black spots. The procedure worked. The silkworm industry was saved, and Pasteur had gained valuable experience into infectious diseases. His next project, a huge one by any standard, was anthrax in French livestock. But he had to take a detour from the pasture to the barnyard before he found the answer to that one.

Chicken cholera, a devastating disease unrelated to human cholera, could wipe out an entire flock within a few days, leaving the farmer bankrupt. It spread by means of contaminated food or direct contact with the excrement of other animals. Pasteur's first task was to isolate the organism which caused the disease. He accomplished this by culturing it in flasks of chicken broth. When he injected healthy chickens with this material, they promptly got sick and died; he knew he had produced a highly virulent germ. He could now use it for his experiments.

Then a stroke of luck occurred. Pasteur seized upon it ("chance favors only the prepared mind!"). Returning to Paris from a trip to the countryside, he discovered that his assistants had injected healthy chickens with material from chicken cholera cultures which had sat on the shelves for weeks. These chickens remained healthy. They next cultured a fresh batch of the bacteria and used it to inject both the chickens which had received the "old" material as well as ones which had not (the control group). The results astonished them: all the birds previously injected survived; those which had not been so injected died, every one of them.

Pasteur instantly realized that the "old" batch of cultures had somehow become *attenuated* while they gathered dust on the shelves. The germs were able to confer immunity, but not cause disease. He then cultured the bacteria in successive flasks of broth, taking a small sample from one, injecting it into fresh broth and, when it turned cloudy with bacteria, repeating the process again and again. He found these serial transfers also weakened the germs' virulence but not their immunogenicity. He now knew he had found a way to protect the chickens. He manufactured great quantities of his new vaccine for distribution to poultry farmers across the country.

In this research on chicken cholera, Pasteur had stumbled onto something more significant than just a way to stop an epidemic of disease in chickens. He knew he was staring at the central mystery of immunity, the same one Jenner had eyed almost a century earlier: how to weaken a germ so it would produce immunity but not cause disease. Jenner had used cowpox to variolate humans and render them immune to smallpox. Pasteur had discovered the same thing with his chicken cholera germ, a biological process called "active immunity." (Pasteur coined the terms "vaccinate" and "vaccine," derived from the latin word for cow, *vaccinus*, to honor his predecessor, Jenner).

In active immunity, the body produces antibodies against the weakened bacteria in the vaccine. When the vaccinated human or animal is then exposed to a wild strain of the disease, it is now armed and ready to defend itself with these new antibodies. Another form of immunity, "passive immunity," results when antibodies from a previously infected animal are injected into a person who's been exposed to a disease. Passive immunity is still used in cases of rabies, hepatitis, and tetanus, among others. Newborns also have passive immunity from the antibodies they get from their mothers in the womb. The problem with passive immunity is that these antibodies are soon lost due to normal breakdown processes in the body. And, unlike active immunity, no new ones are made to replace them. Furthermore, passive antibodies may prevent the development of active immunity. This is why most infant immunizations are delayed until a couple of months after birth, when the baby's maternal antibodies have disappeared.

Anthrax

Pasteur took up the study of anthrax for the same reason he had investigated the silkworm and chicken cholera problems: because of the negative impact the disease was having on the French economy. (He was nothing if not practical in his selection of what to study.) At the time, anthrax was destroying the sheep industry. It was known as the "Black Bane," the "Black Death," or the "Siberian Plague." Whatever it was called, it killed hundreds of thousands of animals annually, as well as an unfortunate few humans whose business brought them into contact with the sheep.

The sick animals died quickly, collapsing in pools of blood, vomit and excrement. They were buried where they fell. Some scientists still thought this indicated the disease was due to bad air or some other environmental factor, even though Koch's discovery of *bacillus anthracis* should have put an end to such thinking. When Pasteur visited sheep farms himself and listened to shepherds and veterinarians, he found that the sickness always returned to the same fields year after year. One field might be completely free of the disease, sandwiched between two or three others rife with it.

While walking through such a pasture where sick sheep had grazed, Pasteur noted an area with a large number of earthworm casts. When he questioned the farmer, the man said he had buried dead sheep there recently. Pasteur knew — from Koch's reports — about the spore form of anthrax. He put two and two together. The earthworms, he reasoned, brought the spores from the dead animals to the surface, where healthy animals might ingest or breathe them. That was why sheep grazing in certain pastures, or in certain parts of the same pasture, were at higher risk for the disease than others.

Pasteur collected some of the earthworms, brought them back to his laboratory, and dissected them. Their intestines were full of earth. And in the earth were — anthrax spores! He injected some of the earthworm intestinal fluid into guinea pigs. They died of anthrax. Pasteur now knew how the disease spread within a herd, and he recommended ways to dispose of dead animals which would prevent the problem in the future. But that wasn't enough. It was time to look at the the the anthrax bacterium itself.

Pasteur began his microbiologic study of anthrax by repeating Koch's experiments, but in a different way. He wanted to be absolutely sure in his own mind that Koch had gotten it right, that *b. anthracis* was the cause of the disease. But Pasteur didn't have Koch's solid culture media technique available to him. Instead, he took a drop of blood from an animal recently dead of anthrax and placed it into a flask of urine. After a few hours growth, a single drop of this liquid was transferred to a fresh flask of urine. And so on. He repeated the process many times until he was certain he had diluted the original bacterial colonies so much that he now had a pure culture of them. A drop of this final dilution was injected into rabbits, who promptly died of anthrax. Pasteur had independently verified Koch's original discovery. The anthrax bacterium was the cause of the disease.

Then chance intervened again, and Pasteur — again — was ready for it. During one of his visits to a sheep farm he found some animals which had gotten sick but survived the infection. These creatures could not be re-infected even when he injected them with pure bacteria from his lab; they were immune. It was about this time that his studies on chicken cholera had shown him how to make animals immune with a vaccine of weakened germs. Why not, he wondered, attenuate the anthrax bacteria as he had done the chicken cholera? Maybe that would lead to a vaccine against anthrax as well, a vaccine which would render the sheep as immune as those which had survived a natural infection.

He tried attenuating his cultures by various means, including letting them age, exposing them to oxygen, and using antiseptic agents such as carbolic acid. He had only marginal results with these. Success finally came when he heated the colonies in chicken broth to a temperature of 107 degrees F. for a prolonged period. This produced a weakened strain of the organism which, when injected into lab animals, caused only a mild form of the disease. But he was certain the animals were now immune. He proved it by challenging them with lethal anthrax doses. They all survived.

Pasteur reported his success. There were many doubters. Then, in 1881, a veterinarian named Rossignol challenged Pasteur in the name of a local veterinary society to prove his anthrax vaccine worked. He offered him a large number of animals for a trial at his own farm of Pouilly-le-Fort near the town of Melun, just south of Paris. Even though he was still in the testing stages of the vaccine, Pasteur accepted the challenge immediately. But his assistants were alarmed and begged him to delay. He would not hear of it and said to them,

> "what succeeded with 14 sheep in our laboratory, will succeed with 50 at Melun."

On May 5, Pasteur arrived at Pouilly-le-Fort with his vaccine. Sensing something big was in the wind, a sizeable crowd had gathered at the little farm. The *London Times* sent a correspondent to report on the progress of the trials, and French newspapers published daily descriptions of the event. There was a festive atmosphere among the onlookers, who included some of the country's most distinguished scientists, veterinarians and physicians.

Pasteur vaccinated 24 sheep, 1 goat and six cows. Another 24 sheep, 1 goat and 4 cows remained unvaccinated.

Twelve days later, May 17, Pasteur gave a second dose of his vaccine to the test animals. Two weeks after that, May 31, all animals were given lethal doses of anthrax.

June 2 dawned overcast and gray. The crowd gathered again to witness the results. Would Pasteur get his comeuppance? Or would his claims be vindicated? The sun broke through the clouds as the great man walked through the crowd toward the penned-up animals.

Eighteen of the unvaccinated animals were already dead, the remainder clearly in the process of dying (one sheep died literally in front of the crowd). All vaccinated animals looked healthy and were on their feet. Pasteur's vaccine was a complete success. Because of lingering suspicions, he repeated the trial at the cathedral town of Chartres later in the year. It was equally successful.

Within a decade, an estimated 3.5 million French sheep had been vaccinated with Pasteur's vaccine. The savings to the French economy were enormous, enough to pay the debt for losing the Franco-Prussian War.

How did Pasteur's attenuation process work? How did he turn a lethal bacterium into a protective one? It has only been in the past dozen or so years, as the genetic structure of anthrax and other microbes have been unraveled, that the answers to these questions have been found. Like all cells, *b. anthracis* contains a nucleus full of DNA. This genetic material is mostly responsible for the cell's reproduction process. But within the cell's cytoplasm are other bits of non-nuclear DNA called *plasmids*. These carry such traits as virulence, antibiotic resistance, and toxin production. *Plasmids* from one cell may communicate with others and thus spread acquired traits from a single bacterium to the entire colony. In this way, for example, resistance to antibiotics is carried from a single germ through the entire species.

Anthrax has two *plasmids*. It needs both to be virulent. One *plasmid* codes for the poly D-glutamic acid capsule, which helps the bacteria resist destruction by the host. The other *plasmid* turns on the production of the deadly toxin.

Pasteur's heat attenuation destroyed only one of the plasmids, the one which produced the toxin. The plasmid which led to the capsule remained intact and was the basis for the vaccine. By modern standards, this was not a particularly immunogenic vaccine. Since the toxin is the killing agent, it would have been better to have engendered immunity to it rather than to the capsule. That's what Sterne did in 1937. He developed a non-virulent strain which produced a low amount of toxin, not enough to kill but enough to evoke an antibody response. Both the Pasteur and Sterne vaccines are used only for animals, and the immunity only lasts about a year. These vaccines are intended to protect animals who've been exposed to a new case, not to maintain continuous herd-wide immunity. (The current vaccine for human use is a cell-free preparation which produces an antibody response to the Protective Antigen (PA) component of the anthrax toxin.)

Pasteur parlayed his success with anthrax into research on swine fever, another economically significant animal disease. By 1886 he had immunized more than 100,000 pigs with the vaccine he had developed.

By now well into his 60's, Pasteur had gained fame for his research on fermentation and for the development of vaccines against chicken cholera, animal anthrax, and swine fever. But, as his critics liked to point out, he had yet to take on a single *human* disease. That was what brought him to rabies, his last great challenge.

The *Rage*

Pasteur's development of a vaccine against rabies was certainly his most famous exploit. But not because the disease caused such high mortality. In fact, relatively few people were bitten by rabid animals, and only a small percentage of those actually developed rabies. There were fewer than 35-40 rabies deaths reported annually in Pasteur's France. But the way both animals and humans died from it was so horrible it guaranteed everlasting fame to anyone who could prevent it.

Perhaps Pasteur's triumph over rabies should be viewed more in terms of the challenges he had to overcome than in the number of lives he saved or the terrifying nature of the disease in the public imagination (dogs howled and gnawed at their cages; humans writhed in convulsions). First, he was unaware rabies was caused by a virus. That meant he never saw it in his microscope or cultured it on growth media. The idea of a virus would not even become apparent until 1898, three years after Pasteur's death, and this from a study of the tobacco mosaic virus. The rabies virus itself was not detected until 1903, eight years after Pasteur's death. Even then, its presence was only appreciated by its effects on the brain and the appearance of small inclusions called "Negri" bodies in brain cells. In 1963, with the newly-created electron microscope, the virus was finally visualized directly.

The word itself, "rabies," is Latin for rage. It is a disease principally of the central nervous system. Confusion and agitation are prominent symptoms, as are convulsions and paralysis. There is no effective treatment. In Pasteur's day, human bites from suspected rabid animals were cauterized with acid or red-hot irons. This was followed by a period of anxious waiting, sometimes for as long as a year. This painful treatment did no good, just as modern antibiotics and other supportive measures are ineffective today: death is inevitable. There has never been a human survivor of rabies who was symptomatic at the time of diagnosis. Prevention is the key to survival.

Rabies virus is maintained in nature in wild animals — called "sylvatic" rabies — particularly in skunks, foxes, raccoons and bats, where it is carried in the saliva. It is very uncommon in small rodents such as rabbits, gophers, and squirrels. Domestic animals are most often infected by the bites of wild animals, and humans are usually infected through their bites and scratches or from saliva contact with mucosal surfaces or open wounds. Possible person-to-person transmission has been reported in several cases from human bites.

Rabies' incubation period is variable, from as short as five days to as long as a year. But the average time is still a relatively long one of two months. Most dogs and cats become symptomatic within 5 days from the time the virus appears in their saliva. This is why suspicious animals are quarantined for 10 days after they bite someone. There has not been a case of the disease in any animal which has remained healthy for this 10-day observation period.

The diagnosis of animal rabies is now made by observing fluorescent antibodies (they literally glow under the microscope) against the virus in the brain tissue of animals who've died suspiciously. Although rabies can now be cultured, it takes too long to be of any practical value for diagnosing and preventing human disease.

Though Pasteur never saw the rabies virus under his microscope or in his culture broth, he detected its presence through its effects; the howling terror of affected dogs. His first goal was to develop an animal model through which he could study the organism. He accomplished this by burring small holes in the skulls of healthy dogs (an ancient technique known as "trephination") and directly injecting into their brains infected spinal cord tissue from sick rabbits. The dogs invariably became ill and died within three weeks. He had found his animal model. Now he could work on attenuating the organism and formulating a vaccine. (Even as a pragmatic physician, my stomach turns over at the thought of these animal experiments, especially when I gaze affectionately at my own labrador retriever named Molly. I can only justify Pasteur's experiments because they resulted in progress against the human form of the disease.)

Pasteur's initial strategy was to attenuate rabies the same way he had done with chicken cholera, through serial passages. But instead of using culture broth, he passed it from animal to animal, rabbits, dogs, guinea pigs and monkeys, making as many as 90 transfers. But the results were variable. In rabbits and guinea pigs, the virus became *more* virulent with each passage, finally levelling off at the 25th one. But monkeys took *longer* to become ill with each transfer. In 1884, Pasteur fashioned a vaccine from the monkey's sera and claimed he had made 23 dogs "refractory" to the disease.

But this method of serial passages was very time consuming and not completely reliable. Furthermore, the vaccine from this technique was intended as a prophylaxis for animals not yet bitten. Pasteur wanted a vaccine for humans who *had been* bitten but not yet developed symptoms. The key was for the vaccine to produce immunity rapidly, faster than the disease could gain a foothold on the nervous system, much quicker than the average two-month incubation period.

Pasteur and an assistant stumbled on the idea of attenuating the virus by air drying. A flask was fashioned in which an infected rabbit's spinal cord was dangled from a cotton plug. Each day a snippet of the cord was mashed into a solution and applied to a dog's brain through the burr hole. Pasteur discovered that after 14 days of drying, the spinal cord specimen was no longer pathogenic. His next step was to inject daily spinal cord preparations into healthy animals, starting with 14 day old ones and continuing until the last injection was as fresh as 1 day old. This last injection would have surely killed the animal if it had not had the 13 prior doses of gradually more virulent vaccine.

In 1885, Pasteur announced to the world that he could now make dogs immune to the bites of rabid animals. But he had not answered the big question: would his technique work on humans, and especially on humans already bitten?

An opportunity to answer that question arose unexpectedly on July 6, 1885, when three people arrived at his lab: nine-year old Joseph Meister, a baker's son, who had been badly mauled by a rabid dog two days earlier. The boy had 14 bites on his thigh, leg and fingers. He was accompanied by his mother and the dog's owner, who had killed the animal when it nipped at him.

Pasteur was extremely nervous about treating young Joseph, especially since he had not yet been able to culture and identify the rabies organism. But the boy's mother, knowing her son faced a certain and horrible death, begged Pasteur until he finally relented. With the help of a physician colleague — who would actually administer the injections — he agreed to treat the lad.

Sixty hours after Joseph was bitten, the doctor injected into a fold of the lad's abdominal skin a syringeful of liquified spinal cord from a rabbit who had died of rabies. The spinal cord had been kept in a flask and air dried for 14 days. Each day a more virulent injection was given to the boy from an animal which had died one day earlier. A total of 11 injections was given, the last one on July 16. Then the mother took her son home. Pasteur chewed on his fingernails with worry. He knew his vaccine was in a race with the disease:

Rabies, with its relatively slow incubation period, is like a local train; the vaccine overtakes it like an express train. . . and keeps it from entering the body.

On July 21, he received word that his vaccine had won the race.

Joseph's wounds were healing and he was well. (Joseph Meister's story doesn't end here. He was later employed by the Pasteur Institute, where he worked for many years. In 1940, when the Nazis occupied Paris, he was ordered to open Pasteur's crypt. Rather than comply, he killed himself.)

In September of the same year Pasteur treated Joseph Meister — 1885 — he treated another lad, Jean-Baptiste Jupille, a 15-year-old shepherd who had been bitten by a mad dog. This treatment also succeeded. Soon bite victims came for the vaccine from all over France, and from the rest of Europe as well. A group of 19 Russians who had been mauled by a wolf made the trip, as did 4 American boys sent by steamship from New York after they had been attacked by a rabid dog.

Within a year of Jean-Baptiste's treatment, 2500 persons from 18 countries had received the vaccine. How much good did it truly do? It's not certain, since it's hard to measure that which *does not* happen, e.g., cases which *do not* occur. How many of those 2500 people would have gotten the disease if they had been left untreated? Who knows? Most dog bites are not from rabid animals, so perhaps 80% of those 2500 patients would have remained well anyway. And even when bitten by a rabid animal, rabies occurs only about 20% of the time. It's probably fair to say that Pasteur's vaccine did prevent the disease in the small percentage of those who would have become ill, perhaps 100 or so people that year.

Pasteur reported that the mortality rate from the rabies vaccine itself was around 0.6% (10 fatalities in the 1700 Frenchmen he treated). Some of these deaths were probably due to severe allergic reactions. No records were kept of non-fatal reactions or vaccine-induced paralysis.

Modern treatment for suspected rabies begins with careful cleaning of animal bites and scratches. Then the nature of the bite is evaluated. If it is deemed high risk — e.g., bites about the head and neck; unprovoked attacks; animals unable to be quarantined — both passive and active immunizations are begun. The former is given as a single dose of Rabies Immune Globulin (RIG). The latter consists of a five-dose regimen of either Human Diploid Cell Vaccine (HDCV), Purified Chicken Embryo Cell Vaccine (PCEC), or rhesus monkey diploid cell vaccine (RVA). These injections are given on days 1,3,7,14 and 28 after the attack.

For bites with lower risk, especially if the animal is a known pet or can be captured and quarantined for 10 days, only active immunization is begun. Pre-exposure immunization can also be given to high risk occupational groups, such as animal handlers, veterinarians, and laboratory workers. And to spelunkers, who have increased risk of exposure to bats.

A direct result of Pasteur's triumph over rabies was the creation of a publicly funded Institute in his name to treat rabies victims. This was later expanded into the internationally-known Pasteur Institute. Its ongoing mission is to promote research on infectious diseases of all kinds.

On his 70th birthday, Pasteur was honored as a national hero with a Grand Jubilee at the Sorbonne. He died three years later, September 28, 1895, from a stroke. He is buried at the Institute named after him. He did not live to see one of the diseases he had struggled so hard to conquer turned into a weapon of mass destruction and biological terrorism: anthrax.

CHAPTER

12

THE DAWN OF BIOLOGICAL WEAPONS

The modern study of germs as weapons began with Japanese experiments during the period of the Second World War. They investigated specific microorganisms for their virulence, for their effects on humans and animals, and for the best means of dispersing them. But long before the Japanese got into biological warfare (BW), generals, terrorists, and assassins recognized the impact such weapons could have on an enemy, even though they may have known nothing about the germs themselves.

Khan Yanibeg's bombardment of the port of Kaffa in 1346 with the bodies of his own dead soldiers may or may not have started The Black Death. But it certainly caused a panic among the Genoese citizens living there, who promptly fled the city. This was precisely the effect Yanibeg wanted. It didn't matter to him whether it was from the plague, from hysterical worry about the plague, or from battlefield casualties. He wanted the city, and now it was his.

But the Khan wasn't the first to use disease — or the fear of it — as a weapon. The Assyrians, one of the cruelest people in an already-cruel world, poisoned the wells of their enemies during the 9th to 7th centuries B.C. The poison was ergot, a black, toxic fungus which grows as a parasite on rye grass. It can poison cattle if they graze on it. The Assyrians probably tossed the blighted rye into wells, and when enemy soldiers drank the water, they developed the classic symptoms of ergotamine poisoning: nausea, vomiting, headaches, seizures, coma and death. And even if the drug didn't kill, it would have rendered the enemy forces so helpless they could be easily defeated. In modern BW parlance, such a weapon is called an *incapacitant.*

Solon, the great Athenian lawgiver of the 6th century B.C., was also a well-poisoner. His choice of weapon was hellebore, an herb which causes cardiac and respiratory depression. Hannibal, the ever-inventive Carthagenian general who gave Rome so much grief during the Punic Wars, hurled clay pots full of venemous snakes onto the decks of his foes' warships in 190 B.C. The serpents may not have killed many, but one can imagine the panic they caused.

The use of fomites — inanimate materials which can transmit infection — also has a long history. As early as the 5th century B.C., Sythian archers harrassed their enemies with arrows dipped in manure or in the decomposing bodies of their own dead. During the French and Indian War (1754-1767), the English gave smallpox-infected blankets to Indians loyal to the French. The result was predictable: a devastating epidemic in the completely susceptible natives. As late as the 1960s, the Viet Cong used infected fomites against U.S. forces in Vietnam: pungi sticks smeared with excrement.

The medieval period was not without its examples of biological warfare. The Spanish, in 1495, tainted wine with the blood of leprosy patients and smuggled it into the French garrison at Naples while they were besieging it. In 1650, a Polish general put saliva from rabid dogs into hollow spheres and fired them against his enemies. The effects of this startling weapon are not known. Yanibeg's use of plague-infected bodies as biological weapons was copied extensively. Peter the Great's Russian soldiers, for example, hurled infected corpses against the Swedes in Estonia in 1710.

The American Civil War also witnessed instances of biological warfare. Confederate forces in Mississippi polluted wells and ponds with dead animals to deny the water to advancing Union troops. And Dr. Luke Blackburn, a fervent Rebel supporter, attempted to infect clothing with smallpox and sell it to Union supply agents.

The use of weapons of mass destruction during WWI was

spectacular in its effects. But they were mostly of the chemical variant: gas. These silent attacks killed, blinded and crippled hundreds of
thousands of men on both sides. The Germans also developed a mod-
est BW program. They infected livestock feed destined for the Allies
with anthrax spores and glanders bacteria (the latter is a bacterial infection of horses and mules which is occasionally transmitted to humans). And German agents innoculated 4500 mules with glanders and
sold them to French cavalry units. But there is little other evidence of
biological warfare during the "war to end all wars."

The carnage from gas warfare during WWI led, in 1925, to a mul-
tinational agreement to ban weapons of mass destruction, including
biological ones. Known as the Geneva Protocol, it prohibited only the
use of germ warfare agents. Basic research, production and stockpiling
were not proscribed. Since there were no plans for inspection, nor
sanctions for non-compliance, the Geneva Protocol was not worth
the paper it was written on. Within a half-dozen years Japan, though
a signatory to the Protocol, was actively engaged in the testing and
use of BW agents. Other countries followed after WWII. The U.S. didn't
formally ratify the Geneva Protocol until 1975. This delay would have
serious diplomatic consequences for America during the Cold War.

Other than the Japanese experiments, biological warfare was not
a prominent feature of WWII hostilities. But when the British learned
the Empire of the Sun was actively engaged in this type of research,
they launched their own limited program in 1941. Commandeering
the island of Gruinard off the northwest coast of Scotland, they dropped
bombs full of anthrax spores on it. Thousands of sheep and cattle
were infected. Two years later an outbreak of anthrax erupted in livestock on the *mainland* coast of Scotland facing Gruinard, probably
from windblown spores off the island. The British abruptly cancelled
the tests in 1943 but continued to monitor the island for the presence
of spores. In addition, they extensively decontaminated the island with
280 tons of formaldehyde and removed much of the top soil. The last
monitoring tests, in 1987, were negative, and the official quarantine
was lifted in 1990, 48 years after the tests were stopped.

Assassinations with biological weapons are hard to uncover. The death of Alexander the Great from anthrax may have been the first such case about which we have any information, though such murders could have been carried out long before this. One definitely documented case occurred during WWII. Reinard Heydrich, Chief of the Nazi secret service, was assassinated with a grenade loaded with typhoid fever bacteria. The Nazis themselves had little to do with biological weapons. Hitler preferred gas. And while many innocent victims perished in Dr. Joseph Mengele's experiments at Auschwitz, this was not research into biological weapons but rather in the service of Nazi genetics.

The United States program during WWII was mostly aimed at developing anti-crop herbicides and experimenting with a few bacteria. The effort was minimal. It was not until after the war, when data from Japanese human experimentation became available to American researchers, that the U.S. BW program got off the ground.

One of the most bizarre attempts to use a biological weapon for political murder took place during the Cold War. In September 1978, a Bulgarian exile named Georgi Markov, who was living in London, was injected while waiting for a bus with a weapon disguised as an umbrella (Fig. 14). The projectile was a pellet thought to contain ricin, a potent poison derived from castor beans. The man died, and although

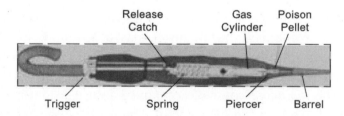

Figure 14. *Umbrella gun*

Source: van Keuren, RT: ***Chemical and Biological Warfare, an investigative guide***, U. S. Customs Service, October 1990.

never confirmed by lab tests, the coroner's inquest ruled poisoning by ricin as the cause of death. A similar attempt had been made ten days earlier against Vladimir Kostov, another Bulgarian living in Paris. In this case, his heavy sweater protected him from complete penetration by the weapon, and the doctors were able to remove the projectile from his back and save his life. They found it definitely contained ricin.

An attempt to use biological weapons for political ends took place in The Dalles, Oregon, in 1984. Seven hundred-fifty-one people developed salmonella gastroenteritis (vomiting and diarrhea) after eating at salad bars which had been poisoned with the bacteria by the Rajneeshee religious cult. The purpose of the bioattack was to lower voter turnout on election day and get the cult's supporters elected to local government offices.

The last major effort to use biologicals as weapons of terror, at least before those U.S. anthrax-by-mail cases of 2001, were the attacks by followers of the fanatical Japanese religious cult Aum Shinrikyo. In 1993, they tried to disperse anthrax spores from Tokyo and Yokahama roof tops. But analysis of the anthrax used in these attacks showed it was closely related to the 1937 Stern strain. This strain is non-pathogenic and is primarily used for animal vaccinations. It is not a risk for humans. Not surprisingly, there were no casualties from the attacks.

Frustrated by their failures with biological weapons, the cult, in 1995, turned to chemical weapons. It introduced sarin, a potent nerve toxin, into the Tokyo subway system. A dozen deaths, hundreds of cases of illness, and untold terror followed.

All these efforts at biological warfare and terrorism, though interesting, are merely side shows and curiosities compared with the main events: the WWII Japanese biological weapons factories at Ping Fan, Manchuria; the U.S. and Russian BW programs during the Cold War; and the Iraqi production of biological weapons in the 1990's. These will be discussed in detail in later chapters.

The Agents of Biological Warfare

The U.S. Army's *Critical Agent List* contains three categories of possible biological weapons. Many of these agents are on another list as well, the *Select Agent List*. This is a list of agents deemed so dangerous they cannot be moved from one lab to another without CDC permission.

Category A Agents

These are agents most likely to cause mass casualties if deliberately dispersed as biological weapons. They are organisms or toxins easily spread through the air or transmitted from person to person. They have high mortality rates; require special public health actions (i.e., vaccinations, quarantine); and are capable of causing public panic and widespread civil disruption. They are:

Bacteria

- anthrax
- plague
- tularemia: a bacterial disease of animals; spread by ticks, mosquitoes, and wild rabbits; can cause sepsis and shock in humans; very hardy, may survive for months in a decaying corpse; no human-to-human transmission; 30% mortality if untreated

Viruses

- Lassa fever: a highly contagious viral infection; spreads to people after contact with infected rodents; muscle pain, hemorrhage and shock are its symptoms
- smallpox: highly contagious viral infection; can be spread by fomites; causes high rate of illness and sometimes high mortality (20%).
- Ebola and Marburg viruses; mortality rates close to 90%; no known cure; spread by contact with blood or body fluids of infected persons

Toxins

- botulism: a neural toxin; can be spread by aerosol or as a food contaminant; extremely toxic

Category B Agents

These agents could be used to contaminate food or water supplies. They are moderately easy to disseminate; cause moderate rates of illness but low death rates; often require specialized lab tests to diagnose; some have been used as biological weapons in the past.

- *salmonella typhimurium*: the agent of typhoid fever
- brucellosis: a disease of animals, principally cattle; causes an

incapacitating human illness with a low mortality rate
- staph enterotoxin: the principal cause of food poisoning
- Q fever: a very incapcitating agent; a single bacterium can cause clinical illness
- *clostridium perfringens:* the agent of gas gangrene
- glanders: a bacterial infection of horses, donkeys and mules; can be transmitted to humans.

Category C Agents

These are emerging infectious diseases. They could be exploited as biological weapons because of their availability, ease of production, ease of dispersion and potential for both high morbidity and high mortality rates.

- yellow fever: a viral infection of the liver
- drug resistant TB: transmissible from person to person
- subacute hemorrhagic fever: a viral illness which causes severe anemia
- Hanta virus: transmitted by infected rodents and their feces; low mortality rate but high likelihood of illness

Advantages of Biological Weapons

The advantages of biological weapons far outweigh their disadvantages. First, many can cause very large numbers of casualties, as Table 2 demonstrates. Anthrax stands out well above the others, a dubious honor.

Release of 50kg. of agent upwind of a population center of 500,000

Agent	No. Dead	No. Sick
Anthrax	95,000	125,000
Tularemia	30,000	125,000
Q Fever	150	125,000
Brucellosis	500	125,000
Typhus	15,000	65,000

Table 2. Mass casualty-generating potential of BW agents

Source: WHO

Another advantage is that BW agents cause illnesses which, in their early stages, are similar to common, benign infections like the common cold, the flu and gastroenteritis. (Four of the 11 inhalation anthrax-by-mail cases of 2001 were initially sent home by their physicians with a diagnosis of "viral syndrome.") Differentiating a BW illness from a garden variety viral disease would be difficult for physicians who have never actually seen a case of BW illness. Furthermore, specialized lab tests such as PCR's and ELISA's might be necessary to make an early diagnosis of agents like Ebola, Lassa and Hanta viruses. Such tests are available only at highly specialized labs. The inevitable delay in getting specimens processed would hinder both patient care and epidemic counter measures.

The favorable cost/benefit ratio of biological weapons is a very distinct advantage to the biowarrior or bioterrorist. In 1969, the U.N. estimated the cost to deploy various types of weapons against civilian targets, as measured by square kilometer of territory attacked:

- $1.00 U.S. for biological weapons
- $600.00 U.S. for chemical weapons
- $800.00 U.S. for nuclear weapons
- $2,000.00 U.S. for conventional weapons

One reason for the attractive cost/benefit ratio of BW agents is their ease of production. Some are found in nature and can be easily collected, cultured and grown in large quantities in production laboratories. Most nations with even a rudimentary pharmaceutical or medical industry could produce these agents in large amounts. And detecting the production facilities would be difficult, since they may appear to be factories engaged in legitimate, peaceful medical research or in the production of products such as vitamins, pesticides, or milk and baby food. This ease of production, difficulty of detection, and favorable cost/benefit ratio has led BW agents to be labelled the "Poor Man's Atom Bomb."

The ease of production of biological weapons has another, more nefarious, side to it. A terrorist could set up a "bathtub" laboratory in an old warehouse or office building or even a large apartment building in the middle of a big city. Fermenters, culture plates, personal protective gear and other equipment and supplies could all be ordered from standard scientific catalogues or on the Internet. These mini labs could be erected quickly and just as quickly taken down and moved if authorities grew suspicious and came snooping around. Richard Preston, in his book *The Cobra Event*, describes a terrorist who does just this, manufactures deadly germs in an apartment and spreads them through the New York subway system.

Ease of dispersion is another big advantage of biological weapons. Bombers and artillery tubes are not necessary. Since many are spread by the airborne route in nature, pilotless drones, crop sprayers or balloons would work as well and be far cheaper and less detectable than conventional munitions. Other agents such as typhoid and botulism can be sprayed, sprinkled onto food, or added to water sources.

During the Cold War years, U.S. scientists performed studies to see how vulnerable America was to biological attack from some of these agents. They used "simulant" organisms, bacteria which are themselves harmless but disperse similarly to harmful ones. A favorite was a bacteria named *serratia marcescens*. It produces a pink pigment when it grows, making it easy to detect. Serratia was covertly sprayed over a number of U.S. cities to test dispersion patterns. The programs were cancelled in 1969 when one man died from it and 10 more became ill with what were probably serratia urinary tract infections.

In another test, *bacillus subtilis*, a relatively innocuous cousin of anthrax, was released into the New York City subway. Winds from the trains quickly dispersed the bacteria throughout the entire underground tunnel system.

Another advantage of biological weapons is the ease with which they can be genetically altered. Microbes do this anyway, through natural mutation. But researchers are now able to cut and splice bacterial DNA to fashion new strains, strains which might be unaffected by current vaccines, resistant to current antibiotics, more virulent, hardier, and more easily dispersed. These genetic changes could also be carried out in small, secret labs using standard microbiology equipment and supplies.

Last but not least are the psychological effects of biological weapons. These could well be more harmful than their actual number of casualties. There is something about germ warfare which makes us shudder with revulsion. Even hoaxes can have major impacts on a community. In 1992, a man sprayed his neighbors with what he claimed were anthrax spores. A massive response was generated, including quarantine for the houses and the neighbors, washdowns of all contaminated surfaces, and many needless visits to local hospitals. Other such hoaxes have severely stressed hospitals and clinics and their limited supplies of medicines, vaccines, and antibiotics.

In addition to the panic and alarm from a real or a phony BW attack, there is the added psychological effect of epidemic hysteria. This is the appearance of patients with psychological symptoms unrelated to a real infection.

Symptoms of epidemic hysteria come in two general forms:

- *Anxiety Symptoms:* dizziness, fainting, nausea, vomiting, weakness, coughing, headache
- *Psycho-motor symptoms:* pseudo-convulsions, pseudo-tremors, pseudo-paralysis (called "pseudo" because while they look like the real thing, they are not)

Patients with these symptoms are not malingering or faking. They truly believe they've been exposed to the infection. Their symptoms, though often bizarre, are the physical expressions of that belief.

Hyperventilation (rapid breathing) is another typical symptom of epidemic hysteria. Weakness of the arm or leg and numbness and tingling in the arms and legs have also been reported during naturally-occurring epidemics. Even hysterical dancing has been noted. In this case, the patient twirled round and round for hours. Another patient laughed uncontrollably, couldn't stop. Another suddenly started shouting obscenities like someone with Tourette's syndrome. And in one case report, a teenage boy was found wandering around in a park in the middle of the night dressed in his bathrobe and slippers. He was diagnosed with hysterical Alzheimer's disease!

Disadvantages of Biological Weapons

There are some disadvantages to biological weapons, more for the military planner than for the terrorist. The principal one is their unpredictability of dispersal, especially if airborne. As the Scots on the coast facing Gruinard Island discovered, the wind goes where it wants, and windblown germs go along with it. For a general on the battle-field, the risk of infectious agents being blown back in his troops' faces would put a serious restriction on their use. A terrorist, however, who's likely to be operating alone or with only a few co-conspirators, would not find this much of a problem.

The durability of BW agents could be a disadvantage in some situ-ations. A force wishing to occupy conquered ground might find the same deadly germs waiting for them when they arrived that they had deployed against their enemy. And if the organism was especially per-sistent — like anthrax spores — it might be years or decades before the land could be occupied. This, again, would not be a problem for the bioterrorist.

There is also the distinct disadvantage that BW agents might be-come part of the natural bacterial flora of the territory against which they were used. If they had been genetically altered to be antibiotic or vaccine resistant, they could be a significant problem to one's own force as well as to the enemy's.

The final disadvantage in using biological weapons is the likely consequences of their deployment. Not only would world-wide cen-sure immediately fall upon the user, but the victim nation might feel free to retaliate in kind, or worse, with nuclear weapons. This fear of retaliation is believed to be the primary reason Iraq did not use its considerable arsenal of BW agents during the Gulf War. This would not be a serious consequence for a shadowy terrorist group like *al Qaeda*.

Anthrax as a Biological Weapon

Anthrax is at the top of everyone's list of BW agents. The same advantages and disadvantages which apply to the others fit it as well, in some cases even more so. For example, the dispersability of anthrax spores is particularly awesome. A 1970 World Health Organization re-port estimated that 50 kilograms of the spores released by a pilotless drone or crop duster over a city of 500,000 souls would result in 125,000 cases of anthrax, with 95,000 deaths. Based on *serratia marcescens* ex-periments, a similar 50 kilogram load of anthrax spores dropped up-wind of a city of 5,000,000 people could yield 250,000 sick and 100,000 dead. This is the same lethality as an atom bomb. The use of subway air vents would be especially effective for dispersing anthrax spores.

This dispersability feature is greatly enhanced if weapons grade anthrax is used. This means that the spores are in powder form — as opposed to a slurry — are highly concentrated, have particles of uniform size, and are treated with something (e.g., talcum) to prevent clumping. The letters sent to Senator Daschle last year contained weapons grade anthrax, about 2 grams worth. This represented between 100 billion and 1 trillion spores.

Except for botulinum toxin — which is even more potent than sarin nerve gas — anthrax is the most deadly BW agent known. A mortality rate of 85% is typical in naturally-occurring epidemics. America was lucky in its one experience with the disease, 2001's bioterrorist attack. Only 5 of the 11 inhalation anthrax cases died. In a massive attack, however, hospitals would be overwhelmed with tens of thousands of cases. Antibiotic supplies, basic support measures, laboratory capability, even hospital beds, would quickly be used up. Mortality rates of *at least* 85% could be expected. In addition, the panic, cases of epidemic hysteria, hoaxes and copy cat attacks would further hobble the health care system, depriving treatment to patients who truly needed it.

Another big advantage of anthrax is its ease of production. With a single seed culture, massive quantities can be grown in a few days with easily obtainable equipment. Since a pinch of anthrax contains about 1,000,000 spores, and only 8,000-10,000 are needed per dose, the killing potential of even a handful of anthrax is terrifying. Furthermore, the durability of the spores guarantees that new cases would continue to occur for many months to come.

Finally, the impact on America of a large-scale anthrax attack cannot be measured just in terms of the number of new tombstones erected or hospital beds filled. Disruption of our entire economy would be more complete than anything we've seen. In the dry language of accountants, it's estimated that it would cost us $26.2 billion for every 100,000 persons exposed, not *infected*, just exposed.

The Second World War brought many innovations to the art of warfare, and an equal number of horrors. The tank, first used clumsily in WWI, became the tip of the spear for Germany's armed forces. The aircraft carrier replaced the battleship in warfare at sea. Germany turned to stealth weapons, notably the development of the submarine. Unrestricted air warfare was used by both sides in bombing runs over non-military population centers like London and Coventry, Berlin and Dresden, Tokyo and Yokahama. By the end of the war, jet planes were replacing propeller-driven ones for dominance in the sky.

Weapons of mass destruction were also developed. America and Germany raced to develop the atom bomb: American won that one. In biological warfare, the Empire of the Sun — and one Japanese scientist single-handedly — led the way into the nightmare future.

C H A P T E R

13

WWII AND THE
JAPANESE UNIT AT PING FAN

Khabarovsk, USSR, December, 1949: I

The twelve Japanese prisoners of war stood before the Soviet mili
tary tribunal in this city on the Soviet-Manchurian border while
the charges against them were read: bacterial warfare against Soviet
civilians and troops during WWII. General Yamada Ōtozoo, Com-
mander-in-Chief of the Japanese Kwantung Army, was the ranking
Japanese officer. Another senior officer was Major General Kawashima
Kiyoshi, commander of several sections of Unit 731 at Ping Fan, a
suburb of the city of Harbin in central Manchuria. Missing was Lieutenant General Ishii Shiro, a medical doctor in the Imperial Japanese
Army, a specialist in infectious diseases, and overall commander of
the notorious Unit 731.

There was little about the twelve prisoners standing at stiff attention that revealed they were from a defeated nation. On the contrary,
their shiny boots, their glittery medals, and the arrogance in their
eyes and postures showed they still saw themselves as a superior race.
If they had lost the war to clearly inferior peoples, it must have been
because they had not fought hard enough, had not been brave enough,
or had been badly led.

The following testimony before the Khabarovsk Tribunal is fictional, but is based on actual events and testimony:

The Soviet Chief Prosecutor rose to question General Kawashima.
He was a man who understood that victory was about arms and power,
not about which was the superior race.

"Tell the court about the special UJI bomb developed at Unit 731," he demanded of the witness.

"It was a 25 kilogram weapon filled with anthrax spores."

"What made it so special?"

"Its outer shell was made of porcelain rather than metal."

"Why porcelain?"

"So it would shatter with a smaller explosive charge."

"Why was that important?"

"It exposed the biological agent inside to less heat and pressure than from a conventional weapon."

"What was the HA bomb?"

"A larger, 40 kilogram, high altitude device. Its casing was made of thinner-than-normal steel."

"And its warhead?"

"Shrapnel as well as anthrax spores."

"How many of these bombs did you and General Ishii produce at Ping Fan?"

"I don't remember. Quite a few, I think."

The Prosecutor took a sheet of paper from an assistant, then turned to the Military Judges to explain. "This is one of a collection of documents taken when General Kawashima and his staff were captured."

He handed the paper to the witness. "What is the date on this document?"

"June 1940."

"It is a list of munitions, isn't it? Specifically, it identifies the number of both UJI and HA bombs stockpiled at Unit 731 that year. Read aloud the total number on the bottom line."

"Sixteen hundred."

The Chief Prosecutor snatched back the paper. "That is correct. There were 1600 of these weapons of death stored at Unit 731. And how did you and General Ishii test these weapons?"

Kawashima refused to answer.

The Prosecutor produced more papers, which he handed one by one to the General.

"What are these documents, General? They all bear your signature."

Kawashima still would not answer.

"Is this not an order for planes to drop rice mixed with plague-infected fleas on the Manchurian city of Changchun to see what effect they would have on the populace there?"

Kawashima maintained a tight-lipped, glaring silence.

The Soviet stabbed at the paper. "Isn't this your signature?"

One after another, the Prosecutor waved the papers in Kawashima's face. "And isn't this an order for similiar experiments on the Chinese city of Chuhsien? And this one for the city of Nanking? And this one for the city of. . ." And on and on he continued until he had read the entire list of eleven Chinese and Manchurian cities used for field testing the BW agents General Ishii had developed at Unit 731.

Ishii Shiro

There is no doubt that the person most responsible for converting Manchuria into one huge biological warfare laboratory during the Japanese occupation was. . . Ishii Shiro.

— From *Factories of Death*
 by **Sheldon Harris**

For the Japanese, the war in Manchuria began in 1905 when it defeated and replaced the Russians as *de facto* rulers there. In 1932, the Japanese Army of the Kwantgung peninsula — a Manchurian province — came to power and swept through the country. It set up several puppet governments, the final one being that of Henry Pu Yi, known to history as the "Last Emperor."

Along with the army's guns and tanks and soldiers came Major Ishii Shiro, an ultra-militarist officer fanatically loyal to the Emperor and his expansionist plans for the country. A medical doctor, Ishii saw a future for himself in the Imperial Army and joined up soon after graduation from medical school. He became proficient in the sciences of bacteriology, preventive medicine, and pathology. In addition, in 1926 he earned a doctorate in microbiology.

Ishii began touting the advantages of biological weapons in the late 1920s and early 1930s. And what better place to study germ warfare than in Manchuria, a conquered nation with an inexhaustible supply of labor, and with many criminals and prisoners-of-war to serve as experimental subjects. He had himself posted to Manchuria in 1932 and remained there until the war's end.

Ishii's initial camp was established near Harbin, the provincial capital of Northern Manchuria. There, in a remote but easily accessible village called Beiyinhe, he constructed buildings for a laboratory, a crematorium and a munitions dump, along with a prison for 1,000 inmates. Those early experiments concentrated on anthrax and plague. The prisoners, mostly bandits and anti-Japanese guerillas, were exposed to these agents then dissected, some while unconscious but still alive. When they were of no further use as subjects, the prisoners who survived the experiments were killed with injections of poison, then dissected and cremated.

The laboratory at Beiyinhe was just a prelude for Ishii. By 1935 he needed much bigger facilities for his schemes. He selected a cluster of 10 villages known as Ping Fan, located ten miles south of Harbin. When completed in 1939, Pin Fan was enormous, 6 square kilometers in area, with 76 structures: laboratories, dormitories, administration buildings, barracks, sheds for test animals and an autopsy/dissection building. In addition, a fully functioning farm supplied the camp with fruits and vegetables, and a brothel staffed with sex slaves ("comfort women") provided relaxation for off duty troops.

The Ping Fan camp was about the size of Auschwitz, with, at its peak, 3,000 Japanese troops permanently assigned there. Ten to fifteen thousand laborers worked at the camp between 1936-1945. One-third of these died of maltreatment. As a cover for his BW experiments, Ishii built an operating lumber mill. The Japanese then winked at one another and referred to their human subjects as "logs."

The Ping Fan Unit was officially known as Water Purification Unit number 731, or just Unit 731. Initially, its guinea pigs were common criminals. But as POW's became available from Japanese military conquests, they included Soviets, Chinese, Mongolians and Koreans, as well as the mentally retarded, European criminals, anti-Japanese guerillas, and possibly Allied POW's: British, Canadians, New Zealanders, Australians and possibly even Americans. (In another of history's great ironies, some of the Americans who survived the Bataan Death March ended up at Ishii's camps.) The germs tested on these victims were anthrax, plague, cholera, typhoid, glanders, tetanus and gas gangrene. Ishii increased his production capability until almost 40,000,000 billion pathogens were being produced annually.

Though Unit 731 was Ishii's largest germ warfare plant, experimentation and production went on at other locations as well. While most laboratory experiments were conducted at Ping Fan, Anda, a facility 2 hours' drive north, was used for above-ground field tests. Anthrax and plague in particular were tested on prisoners staked to the ground there.

Another BW unit was established at Changchun, a city of 500,000, about 150 miles south of Ping Fan. This was the headquarters of the Kwangtung Army. Known as Unit 100, anthrax, plague and glanders were used in large field trials against civilian populations. Another BW factory was established at Nanking. Known as the Tama unit, it experimented with many BW agents in the laboratory, in field tests, and on civilian populations.

Khabarovsk: II

The next witness was a middle-aged man wearing the insignia of a Lieutenant in the Japanese Army. He had been barely twenty-two years old when he first came to Manchuria in 1933, but had remained there until the end of the war.

"You were assigned to duties at both Unit 731 and at the Anda field testing site, is that correct?" the Soviet prosecutor asked grimly.

"Yessir."

"What were your duties at the Anda station?"

"I was part of the security force. We escorted prisoners to the testing sites, guarded them while they were there, then brought them back to their barracks. I had nothing to do with the experiments themselves."

"But you did witness many experiments firsthand?"

"Yes."

"Tell the court specifically how they tested anthrax."

"The doctors wanted to know the infectious range of the weapons: how far from where the weapon was detonated would humans still become infected. We staked the prisoners to the ground in groups of ten. Then bombs filled with anthrax spores were detonated at various distances from them."

"Who were the 'experimental subjects'?"

"Mostly Chinese prisoners-of-war. But the scientists also wanted to see how different ethnic groups would react to the disease. POW's from other nations were also used as experimental subjects."

"But among yourselves — between you and your men — you didn't refer to them as 'experimental subjects,' did you? Or as prisoners-of-war? Or even as 'guinea pigs,' which is what they were? What did you call them?"

"*Maruta.*"

"Which means what?"

"'Logs,'" the Lieutenant responded promptly, without the slightest trace of shame.

"You referred to these people, these human beings, as 'logs'? Or collectively as so much 'lumber'?"

"That's correct."

"What happened to the prisoners after they were tested?"

"They were taken to special rooms and observed by the doctors."

"Then what?"

"When they died, they were autopsied."

"Were all the victims dead when they were autopsied?"

A crack appeared in the Lieutenant's composure: he hesitated. "No, some were unconscious but still alive."

"How do you know that?"

"Because I saw them move when the doctors made the cuts."

The prosecutor exploded. "They were cut open while they were still alive!?"

Red-faced, the Lieutenant would only nod.

"What anesthetic was used?"

The Lieutenant mumbled something unintelligible.

"Speak up. The court can't hear you. What type of anesthesia was used?"

The answer came out barely above a whisper from the now-pale witness.

"None. The scientists wanted pure specimens of live tissue to study. They didn't want them drugged. When they were finished, we disposed of the bodies."

The interrogator appeared incredulous. But like the good prosecutor he was, he already knew the answers before he asked the questions. "Not all prisoners got sick from the experiments, did they?" he asked. "What happened to those who didn't?"

"'The doctors said they had been 'contaminated' and were of no further value."

"What happened to them?"

"They were sacrificed."

"Sacrificed?"

"Killed."

In addition to the HA and UJI bombs, Ishii also experimented with artillery shells as delivery vehicles for his biological weapons. One was a conventional gas shell with a warhead packed with bacteria. Another was a 75 mm. high explosive shell full of bacteria instead of explosives. Neither weapon proved practical for operational use. Ishii also experimented with aerial spraying as a way to disperse bacteria: for example, as an anthrax slurry misted over the "logs."

In the Ping Fan laboratories, various fomites were tested. Prisoners were forced to eat food laced with germs. These included chocolates filled with anthrax and cookies contaminated with plague. Drinks were also poisoned with germs and given to the "logs"; even fruits and vegetables were injected or sprayed with biological agents and given to the prisoners. These fomite experiments were put into operational use in Manchurian and Chinese cities. Nangking children, for example, were given, as special treats, anthrax-filled chocolates as well as sweet cakes laced with typhoid. Fountain pens smeared with typhoid were also dropped along roadways for enemy soldiers and civilians to pick up.

Khabarovsk: III

The next witness, Kurushima Yuji, identified himself as a low-level technician and clerk. He said he was the custodian of Unit 731's experimental records.

A prosecutor asked him, "Besides anthrax, what other diseases did you experiment with at Unit 731?"

"Plague, brucellosis, botulism, gas gangrene and cholera."

"And you tested them all, in some way or other, on humans as well as animals?"

"Yes."

"Between 1941 and 1945, how many prisoners died from the experiments at Unit 731?"

"About six hundred per year."

"But that number doesn't include the deaths at Ping Fan during the years 1939 to 1941, does it?"

"No."

"Nor the 5,000-6,000 killed in the biological warfare units in Mukden and Changchun in Mongolia, or at Nanking in China?"

"No."

"Nor the tens of thousands who died at Canton, Beijing, and Shanghai in China, or in Manchuria, Mongolia and the Soviet Union during field trials with biological agents?"

The defendant hung his head and refused to answer.

But the prosecutor was not done with him. "Nor the deaths from Manchurian wells you poisoned with typhoid and anthrax?"

No response.

"Nor the civilian casualties from plague-infected rats released into Manchurian cities?"

Still no response.

"Nor the illness from beans and rice laced with plague you scattered by airplanes to starving civilian populations?"

Nothing.

The prosecutor took a deep breath, calmed himself, then continued. "Did any of the prisoners at Ping Fan survive the end of the war?"

"No."

"No one left the compound alive?"

"No."

"In its thirteen year period of operation, no prisoner escaped death?"

"None."

In his summary, the Chief Prosecutor pointed out that the biological weapons developed at Unit 731 by General Ishii were all used tactically against the Soviet Union in 1939, against Chinese cities during 1940-1944, and against Chinese troops in 1942. As the Kwangtung Army retreated from Manchuria at war's end, it destroyed all the BW camps. The prisoners were killed. No one was left alive. In a final act of vengeance, plague and anthrax-infected animals were released from their cages into the surrounding countryside. Epidemics of these diseases recurred in both the human and animal populations for years afterward.

The twelve Japanese defendants at the Khabarovsk trial were all found guilty and given sentences ranging from two to twenty-five years at hard labor. None was sentenced to death.

The final itemized butcher's bill for the Japanese BW program during WWII has been estimated as follows:

- 3,000 deaths from the experiments at Ping Fan;
- uncounted thousands of deaths at Beiyinhe;
- around 5,000 dead from experiments at other BW camps;
- tens of thousands of prisoners massacred at war's end to prevent them from falling into Chinese or Soviet hands;
- 30,000 who perished after the war in the epidemics around Ping Fan from the release of infected lab animals

The Cover Up

The Japanese war crimes trials held in Tokyo at the end of the war involved a genuine conspiracy of silence. . . Allied prosecutors from a half dozen countries. . . remained silent. . . the Chinese. . . must have lived in hope of gaining something. . . for their silence. . . The Russian authorities allowed themselves to be silenced.

— *Factories of Death*
   by **Sheldon Harris**

The end of WWII marked the beginning of the Cold War. Even before the guns had grown cold, the Soviets blockaded Berlin (1948), forcing the Allies to supply sectors of the city via the famous Berlin Airlift. American scientists at Fort Detrick, the Pentagon, and the White House were desperate to match the Soviets in the new arms race. That included biological weapons as well as conventional and nuclear ones. If a few Japanese prisoners had to forgo punishment for war crimes in exchange for precious BW research data, that must have seemed a fair trade at the time. In retrospect, it was an abomination.

Almost as soon as Japan surrendered in 1945, scientists at Fort Detrick were on their way to Japan to look at data from the BW experiments at Unit 731. Ishii himself was interviewed in his Tokyo home 25 times (he was never arrested). The consummate con artist, he convinced Allied authorities that his operations were very small in scale and that he only used animals; no humans were ever used as test subjects. Furthermore, he claimed, no one in the Japanese high command — certainly not the Emperor — ever knew about his research activities. He portrayed himself as a rogue scientist, and the Allies bought it. At least at first.

But by the end of 1947, American investigators had accumulated mountains of evidence about Unit 731 and the other BW camps run by Ishii. However, they were more interested in getting the data from these experiments than in prosecuting Ishii and his cronies. The U.S. scientists knew they would never be able to get similar human experimental data back home because of the legal and ethical prohibition against such research in America. They made a deal with Ishii and his top lieutenants, a deal sanctioned by the American government: immunity from prosecution and a small monetary payment in exchange for the data. What they were after were the following:

- reports of every biological weapon Ishii had ever studied;
- all the microscope slides of autopsies on BW subjects;
- reports of all the autopsies;
- photograhps of autopsy material;
- reports of the field trials of biological agents.

From the beginning, media stories about General Ishii's experiments on POW's were suppressed. Only a couple — 1946 reports in the *New York Times* and the *Pacific Stars and Stripes* — made it into print. The public knew nothing about Ishii and his death camps.

But the Soviets knew plenty from their own captured Japanese prisoners. They were preparing their war crimes trials in Khabarovsk, and in 1947 they requested the U.S. to provide them access to some of the biowarfare data. The Americans stalled. When the Soviets officially requested that Ishii and others be turned over to them for prosecution for war crimes against Soviet troops and citizens, they were refused outright.

The Tokyo war crimes trials ran from 1946-1948. Two thousand judicial proceedings were held, in which 5,700 Japanese nationals were tried. Neither Ishii nor any of his associates ever appeared before these tribunals. They were protected by grants of immunity. Many of these men went on to successful post-war careers in Japan. None ever admitted his guilt. Ishii himself lived out a comfortable retirement in Tokyo, surrounded by his children and grandchildren. To this day, the Japanese, as a nation, have never accepted responsibility for their behavior toward conquered nations during WWII, and especially for the notorious biological warfare experiments conducted in Manchuria and China.

The most complete account of Japanese BW experiments during WW II is Sheldon Harris's *Factories of Death*, Routledge, London, 2002. It is simply without parallel. I have referred to it extensively for this chapter.

CHAPTER 14

AMERICA'S BIOLOGICAL WEAPONS PROGRAM

In 1943, a sleepy old Army post in western Maryland, close by the peaceful splendor of the Catoctin Mountains, was activated as America's first biological weapons facility. Known as Camp Detrick, it was near enough to Washington, D.C. and the Pentagon for easy access by military and civilian leaders, yet far enough away should there be a biological accident. The camp's rural setting gave it anonymity, and, for a time, kept out the nosy public and the prying eyes of the media.

Camp Detrick quickly grew into a large complex with 250 buildings and living quarters for 5,000 people. It was renamed Fort Detrick in 1956 and became America's pre-eminent site for the production and testing of biological weapons. When the dirty secrets from Japanese experiments in Manchuria during WWII became available to U.S. scientists, three other facilities were created or expanded to assist Detrick in its mission:

Horn Island. Located ten miles south of Pascagoula, Mississippi, this site was principally used for testing BW agents, mostly botulinum toxin.

Granite Peak, Utah. 35 miles from Dugway Proving Grounds in Utah, this site contained an enormous expanse of high desert and shrub brush. It was completed in 1945 and used to field test all types of BW agents.

Vigo, Indiana. Built near Terre Haute, this facility was used to manufacture BW agents, particularly anthrax.

One of Detrick's earliest operations was a germ production line begun in 1946 (Figure 15). It used chicken eggs as culture media, innoculating them with brucellosis or Venezuelan Equine Encephalitis (VEE — a usually non-fatal central nervous system infection). But the work was done by hand and yielded only a small amount of bacteria or virus. It was considered a pilot program, with a capacity for barely 2,000 eggs per run.

Figure 15.

WWII-era germ production line at Camp Detrick

Source: U.S. Army

Munitions studies of biological weapons were also begun during WWII. Large (110 lb. and 115 lb.) and small (10 lb.) bombs were tested using anthrax simulants. Shotgun shell bombs were similarly tested. The smaller weapons proved to be most successful when used as clusters inside larger bomb casings. Five thousand anthrax-filled bombs were produced at Camp Detrick, and a production order for 1,000,000 more went out to a contractor but was cancelled at war's end.

Some anti-crop agents were developed by the U.S. during WWII, such as a rice fungus designed to be dropped as a bomb and an airplane-sprayed defoliant. No U.S. biological agent was ever used on the battlefield or over enemy territory during the war.

After WWII

The Korean War began in 1950 with the invasion of South Korea by its communist-led and Chinese-backed neighbor, North Korea. Led by General Douglas MacArthur, the United States was soon involved in the shooting as the largest contingent of a United Nations force. Hostilities ceased in 1951, but a formal armistice was not signed until two years later. Even before the ink was dry, the USSR, China and

North Korea were accusing the U.S. of waging biological warfare against North Korea.

In 1952, an International Scientific Commission was formed to investigate these charges. Dominated by scientists from communist bloc countries, the commission concluded that the U.S. had in fact used such weapons, though the charges were never substantiated. When the Americans attempted to form an independent commission to investigate, it was rejected by the Soviet Union. In the end, nothing was ever concluded, and the U.S. vigorously denied the accusations. However, America's failure to ratify the 1925 Geneva Protocol, its known collaboration with Japanese biological war criminals, and its ongoing program of BW experimentation cast doubt on these denials and cost the U.S. diplomatic credibility for years to come.

During the Korean War era, construction and testing continued apace at Camp Detrick. A 4-story tall metal sphere — nicknamed the "8-ball" — was built for exploding biological weapons and creating aerosols and mists whose dispersion patterns could then be measured. Another building, designated Building 470, was also constructed. It was 8 stories tall and windowless. It was used for making anthrax spores.

At Dugway, aerosol tests were carried out to determine how to deploy offensive biological weapons against the Soviet Union. All in all, 173 such tests, using non-infectious aerosols, were carried out there.

Other tests were done to study how weather conditions might affect the dispersal of BW agents. In one experiment, a car was driven through a Minneapolis suburb on a cold, clear night and released a mist of biological simulant. The investigators discovered that if a temperature inversion layer was present during the spraying, the agent would be trapped between the layers and spread further across the city. The simulant stood for anthrax spores.

In 1956, the same year Camp Detrick was officially named Fort Detrick, a facility was opened at Pine Bluff Arsenal, Arkansas. Its mission was to make bacterial agents by culturing them in chicken eggs. But the time consuming hand labor of egg innoculations started at Detrick 10 years earlier was now replaced with assembly line efficiency. Tularemia, Q fever and VEE were produced in a streamlined process which would have made Henry Ford proud. One hundred twenty gallons of Q fever could be manufactured weekly from a run of 120,000 eggs; 500 gallons of VEE from a 300,000-egg run.

Animal studies were carried out at both the Fort Detrick and Dugway sites. In one experiment, an F-100 jet plane was fitted with spray tanks and nozzles. Flying across the desert at subsonic speed, it sprayed Q fever bacteria over a large number of animals, who were then brought back to the labs for evaluation. The tests were considered highly successful.

Human testing was also started at Fort Detrick and Dugway. Seventh Day Adventists — known as conscientious objectors for refusing to bear arms — were persuaded to serve their country instead by volunteering for these tests. Q fever germs in various concentrations were exploded into the 8-ball as the volunteers inhaled them through rubber hoses connected to the sphere. If they became ill, the Adventists were treated and monitored carefully. All survived. (I have an acquaintance who served in the Army Signal Corps at Detrick from 1970-1971. Some of his friends were those same Adventist volunteers. They told him bluntly that it was their job to breathe various germs and report any symptoms of illness. My acquaintance was incredulous!)

On July 12, 1955, human testing took on a new dimension: field experiments at Dugway. A mist of Q fever germs was sprayed into the air over a group of Adventists positioned a half mile away, anxiously waiting to see what would happen. The test showed that Q fever could be aerosolized effectively and disseminated widely.

The Cold War

The development and testing of biological weapons continued through the 1950s and 1960s under Presidents Eisenhower, Kennedy, Johnson and Nixon. Ike was especially interested in *incapacitants*, agents which incapacitated an enemy but wouldn't kill him. Germs like Q fever, tularemia and VEE were perfect alternatives to other more lethal weapons of mass destruction like nuclear bombs, or chemical agents such as nerve gas.

In one test, a potent mixture of staph enterotoxin, VEE and Q fever was mixed together. This cocktail was tested at Dugway and manufactured in quantity — thousands of gallons — at Pine Bluff Arsenal. It was seriously considered for use against the Cubans during the Cuban Missile Crisis of 1962. Estimates were that barely 1-2% of the population would die from the cocktail, mostly the elderly and those with other health problems. The rest would just be very sick for a few days, easily overcome in any U.S. invasion of the island.

Under President Kennedy, new and better spray and aerosol devices were built to disperse BW agents over wide areas. Field tests of the devices — in some cases with simulants, in other scenarios with the real thing — were carried out in Okinawa, Panama and the Pacific Islands, as well as in Alaska to gauge their effectiveness in cold climates similar to the Soviet Union's.

The Johnson Atoll Field Trials, carried out from 1964-69, were among the largest open air tests ever attempted. Monkeys caged on barges strung out south of the Atoll were sprayed with a variety of BW germs. The animals were then taken to the island lab for monitoring and evaluation. In one test, a jet plane screamed across the water and sprayed a 32-mile long plume of germs over the monkey barge line. These tests showed that the agent could travel up to 60 miles before losing its infectivity.

For sheer geographic magnitude, however, the program of open air testing during the late 1950s known as Operation Large Area Coverage takes the prize. Both simulants and small amounts of actual agents were occasionally used. But to test how massive an area could be contaminated with a BW agent, microscopic particles of fluorescent zinc cadmium sulfate were released into the air stream and tracked. The particles were collected along their route at Civil Aviation Authority sites and Weather Bureau stations.

In one test, in 1957, the particles were dropped along a corridor from South Dakota to Minnesota and tracked all the way into Canada and upper New York state. The following year, the particles were detected as far away as the Gulf of Mexico. Two other tests dispersed the particles along a route from Ohio to Texas and from Illinois to Kansas. These experiments proved the feasibility of disseminating biological agents across vast tracts of land and civilian population centers.

Conventional delivery systems for BW agents were not ignored either. The Pentagon modified Pershing, Sergeant and Regulus missiles to carry germ payloads. Tested with simulants or chemicals, the agents were released high in the atmosphere — ten miles or more — as a fine mist, which then dispersed across an area as wide as 60 square miles.

Safety in the BW worksite

During the heyday years of America's offensive BW program, concern for the safety of the technicians and scientists who developed and tested these agents was of prime importance. For the most part, Fort Detrick was a safe place to work. From 1943-1969, a total of 456 cases of occupational infections were reported there. This represented only 10 infections per 1 million hours worked, a rate less than that for other laboratories and well within the standard set by the National Safety Council for laboratory workers in general. Three of these infections ended in death: two from anthrax and one from a viral encephalitis. Forty-eight occupational infections, with no fatalities, were reported during the same period from the other BW production and testing sites.

This concern to protect workers who manipulate cultures of organisms in the laboratory or perform experiments with hazardous germs grew into a series of guidelines known as Biosafety Levels 1-4. These levels are arranged in a hierarchy of requirements for administrative controls, laboratory practices, facility barriers and personal protective equipment. Basically, the more harmful the biological agent, the higher the safety level needed. The BSL Levels are summarized in Table 3.

CDC Summary of Biosafety Levels for Infectious Agents

BSL-1
- Agents: not known to cause disease in healthy people
  ex: water testing labs for coliform bacteria
- Practices: standard biological techniques; prohibition against smoking and eating in the lab
- Barriers: None
- Facilities: open bench with sinks

BSL-2
- Agents: associated with human disease; possibly bloodborne exposure; ex: hepatitis B, whooping cough, VEE, plague, anthrax, tularemia, Q fever when used in diagnostic tests and cultures
- Practices: BSL-1 plus limited access, "sharps" precautions, bio-hazard warning signs and disposal procedures;

immunizations, e.g., against hepatitis B, plague, anthrax
- Barriers: lab coats, gloves, face masks
- Facility: BSL-1 plus autoclave for sterilization

BSL-3

- Agent: high potential for aerosol transmission; disease may be lethal; ex: tularemia, Q fever, anthrax, botulinum, plague when used experimentally, in pure cultures, or likely to be aerosolized
- Practices: BSL-2 plus limited access, decontamination of clothing and waste
- Barriers: lab coats, gloves, respirator with HEPA filter
- Facility: BSL-2 plus physical separation from access corridors, exhaust air not recycled; negative airflow into labs

BSL-4

- Agent: dangerous germs with potential for life threatening disease; ex: Ebola, Marburg, Lassa viruses
- Practices: BSL-3 plus clothing change before entering; chemical shower on exit; all material decontaminated
- Barriers: full body, air supplied suit
- Facility: separate building, dedicated supply/exhaust/ decon system

Towards a Biological Weapons Prohibition

Except for the Viet Cong pungi sticks previously mentioned, the Vietnam War era was not a time for biological weapons. The U.S. charged the Soviet Union and its puppet regimes with using "yellow rain" (toxins made from a fungus species) in Laos, Kampuchea and Afghanistan, but the allegations were never substantiated. For its own part, the U.S. concentrated on chemical rather than biological weapons. Agent Orange, a potent herbicide, was used as a defoliant to uncover supply routes along the Ho Chi Minh trail from North Vietnam. The controversy about the effects of this agent on the health of U.S. troops exposed to it is ongoing among both politicians and scientists.

Fort Detrick and the other U.S. BW facilities continued to develop and stockpile germs for offensive warfare. These included both lethal (anthrax, botulinum toxin, tularemia) and incapacitant agents (brucellosis, Q fever, staph enterotoxin, VEE), as well as agents for use against enemy agriculture (rice blast, rye stem rust, wheat stem rust).

Smallpox was intensively studied during this period. It was grown in chick eggs and tested on rhesus monkeys. A breakthrough came with the ability to freeze dry the virus. This allowed it to remain for years in storage without losing its potency. In addition, the dried agent could now be made into a fine powder, which gave greater airborne dissemination. Since the incubation period of smallpox is around 1-2 weeks, the military concluded it would be a perfect weapon for bioterror; the terrorists could release the agent and be long gone before any symptoms showed up in their victims.

By the mid-1960s, opposition to the Vietnam War was growing. The tide was turning against biological weapons as well. The public had discovered Fort Detrick, and crowds of protesters regularly lined up to picket it. Security was beefed up. The Pentagon reviewed the role of biological agents as weapons of war and concluded that, while they may have limited value in small-scale operations or raids, they would not be effective on the battlefield or for projecting American military might around the world.

In July 1969, Great Britain recommended a prohibition on the development, production and stockpiling of bacteriologic and toxic weapons and put forth a plan for investigating alleged violations. In September of the same year, the Soviet Union also submitted a BW disarmament proposal, but without a plan for inspections. It also called for a UN-sponsored disarmament convention. A month later, the World Health Organization questioned the role of BW agents. Not their effectiveness — that was never in doubt. It was the unpredictability and lack of control over such weapons that frightened the WHO.

In a dramatic gesture a few weeks later, President Richard Nixon pre-empted everyone by anouncing on November 25 that the United States was unilaterally renouncing "the use of lethal biological agents and weapons of biological warfare. The U.S. will continue its biological research into defensive measures," the President concluded. In an act of supreme irony, Nixon chose Fort Detrick as the place to make his announcement. Immediately after this, U.S. stores of biological pathogens were destroyed, the equipment used to produce them dismantled, the scientists and technicians let go or transferred to other positions.

In 1972, the International Biological Weapons Convention (BWC) was signed by 103 nations, one of whom was the USSR. Another was Iraq. It specifically prohibited the development, possession and stockpiling of biological agents in "quantities that have no justification for prophylactic, protective or other peaceful purposes." It also prohibited the development of delivery systems for dispersing BW agents, as well as the sale of BW technology to other countries.

By the time the BWC was signed, the U.S. program was already gone, vanished. Most of Fort Detrick's useful facilities were turned over to other agencies, such as the National Cancer Institute. The United States Army Medical Research Institute of Infectious Diseases (USAMRIID) was born at that time, the only remnant of the once mighty biological weapons program. USAMRIID's mission was, and continues to be, to develop vaccines and tests for defense against BW agents and to investigate virulent pathogens which might be used as BW agents. A BSL-4 facility was built to handle exotic diseases like Ebola, Marbug and Lassa fevers.

In addition, USAMRIID contains a 16-bed clinical research ward at BSL-3 safety level and a 2-bed area where patients can be isolated under BSL-4 conditions. Health care providers in these clinical areas wear the same protective devices as those in purely research settings. The level of confinement depends upon the organism suspected of causing the patient's illness.

USAMRIID also has an Aeromedical Isolation Team for transporting patients suspected of infections with highly contagious, life-threatening illnesses requiring BSL-4 isolation. This team, capable of transporting two patients at a time, remained on constant alert during the 1995 Ebola epidemic in Zaire to evacuate any U.S. citizens who might have become infected there.

Finally, USAMRIID provides support to federal, state, local and international agencies on diagnostic tests and epidemiologic investigations of highly contagious epidemics. It has, for example, assisted with immunizations against VEE, provided lab support for the Legionnaire's outbreak in Philadelphia in 1976, helped manage patients with viral hemorrhagic fever in Sweden during the 1980s and assisted with the outbreak of Ebola in monkeys imported to Reston, Virginia in 1990.

After the BWC

The Biological Weapons Convention was ratified by the U.S. Senate in 1974 and signed into law by President Gerald Ford the following year. But not only was the BWC *not* a deterrent to the development and sale of BW agents, it was, in some cases, a stimlulus for it. The Soviet Union, chronically paranoid about the U.S. and its military intentions, believed America would not honor the BWC treaty. It immediately embarked on a program of massive BW development and testing. Iraq, with equipment and seed cultures easily obtained from countries which should have known better, followed suit, beginning in the late 1980s. Iran, Libya, North Korea and probably Cuba began to investigate biological agents about the same time.

Two loopholes in the BWC made cheating inevitable. First, the treaty never specified what constituted "defensive" research as opposed to the offensive variety. Presumably, even massive amounts of a germ *could* be required to test protective gear for troops, challenge environmental detectors, make vaccines and develop new antibiotics. This was all perfectly legitimate under the terms of the treaty. But those same massive quantities could, with the snap of the fingers, be put to offensive or terrorist uses.

The second loophole was that there was no means specified to identify cheaters, and what to do with them when caught. The UN ran into this very loophole when it sent a team (UNSCOM) to snoop around Iraq for biological weapons after the Gulf War.

Vaccine Fiascos

Even before the Gulf War, which began in January 1991, the U.S. knew the Iraqis had developed weapons of mass destruction, particularly biological ones such as anthrax. To guard against an Iraqi BW counter attack, 150,000 U.S. troops heading to the Middle East were immunized against anthrax. Thirty million doses of cipro were also stockpiled for possible use by the 500,000 troops eventually committed to Operation Desert Storm.

Then, in 1992, an intelligence bombshell exploded. Ken Alibek, head of Russia's BW program — known as Biopreparat — defected to the United States. He laid out for his interrogators the entire Russian menu of research and development and the locations where these operations were carried out. The Soviets, Alibek testified, were annually producing thousands of tons of anthrax, smallpox, tularemia, botulinum toxin and plague. At first, the Americans didn't want to believe him. It seemed incredible that Russia could have had such a massive program going on undetected for years right under their noses. But Alibek's credentials were so impeccable, his knowledge so detailed, that the scientists who questioned him finally, grudgingly, accepted his veracity.

Based on Alibek's admissions, it was clear that much more anthrax vaccine was going to be needed for U.S. troops, and quickly. The problem was that this particular vaccine had always been intended only for small scale occupational use in persons whose jobs put them at high risk of anthrax exposure. The vaccine had never been intended for protection against biological warfare. Even the recommended 6-shot schedule was based on guesswork; when some previously immunized wool workers developed the disease after just three injections, the number was arbitrarily bumped up to 6.

Furthermore — and this may have been the most startling revelation to the military planners — the vaccine had never been tested against the airborne spread of anthrax spores under battlefield conditions. It was a long stretch from occupational contact with a diseased sheep or cow to clouds of spores released against troops in combat. There was simply no evidence the troops would be protected even if immunized. Despite these misgivings, the Pentagon, in 1995, placed a sharply increased order for vaccine with the Michigan Department of Public Health Laboratory in Lansing, the country's only supplier of the vaccine since 1925.

Compounding the supply problem was that most of the pharmaceutical companies which had always produced vaccines were getting out of that part of the business. It had become too costly to develop and produce a vaccine which might be used only in small quantities, maybe not even enough to cover expenses. And a few unfortunate cases of vaccine-induced sickness — almost unavoidable — could spark lawsuits which would turn the company's profit/loss statement into a sea of red ink.

In 1997, the same year Secretary of Defense Cohen terrified the country with his 5 pound sack of sugar, the Pentagon announced it would immunize all its 2.6 million troops against anthrax. This seemed like an act of folly. The military simply chose to ignore the current vaccine supply problems and assumed that if it threw enough money at them, they would be fixed.

Things began to unravel fast. It became quickly apparent that the Michigan lab could never produce the vaccine in anything close to the Pentagon's demands. The other shoe dropped when the Food and Drug Administration discovered the Michigan facility could not pass inspection. The equipment was old, some of it actually rusting; cleaning processes were inadequate; and the operations procedures were generally out of date.

A year later, the Michigan lab finally got out of the anthrax vaccine business altogether. It sold out to a new company called BioPort. That same year, 1997, the military changed its policy again. With only 260,000 of the 2.6 million troops vaccinated so far, there was little chance for the all-force immunizations originally planned. The Pentagon finally accepted reality and scaled back. From now on, it said, only forces headed for the Middle East or South Korea would be immunized. If any vaccine was left over, other troops scheduled for overseas deployment would receive it.

Then even those plans went up in flames. BioPort could not meet FDA standards either! It closed its doors in late 1999. It was at this time that some service men and women refused the anthrax immunizations, claiming they had become ill from them. A lawyer filed suit against the government on their behalf. To make matters even worse — if that was possible — some reservists threatened to quit the service rather than take the shots. The all-force vaccination program was put on hold, and only troops likely to be going into areas with a known BW risk (i.e., Marine Expeditionary Units, Delta Force, Army Rangers, Navy SEALS) were required to get immunized.

But things have improved recently. All soldiers, sailors, marines and airmen deployed to Operation Iraqi Freedom in March, 2003 have been immunized. And BioPort, which has resumed vaccine production, has a government contract to produce 4.6 million doses for the Pentagon, though it may be years before such a quantity is available.

The Pentagon has one more plan for anthrax. It intends to develop a more potent, genetically altered strain of the germ, one similar to the kind Ken Alibek revealed the Russians had produced in massive quantities. The justification for developing this new strain is to see whether the current vaccine would be effective against it. If not, why continue to forcibly immunize troops who would not be protected? But some believe this plan is a thinly-veiled effort to hide an offensive program under the guise of a defensive one.

Miscellaneous Projects and Programs

In 1998, President Bill Clinton read *The Cobra Event*, Richard Preston's novel about a genetically altered viral bioweapon. Clinton was genuinely concerned about the threat of biological weapons and approved a number of projects aimed at preparing the U.S. against an attack with one or more of these agents. These programs included increasing supplies of vaccines and antibiotics at the National Pharmaceutical Stockpiles, research into new antibiotics and vaccines, recombinant DNA studies of potential biological weapons, and training for emergency responders on how to recognize and manage a bioterrorist attack. Two other covert projects of the Clinton era deserve mention.

In 1997, Project Clear Vision was launched. Based on information from Ken Alibek, the CIA constructed a model of a bomb — a "bomblet" — similar to the type built by the USSR to carry biological weapons. The CIA feared such a bomblet was now being sold on the black market to terrorist groups or governments known to sponsor terrorism. By mid-2000, tests of the bomblet in a wind tunnel demonstrated how readily the biological agent could be dispersed over the target after it was released.

The second project was very sobering. Called Bachus, it was undertaken by the Defense Threat Reduction Agency (DTRA). Its purpose was to demonstrate how easy it was to build a secret germ warfare plant from commonly available materials. Funded with a paltry $1.6 million, and using supplies ordered from scientific catalogues, the Bachus team chose a spot in the Nevada desert and had the plant operational within weeks. They demonstrated they could manufacture 2 pounds of anthrax per test run. The project went undetected by U.S. intelligence agencies.

Both Clear Vision and Bachus used simulants for their production and testing. But they could just as easily have used the real thing.

The current state of America's preparedness for biological weapons and bioterror will be described in a later chapter. But it is appropriate at this time to turn to what has been the major stimulus for U.S. research and testing for more than a half a century: the spectacular successes and equally horrific failures of the Soviet bioweapons program.

C H A P T E R

15

BIOPREPARAT

In the Soviet Union, thousands of people were involved in develop-
ing an anthrax biological weapon. Here in the United States, maybe
two or three people were involved in developing protection against
anthrax.

— **Ken Alibek**, Russian defector
Frontline interview, PBS, 1998

The most remarkable thing about the Soviet Union's offensive biological warfare program, at least before it signed the BWC treaty,
was how closely it paralleled America's. Both sides got their hands on
captured Japanese experimental data from WWII, the Russians when
they overran Manchuria and seized Ping Fan itself. Both programs focused on the same half-dozen biological agents: anthrax, plague, tularemia, botulinum toxin, Q fever, brucellosis and glanders.

The same types of experiments — with animals and humans —
were carried out by both sides to test aerosolization of the germ agents.
Some were done in test chambers, some in the open; some with
simulants like *serratia marcescens* and *b. thuringiensis*, some with real
germs. In one experiment, simulants were sprayed over the city of
Novosibirsk, reminiscent of tests carried out over San Francisco. And
in another experiment, eerily similar to the one in New York City,
simulants were released into the Moscow subway system to study their
dispersion. Finally, both countries studied ways to load these agents
into missiles, artillery shells and bombs.

It was only after the BWC was signed in 1972 that the two countries' offensive BW programs diverged. The U.S. shifted to *defensive* and peaceful uses for biological research. The USSR massively accelerated its program of research, production and testing of *offensive* biological weapons.

Soviet BW programs before 1972

The earliest Soviet studies of biological agents as weapons of war began in the late 1920s and 1930s with typhus. Napolean's retreat from Moscow in 1812 was plagued by epidemic typhus. And Russian generals must have seen how this disease could spread among troops during the trench warfare of WWI, rendering entire army regiments combat ineffective. In 1928, barely three years after the U.S.S.R. signed the Geneva Protocol, its scientists were ordered to turn typhus into a battlefield weapon.

The work began at the Leningrad Military Academy, where chicken eggs were used to culture the organisms. By the early 1930s, a powdered form of the germ had been produced for use as an aerosol on the battlefield. Later in the same decade, a facility in the White Sea — Solovetsky Island — was producing typhus, Q fever and glanders for use as biological weapons. Since Solovetsky Island was part of the vast Gulag Archipelago of prison camps begun under Stalin, some of the prisoners may have been used in these early BW experiments, though the Russians have never admitted it.

The combat use of a Soviet biological agent may have occurred during WWII as German troops prepared to assault the city of Stalingrad in 1942. An outbreak of tularemia spread through the defending Russian forces. Thousands of Russian soldiers and civilians became ill, along with German Panzer forces.

Tularemia was not prevelant in that area before this. But a bacteriologic weapons facility had just been completed near the city of Kirov that same year. It is very likely that the tularemia which infected the German and Russian troops had been developed at the Kirov facility and was intended for use against the Germans. Either a change in wind direction, or infected rodents passing through the battle lines, had carried the agent back upon the Russian troops and civilians. Additionally, many cases on both sides were the result of the pneumonic form of the disease, which is carried from person to person by coughing, sneezing and other droplet spread.

The Soviets also profited from the Japanese design of BW facilities during WWII. In 1946, using blueprints captured at Ping Fan, they built a bioweapons factory at Sverdlovsk near the Ural mountains in Siberia. Known as Compound 19, its principal purpose was to manufacture anthrax, but it also assembled and tested all types of munitions for BW agents. Thirty-three years after its construction, something went very wrong at Compound 19.

Soviet BW Programs After the BWC Treaty: 1973-1988

From those early experiments in the 1920s until the BWC was signed in 1972, most Soviet bioweapons research and development was carried out at a dozen or so military facilities. These included:

- The Scientific Research Institute of Microbiology in Kirov;
- The Center for Military-Technical Problems of Anti-bacteriological Defense in Sverdlovsk (Compound 19);
- The Center for Virology in Zagorsk;
- The Scientific Research Institute of Military Medicine in St. Petersburg;
- Vozrozhdeniya Island (known familiarly as "Renaissance" or "Rebirth" Island) in the Aral Sea.

The names of these facilities, all supposedly engaged in legitimate biological research and testing, are laughable, even beyond the Soviet hyperbole. They were merely legal-sounding covers for facilities engaged in the study, production and testing of BW agents. The Kirov facility, for example, developed typhus, Q fever, tularemia, brucellosis, and anthrax and stockpiled plague. The Sverdlovsk site produced, stockpiled and performed research on antibiotic-resistant strains of anthrax. And the Zagorsk Institute looked at every conceivable type of virus as a potential biological weapon, particularly smallpox.

These military facilities all reported to and were funded by the 15th Directorate for Biological Protection of the Soviet Ministry of Defense. Eight other sites were developed under the control of this Directorate, some to work on agents harmful to livestock and plants, others to test BW munitions, still others to conduct large-scale field trials of biological agents.

As soon as the BWC treaty was signed, the U.S.S.R. began a massive BW program. To carry it out clandestinely, the Politburo created and funded a civilian arm of the program to match the military one. Known as Biopreparat (Chief Directorate for Biological Preparation), and headed by a General in the Soviet Army, biological weapons were developed within facilities supposedly conducting regular pharmaceutical and medical research. Though in appearance civilian, Biopreparat was in fact managed from top to bottom by the military, by the same 15th Directorate which administered the purely military sites.

When fully developed, Biopreparat boasted 52 different sites, but never more than 10-15% of these facilities, their equipment, or the personnel were ever actually engaged in legitimate research. Almost 50,000 scientists and technicians were employed by the two arms of the Soviet BW network. They turned out biological weapons not by the ton, but by the hundreds of tons (Table 4).

Table 4: *Soviet Production of Biological Agents*
(tons per year)

tularemia   1,000-2,000
anthrax   4,000-5,000
Venezuelan equine encephalitis   (VEE) 100-200
bubonic plague   1,000-2000
smallpox   100
glanders   1,500-2,000

Source: Compiled from a variety of government publications

Some of the larger Biopreparat facilities were:
• The Center for Applied Microbiology at Oblensk;
• The Vector Program in Koltsovo, Siberia. Here, dangerous emerging viruses like Ebola and Marburg were developed as offensive biological weapons;
• The State Institute of Ultrapure Biological Preparations in Leningrad;
• The Scientific, Experimental and Production Base in Stepnogorsk, Kazakhstan.

An early Biopreparat project, known as Enzyme, was begun in 1973. Authorized personally by Secretary Brezhnev, its purpose was to use data from the fledgling new field of recombinant DNA technology to modify existing BW agents and make them resistent to current antibiotics and vaccines. Project Enzyme also modified BW agents for delivery by missiles, particularly the huge Soviet SS-11 and SS-18 ICBMs. With MIRVed warheads, these weapons could reach multiple U.S. targets.

In 1983, the Soviets built a plant at Stepnogorsk in northern Kazakhstan. Its principal job was to make anthrax. Using 20,000 liter fermenters, it turned out more weapons-grade anthrax than had ever been done before, principally due to innovations by Ken Alibek on how to stabilize the spores once they were produced.

Ironically, the Soviets began this large-scale production not unlike the way Louis Pasteur obtained his pure cultures of the organism 100 years earlier: by serial transfers of bacterial cultures. The process started with a few grains of freeze-dried anthrax in a stoppered vial, to which nutrient media was added. This was incubated for 1-2 days, then several samples of the mixture were transferred to other flasks and incubated 24-48 hours longer. The liquid cultures were siphoned off and oxygenated with air bubblers. Next, the liquid was piped into the large fermenters for another 24-48 hours of incubation. Huge centrifuges spun the fluid to concentrate it, and additives were mixed in to stabilize the spores. The final product was filtered and prepared for the bioweapons carriers. The equipment used for this production line was the same kind originally developed for bottling soft drinks.

By 1987, 4500 tons of anthrax were being produced annually. And the dispersability of this strain was several times greater than prior ones: only 5 kilograms of it were needed to cover a square kilometer, versus 15 kilograms needed for the same coverage with previous strains.

It was during this period that large field tests were carried out using aerosolized anthrax simulants, particularly the harmless anthrax cousin, *b. thuringiensis*. It was sprayed on animals from planes and exploded over them by artillery shells near the vast military proving grounds at Rebirth Island. Ballistic missiles filled with simulant were tested over Pacific Ocean sites as well. *Serratia marcescens* was used to test dispersability of BW agents in the Moscow Metro subway system.

Rebirth Island

In the opening sentences of his book, *Biohazard,* Ken Alibek, head of Biopreparat from 1988-1992, describes a typical experiment at this Aral Sea facility:

> *. . . one hundred monkeys are tethered to posts set in parallel rows. . . far in the distance, a small metal sphere lifts into the sky then shatters in an explosion. . . a cloud the color of dark mustard begins to unfurl toward the monkeys. They pull at their chains and begin to cry. Some bury their heads between their legs. A few cover their mouths or noses, but it is too late; they have already begun to die.*

— **Ken Alibek**
   Biohazard, p. IX

Surrounded by semi-arid desert, this island in the middle of the Aral Sea in Central Asia was — like the U.S. Army's Dugway Proving Gound — the Soviet Union's principal site for open-air testing of aerosolized biological weapons. Anthrax, tularemia, brucellosis, typhus, Q fever, smallpox, botulinum toxin and VEE were all tested there. The animal subjects were of every size and species: horses, monkeys, sheep, donkeys, mice, guinea pigs and hamsters.

From these and other tests, the Soviets evolved a comprehesive offensive BW strategy. Tularemia and VEE were the principal agents for tactical battlefield use. They would quickly incapacitate enemy troops and be gone by the time their own forces arrived on the scene. Anthrax, Marburg and brucellosis were reserved for rear areas. They would kill or make very sick the enemy's reserve units and command and control forces. Smallpox and plague were considered strategic weapons. They were intended for enemy cities, delivered by ICBMs. Their job was not just to kill, but to sow terror and panic among the civilian population and lower its will to fight.

During the 1970s and 1980s, local Kazakhs paid a high price for Rebirth Island's activities. Fishermen and other residents suffered recurring outbreaks of plague from the airborne tests done there. In 1992, this testing was stopped.

Alibek

Born Kanatjan Alibekov, Ken Alibek was from Kazakhstan on the wind-swept steppes of Central Asia. His grandfather had been a leading member of the Kazakh Communist party in the 1920s and 1930s. His father was a policeman in the town of Alma-Ata, capitol of the Soviet Republic of Kazakhstan. Kanatjan grew up in Alma-Ata until he went off to the Tomsk Military Medical Institute in 1973 to begin his training as an army doctor.

He first became interested in biological warfare when, as a school project, he analyzed the tularemia outbreak among Russian troops at Stalingrad in 1942. He was never able to prove it, but he was convinced the epidemic was from Soviet germ warfare operations gone astray. That project hooked him, and he focused all his energy on learning epidemiology and lab research techniques in microbiology, the basic sciences of BW.

When he graduated from Tomsk in 1975, he was ready for his first assignment. It was to a bioweapons facility at Omutninsk, a city near Kirov. There he learned to translate the "simple lab techniques of medical school into complicated industrial procedures in biochemistry and microbiology." It was here also that he practiced the techniques of animal experimentation with deadly biological agents on a large scale. These skills would soon be put to even bigger uses when he was transferred to the bioweapons facility at Stepnogorsk in 1983.

Figure 16. *Anthrax fermenters at Stepnogorsk*

Source: Defense Threat Reduction Agency

Over 800 colleagues worked with him at Stepnogorsk. The site was large, with 25 buildings, one of which was an aerosol chamber for testing BW munitions. Building 221 was the main anthrax production site. It held 10 of the 20,000 liter fermenters. (Figure 16). At peak output, they yielded 300 tons of anthrax per production cycle, almost 2 tons per day from this plant alone, 4,500 tons annually from all plants combined. This was truly the industrialization of anthrax.

It was at Stepnogorsk that Alibek created a weapons-grade strain of anthrax. The "Alibek" strain (known to him and his colleagues as Strain No. 836) began with a procedure to grind up the spores and coat them with a plastic resin. Through careful testing, Alibek discovered that this process kept the spores airborne 4 times longer and greatly lengthened their survivability during periods of dormancy. The Alibek strain was also more infectious: fewer spores were needed to start an infection than with other strains.

After the grinding and coating process, the spores were packed into cantaloupe-shaped balls for loading into the warheads of ICBMs. (Other "cantaloupes" were loaded with plague, smallpox and Marburg germs and also packed into missiles). Alibek calculated he needed 400 kilograms of dry anthrax for ten SS-18 missiles. A single fermenter produced sufficient spores for one missile. Alibek was soon able to fill enough missiles with anthrax to target every U.S. city. If launched, they would have killed 100-150 million Americans. And Stepnogorsk was only one of 6 plants producing anthrax and other BW weapons.

In 1988, perhaps because of his success at Stepnogorsk, Alibek was appointed Deputy Chief of Biopreparat. He didn't know it at the time, but the agency's halcyon days were already behind it. And his own life, both the professional and personal aspects of it, was heading into an uncertain future just over the horizon. But for a few years more, the list of Biopreparat accomplishments continued.

One project had begun in the 1970s in the small Siberian town of Koltsovo. Known as Vector, its purpose was to develop viral agents as biological weapons. By the late 1980s, Vector had obtained specially designed viral reactors. Five feet tall, they mixed the cultures automatically — like a washing machine — and piped out waste products through one set of tubes, the finished bioweapon through another. By 1989, Vector had Marburg virus ready for use by the Ministry of Defense. Lassa and Ebola viruses were also worked on but never brought to completion. In all, Vector was the repository for over 15,000 viral strains. But its real prize was smallpox.

The first case of smallpox probably occurred in China in the 12th century B.C. The last recorded case, 3,000 years later, was in Africa in 1977. The disease was declared officially eradicated by the WHO in 1980. After this, the only "approved" sources of smallpox were small stores kept in Moscow and at the CDC in Atlanta. Routine U.S. immunizations were discontinued in 1972. Americans, year after year, became more and more susceptible to the disease. The Soviets saw this as a military opportunity.

In 1990, the Soviet "legal" stores — those approved under the BWC — were transferred from Moscow to Vector. This was done to provide cover for the massive illegal smallpox production going on at Vector, between 80-100 tons annually. Some of it was destined for the "cantaloupes," then to be loaded into SS-18 missiles and targeted at American cities.

Another Biopreparat site was in St. Petersburg, the wonderfully named Institute for Ultra-Pure Biological Preparations, headed by Vladimir Pasechnik. Pasechnik added two innovations to Biopreparat's germ producing program. First, he invented a method for powderizing viral and bacterial cultures using jet blasts of air. This replaced the older, more time-consuming and inefficient ball bearing milling process.

Ultra-Pure's second success was in modifying cruise missiles to carry BW agents. Unlike ICBM's, cruise missiles (like the U.S. Tomahawk) travel at subsonic speeds close to the ground, thus avoiding enemy radar. Pasechnik adapted aerosol sprayers to fit these missiles. As they flew along, guided by on-board radar systems at levels as low as 50 feet, they could spray clouds of deadly germs over their targets.

A third site for continuing BW research and production was the

Institute of Applied Microbiology in Obolensk, just south of Moscow. Plague, tularemia, glanders and anthrax were studied there. But what made the Obolensk facility unique was its efforts to genetically engineer BW agents to make them resistent to antibiotics. Plasmids, those small loops of non-nuclear bacterial DNA, were used to carry other bits of DNA into bacterial cells, making them antibiotic resistant. For anthrax, they chose a plasmid from its close cousin *b. thuringiensis*. This plasmid, when introduced into *b. anthracis*, carried the DNA to make anthrax resistant to tetracycline antibiotics, the recommended one at the time. The Obolensk scientists accomplished the same bit of genetic engineering for plague bacteria.

The other noteworthy project at Obolensk was the creation of a new biological weapon targeting the nervous system. This was done by injecting DNA from a neural toxin into plague bacteria and turning it into a "super germ." When infected, the victim would get all the symptoms of plague but would have, in addition, convulsions and paralysis from the neural toxin.

Collapse

Nineteen eighty-nine was a bad year for the Soviet Union. The Berlin Wall, that symbol of Soviet oppression, came crashing down. When the dust finally settled a couple of years later, not only was East Berlin gone, but so were most of the Soviet Socialist Republics. Spent into bankruptcy by an arms race with the West, the bits and pieces of the Soviet Union struggled to find their way in the new world order.

Nineteen eighty-nine was also a bad year for the Soviet bioweapons program. Vladimir Pasechnik, one of their most senior BW researchers, failed to return from a trip to Paris. He soon turned up in Britain, a defector. Pasechnik explained the work he had done with recombinant DNA techniques to create antibiotic resistant germs; he gave the Americans their first look at how far Soviet BW science had progressed and the "superbugs" it was now capable of producing in mass quantities. But the U.S. intelligence community could not, or would not, believe what they were hearing from this former head of the Ultra-Pure Institute.

Pasechnik's reasons for defecting are murky. Apparently, it was not because he had suddenly found a conscience. Nor was it a simple rejection of communist ideology. And it certainly was not treason for profit. It was, in all probability, a much more human reason. Pasechnik was having a crisis in his personal life — a mid-life crisis — and that is what drove him into the arms of the West.

If Pasechnik's reasons for deserting were nebulous, the consequences of his flight were not. Embarrassed by the leak of its secret BW program, and diplomatically compromised, the Kremlin, in 1990, ordered all offensive BW research and development to cease, all production discontinued, all stockpiles destroyed. Many of Biopreparat's facilities and equipment were eventually returned to their advertised purpose: legitimate pharmaceutical and medical research.

The BWC treaty had encouraged mutual visits between adversaries to assure compliance with the treaty. The U.S. decided to cash in on that. Under the cloak of secrecy, a joint U.S./U.K. team visited a number of Biopreparat facilities in January 1991. These included Obolensk, Vector and the Ultra-Pure Institute in St. Petersburg. Despite Soviet efforts to conceal the real work that had been going on at these sites, the visitors were not fooled and easily spotted the equipment for large fermenters, oxygen aerators and testing chambers for military BW weapons.

Later that same year, in a tit-for-tat, a Soviet team visited the U.S. The Soviets had not believed a word of President Nixon's promise in 1969 to stop all offensive BW work. They expected to find as much evidence of it in the U.S. as the U.S. team had found in their own homeland. But they didn't. They toured Fort Detrick and USAMRIID, Dugway Proving Grounds, and Pine Bluff Arsenal. All they uncovered was the peaceful and defensive work which the Americans had promised. Ken Alibek and the other Soviet team members were as stunned as the American team visiting the U.S.S.R. had been, but for different reasons. The Soviets realized they had spent 30 years preparing for an attack which could never have happened; they had developed a massive BW capability in response to a threat which didn't exist, except in their own paranoia. In the process, they had contributed to the financial collapse of the U.S.S.R. and the bankruptcy of the communist cause.

The following year, May 1992, Russian President Boris Yeltsin finally admitted the existence of the Soviet offensive BW program. But he pledged that, from then on, Russia would comply with the terms of the 1972 BWC treaty. That was the same year Ken Alibek defected to the U.S. and confirmed everything Vladimir Pasechnik had told the Americans and much more.

In 1991, Kazakhstan, along with the rest of the Central Asian Republics, broke away from the U.S.S.R. A few years later, to improve relations with the West, the Kazakhs invited an American team to visit their BW facilities. The team toured the plant at Stepnogorsk and saw the remenants of the massive 20,000 L anthrax fermenters, confirming what Alibek had been telling them all along. They also visited Rebirth Island ("Voz" to the Americans), examined the former Soviet BW testing ground, and collected soil and other samples, which proved that large scale testing of anthrax, plague, glanders and other germs had taken place there.

In 1998, Alibek went public and told the media the story he had given in secret. The U.S. Congress was aghast and began to take seriously the problem of biopreparedness.

Defusing the Threat

Recognizing that the collapse of the Soviet Union had turned thousands of former Soviet bioweapons scientists and technicians out of work, the U.S. Department of Defense established the Defense Threat Reduction Agency (DTRA) in 1991. Its purpose was to reduce this threat by helping Russia find peaceful uses for this technology and employment for its BW scientists.

DTRA estimated there were close to 15,000 of these under or unemployed bioweaponeers who could be recruited by terrorist groups or rogue states. They might, for the right price, be tempted to sell not just their expertise but weapons-grade germs outright. Furthermore, DTRA learned, much of the infrastructure of the Soviet BW program was still intact in Russia (i.e., the buildings and equipment), despite the Kremlin's 1990 order to tear it all down. This equipment could easily be turned back into offensive uses if the wrong people got control of the government again.

Under DTRA, the U.S. government authorized increasing amounts of money for collaborative projects with Russian scientists to reduce their incentive to link up with terrorist groups or states. In some cases, BW producing equipment was destroyed outright. In others, it was modified with U.S. funds for medical and pharmaceutical purposes. The 2000-2004 U.S. budget contains $1.9 billion for biopreparedness, of which $220 million is earmarked for these collaborative threat reduction projects with the Russians, an amount substantially up from the previous budget.

In the year 2000, the U.S. General Accounting Office (GAO) prepared a report on the effects of these threat reduction projects. It found much of the threat still exists. During a visit by a U.S. team in 1999, six non-military Russian BW sites were inspected. (All Russian military sites remained closed to the team.) Nonetheless, the Americans still found plenty to worry about. For example, at Vector they found two large aerosol chambers used to test the spread of BW agents, though the Russians maintained that neither chamber had been used for years. The report also concluded that thousands of strains of deadly pathogens, some genetically engineered for antibiotic resistance, were still kept at the Vector and Obolensk sites.

The 80 year partnership of the Soviet Union with biological weapons was dizzying in its accomplishments. But it had failures as well. One of these was monumental. It was made much worse by the cover up which went along with it. It all happened 23 years ago in a quiet Siberian backwater town known as Sverdlovsk and at a military bioweapons facility called Compound 19.

CHAPTER
16

ACCIDENT AT SVERDLOVSK, APRIL 1979

A Biological Chernobyl

Sometime in the evening of April 2, 1979, a plume of dust and anthrax spores spewed forth from a chamber at Military Compound 19 in this city and headed southeast at about 4km/hr, carried on the prevailing winds coming off the nearby Ural Mountains. Within forty-eight hours veterinarians reported the first cases of anthrax in sheep and cattle. The vets were very familiar with this disease. In fact, the cutaneous form of anthrax was so prevalent in the livestock of the region that it had long been known as the "Siberian Ulcer."

The first human case occurred on April 6 in a night shift worker at a ceramics factory a few blocks downwind from the military compound. Within a few days, that patient and five others, all night shift workers at the ceramics plant, had been admitted to local hospitals with inhalation anthrax, though the doctors and nurses didn't realize at the time that's what they were dealing with. All these workers would be dead within a week. Soon, other workers on duty that night in the vicinity of the ceramics plant became ill, most of them dying as well. The epidemic picked up speed over the next few days and peaked six days later, April 10, when eleven cases were admitted. It ended with one final, solitary hospital admission six weeks later on May 18.

The city of Sverdlovsk is better known by its modern name:

Yekaterinburg. Located on the eastern slope of the Urals just north of Kazakhstan, it is technically in Asia, since the Urals are the map-maker's boundary between Europe and Asia. It was there in 1918 that Tsar Nicholas II of Russia, last of the Romanov Emperors, was brought with his wife and family and murdered by the communists on the night of July 12 in the basement of the Ipatiev House. The house was later destroyed and a shabby memorial erected over its ruins. Even today an occasional flower of remembrance is placed there by some one nostalgic for the good old days of Imperialist Russia.

Sixty-one years after the Romanov tragedy, another one of epidemic proportions came to the area: inhalation anthrax. It was first suspected by U.S. intelligence agents from signal intercepts and satellite photographs of roadblocks and decontamination trucks around Military Compound 19. The photographs in particular raised alarm that research and production of biological weapons was taking place there and that something catastrophic had happened in early April of that year. A visit by the Soviet Minister of Defense a few weeks later raised CIA eyebrows even higher.

The first press report of something unusual happening in the Sverdlovsk region was an article in a West German magazine heavily subscribed to by Russian emigrees. The article claimed there had been an explosion in a military weapons facility in Sverdlovsk and that clouds of deadly bacteria had been released, with thousands of residents dying from it.

It took almost a year, under the incessant drumbeat of criticism by the West, for the Soviets finally to admit that an epidemic of anthrax had in fact broken out in the Sverdlovsk area. But they vehemently denied it was related to biological weapons production or testing at Compound 19. Instead, on June 12, 1980, TASS, the Official Soviet news agency, declared it was only a "natural outbreak of anthrax among domestic animals." Any human cases were either of the cutaneous variety from handling the infected animals, the Soviets staunchly maintained, or gastrointestinal anthrax from improper handling of meat products, particularly sausages made from the infected cattle and sold on the black market. That remained the official communist explanation for another twelve years.

Compound 19

Built in 1946 to specifications from captured Japanese blueprints, Compound 19 was, in 1979, the busiest production plant of the Soviet 15th Directorate. It produced anthrax by the ton, operating in three shifts around the clock. When fully fermented, the anthrax spores were ground into fine powder for use as an aerosol agent. To keep the spores from escaping into the outside world, large filters were fitted over the exhaust vents. But the filters frequently became clogged with dust. Standard operating procedure called for the machinery to be shut down while the filters were removed and cleaned. Once the filters were reinserted, production could resume.

On April 2, 1979, standard operating procedure was apparently not followed, at least not completely. A technician stopped the machinery and removed a clogged exhaust filter in the anthrax drying plant at Compound 19. He cleaned the filter and made a note in the log that it needed to be replaced. But when the night shift came on, they didn't realize the filter was still out. They started the machinery with a hole where the filter should have been. For several hours, anthrax spores and dust were blown through the exhaust pipes into the night air. No one thought to notify the Sverdlovsk medical authorities or the regional public health officials.

Tainted Meat

In support of the official explanation that infected meat was the cause of the epidemic, Dr. Pyotr Burgasov, the Soviet Deputy Minister of Health and the official in charge of the public health response to the epidemic, offered two pieces of evidence: the veterinary, and the pathological. The veterinary evidence centered on the fact that an epizootic of anthrax in sheep and cattle had broken out in the area in the spring of 1979, during the month of April in fact. This was the putative source of the tainted meat, Burgasov claimed. And the region's veterinarians confirmed that such an animal outbreak did occur at that time.

When questioned, Burgasov was unequivocal: the animal epidemic definitely PRECEDED the human one. Of course, that would have to be the case — an absolute prerequisite — if the tainted meat hypothesis was to have any credence.

The second piece of evidence offered by Burgasov came from

autopsies performed on forty-two victims of the epidemic by Dr. Faina Abramova, Chief Pathologist at the main Sverdlovsk hospital. Thirty-nine of these post-mortems demonstrated disease in the gastrointestinal tract, particularly in the small intestine. Burgasov seized on this, claiming it was exactly what one would expect in a food-borne epidemic from tainted meat which had been improperly processed, handled, cooked, and illegally sold.

But the official Soviet explanation for the epidemic never sat very well with international infectious disease experts, especially the Americans. The tainted meat hypothesis left too many questions hanging. But in the dark days of the Cold War, answers to these questions were not readily forthcoming.

Casualty Lists

The epidemic's vital statistics — total number of cases, case fatality rate, incubation period, etc. — were revised and debated for years, another result of the prolonged cover-up. Ken Alibek, for example, thinks the epidemic began on Friday, March 30, not 3, 4, or 5 days later as other writers maintain. Alibek believes these later dates are simply manipulations of the data by communist officials.

The total number of deaths and the case fatality rate have also varied considerably. Inglesby, et.al., in a May 1, 2002 *Journal of the American Medical Association* article, suggests there may have been as many as 250 cases, with 100 deaths. Another report by a Sverdlovsk hospital physician claims 358 people became ill, with 45 deaths. Still another claims 48 deaths among 110 patients.

The failure of communism in 1989 opened up possibilities for further investigation of the Sverdlovsk incident, an opportunity dramatically enhanced when Boris Yeltsin, the new President of Russia, admitted in 1992 that the military facility in Sverdlovsk had indeed been working on offensive biological weapons, though he refused to admit it was responsible for the 1979 anthrax outbreak. (Another irony of history is that Yeltsin had been the Communist Party Chairman in Sverdlovsk at the time of the epidemic and helped maintain the cover-up. When questioned about it years later, he claimed the military had deceived him about the cause of the outbreak.)

After lengthy negotiations with Russian authorities, a team of American investigators was formed to come to Russia and take a closer look at the Sverdlovsk epidemic. The team was headed by Dr. Matthew Meselson, a Harvard biologist. His wife, Jeanne Guillemin, was the team's anthropologist. Her role was to interview the survivors and the relatives and friends of the deceased in a sort of posthumous case contact investigation. Other team members were Dr. David Walker, a pathologist who would review Dr. Abramova's original autopsy material; Dr. Martin Hugh-Jones, a veterinarian who would look at the data on the animal outbreak; Alexis Shelokov, a translator and vaccine expert; and Dr. Olga Yampolskaya, an infectious disease expert and the lone Russian on the team.

Meselson's American team members arrived in Moscow on June 2, 1992, were flown to Yekaterinburg shortly thereafter, and set about their investigation immediately. They published their findings in *Science*, November 18, 1994. In summing up their work, it is safe to say that it resulted not only in carefully documenting the epidemic's "vital statistics" but also in refuting the two key pieces of evidence supporting the contaminated meat hypothesis. Guillemin subsequently published a complete description of the investigation under the title, *ANTHRAX: The Investigation of an Epidemic*, University of California Press, Berkeley, 1999.

The American team used a variety of data sources in its investigation:

- the official KGB list of 68 people who died during the epidemic;
- household interviews with the relatives and friends of 43 victims who died and 9 who survived;
- the grave markers of 61 victims;
- autopsy reports of 42 victims;
- the clinical case histories of 5 victims;
- hospital lists of 110 patients screened for anthrax.

Using these sources, the Meselson team concluded that 96 people became sick during the epidemic, 77 with inhalation anthrax, 18 with the cutaneous form of the disease. Sixty-six of the inhalation cases died and 11 survived. (Two of the 68 names on the KGB list were thought to have died of causes other than anthrax.) Assuming these final numbers are correct, they yield a case fatality rate of 86%, which is consistent with the historical record for anthrax outbreaks.

Fifty-five of the 77 cases were men, with a mean age of 42 years, the youngest being 24 years. Twenty-two cases were women, with a mean age of 55 years; only 2 women were under 40 years of age. This preponderance of male cases probably reflects their larger make-up of the workforce. And the absence of children in the caseload is under-standable, given the presumed time of exposure: most children would not have been outdoors when the plume of spores was released.

A high percentage of the inhalation cases had a brief period of remission following initial flu-like symptoms. This has been a typical finding in other anthrax epidemics (i.e., Woolsorter's Disease), but not in the 2001 U.S. cases. After this brief remission, sudden collapse and death followed quickly. The mean time between the onset of symp-toms and death was just 3 days.

Calculating the incubation period — the time from first exposure to the onset of symptoms — is problematic, in part due to disagree-ment over the date the plume of spores was actually released from Compound 19. But arriving at some sort of reliable figure for this in-terval is extremely important; current recommendations for vaccine use and the duration of prophylactic antibiotics depend upon it.

Assuming April 2 as the date of exposure, 37 of the 66 fatalities began their illnesses within the next two weeks. The longest incuba-tion period was 43 days, with a mean of 3-4 days and a mode of 9-10 days. As explained previously, this long "tail" to the epidemic is prob-ably due to anthrax spores remaining dormant in the lungs for a pro-longed period before regerminating into bacteria again and causing symptoms. This assumption has been validated by experimental data from monkey testing. And it is this data which has led to the recom-mendation for a 60-day course of prophylactic antibiotics for those exposed in the U.S. postal attacks of 2001.

But suppose this was not a single-source epidemic, that not every-one was exposed on April 2? Many of the spores must have fallen to the ground or onto the trees and roofs of other buildings in the neigh-borhood. The area near Compound 19 had many unpaved streets. Dust kicked up by vehicular or foot traffic could have led to exposures later than April 2, although cases from these exposures were more likely to be of the skin form than the inhalation variety.

Even the public health response could have contributed to these later exposures. Buildings and trees in the area where most patients lived were washed down by local fire brigades, further contributing to the spore load in the soil and to the dust in the streets. This clean-up might also have re-aerosolized some spores. (As she plodded to her interviews, watching the dust swirl around her feet, Jeanne Guillemin had these same thoughts.) If some cases were exposed later than April 2, the average incubation period would be shorter, as would the "tail" of the epidemic; it might even disappear.

The symptoms of the disease were exactly like those seen throughout history, even in the 2001 U.S. mail attacks. Fever, cough and shortness of breath were almost universal. Vomiting, chills, weakness, headache and chest pain were likewise prominent.

The first name on the KGB list of victims was Spiridon Zakharov, a 44 year old man who worked in the pipe shop of the ceramics factory. His wife reported that he got sick on April 6 but went to work the next day anyway. He collapsed at work and was taken to the hospital. He died there two days later.

Mikhail Markov was the second name on the KGB list, also a worker in the ceramics factory. He developed a cough on April 6 and was told by the factory doctor that he just had the flu. He felt better the next day and went to work. But the following day he worsened, developed fever, chills and headaches. He was taken to the hospital, where he died that night.

Hospitalized patients were treated with a variety of antibiotics, anti-anthrax globulin, intravenous fluids and respiratory support. Public health officials mobilized a response to the epidemic by the end of the first week, interviewed close contacts of the patients and gave them prophylactic antibiotics and anthrax vaccine shots.

Guillemin and the U.S. team also demonstrated that all human cases occurred along a narrow corridor one kilometer wide by four kilometers long, a distribution pattern consistent with the air-borne spread of anthrax spores. (Sporadic animal cases continued to be reported for weeks as far as fifty kilometers downwind.)

Ivan Vershinin's name is in the middle of the KGB list, number 28. His son Aleksander described the circumstances of his death. His father worked at the ceramics factory and became ill on April 11, complaining of difficulty breathing. He was taken to the hopsital but died that night. His death certificate listed "sepsis" as the cause of death.

One of the last names on the KGB list was Fagim Dayanov, number 61. A 43-year-old male, he didn't work at the ceramics plant but at another factory nearby. On May 3 he was sent to clean the factory's roof. Though he had a fever the next day, he went to work anyway, but stayed home the next day. His condition worsened the following day, and he was taken to the hospital. It was May 6. Despite intensive treatment, he died there on May 10.

One of the Russian experts the American team interviewed was Nickolay Babich, who, in 1979, was head of the Sverdlovsk Epidemiological Station. He was on the scene during the whole course of the outbreak. He categorically denied the tainted meat hypothesis.

And what about the reports of an epizootic of anthrax in sheep and cattle in the south of the region preceeding the human outbreak?

"There was none," Babich stated flatly. "I believe the animal deaths occurred only AFTER the epidemic began."

Dr. Walker, the team pathologist, reviewed Dr. Abramova's original autopsy data and slides. His conclusions also helped disprove the tainted meat explanation. First, he noted that all forty-two cases autopsied had unmistakeable evidence of INHALATION anthrax: hemorrhagic destruction of the thoracic lymph nodes and a bloody inflammation of the mediastinum. Furthermore, anthrax bacteria were seen on stained microscope slides of tissue taken from the thoracic lymph nodes.

He agreed that thirty-nine of these cases did have lesions in their small intestines. But these were caused by bloodstream spread of the bacteria from the lungs to the GI tract, NOT from a primary, gastrointestinal infection. This finding was consistent with the observation that none of the 96 cases had the kinds of gastrointestinal symptoms one would expect if this had been a food borne epidemic: bloody vomiting, bloody diarrhea, severe abdominal cramps and oral or pharyngeal sores and ulcers.

In addition to knocking down the official Soviet explanation that the epidemic was caused by infected meat, the team was also able to gather some positive information supporting their own suspected inhalation cause for it.

Noteworthy was an interview the team conducted with General Valentin Yestigneyev, the Scientific Director of the Military Compound in Sverdlovsk in 1979. The General admitted that anthrax research had been going on at Compound 19. In a typical experiment, he explained, two monkeys would be secured in an aerosol testing chamber, about 3 cubic meters in size. They would then be sprayed with 5 milliliters of anthrax suspension.

And how many spores would that be?

About 5 billion, the general answered.

(The interviewer's eyes must have grown wide at that. Five billion spores! An enormous dose.)

But the general quickly assured the team that special filters were in place to keep aerosol emissions from escaping into the outside world. The air, before being vented from the chamber, went through two cascades of 30% hydrogen peroxide, then through two filters each ten centimeters thick, before being discharged. This same procedure was followed for all exhausted air at Compound 19.

"It was practically impossible that the filters didn't work," the general insisted.

And maybe he was right. Maybe the filters in the aerosol test chamber hadn't failed after all. But somewhere in Compound 19 a filter did fail, maybe in the anthrax drying room, as Alibek contends. Maybe the filter there was clogged, was removed for cleaning and not replaced before the air was vented. Or maybe the concentration of hydrogen peroxide wasn't what it should have been; or perhaps the air didn't go through all the filters. No one will ever know for certain what went wrong. But the result was that everyone living within that narrow downwind corridor — humans and animals alike — were suddenly exposed to a lethal dose of airborne anthrax spores. (It is a great irony that the Sverdlovsk epidemic, a modern one, was due to the ancient Greek idea of miasma: bad air!)

For the Soviets, the accident at Sverdlovsk caused them to switch their anthrax production to the plant at Stepnogorsk, whose capacity was rapidly expanded under the leadership of Ken Alibek.

In 1998, scientists at the Los Alamos National Laboratory used the recently-developed PCR test to examine tissue samples from the forty-two autopsied Sverdlovsk victims. Four distinct strains of anthrax were identified. This was considered inconsistent with a food-borne epidemic, where one strain should have predominated. But it was considered quite in line with an accident at a laboratory performing research on the offensive uses of anthrax, where many strains might have been involved.

If anything good came out of the many deaths in the Sverdlovsk epidemic, it was the careful description of the characteristics of inhalation anthrax by the U.S. team. Textbooks of infectious disease now use the findings of Guillemin and her colleagues as the basis for their own descriptions of the incubation period, the case fatality rate, the typical signs and symptoms, and the pathological findings of inhalation anthrax.

C H A P T E R

17

SADDAM

Beyond al-Qaeda, *the most serious concern is Iraq. Iraq's biological weapons program remains a serious threat to international security."*

— **John Bolton**, U.S. Undersecretary of State
for Arms Control, November 2001

Countries currently believed to possess offensive biological weapons or the capability to produce them are Libya, North Korea, South Korea, Taiwan, Syria, Israel, Iran, China, Egypt, Vietnam, Cuba, India, South Africa and Russia. Ranked in terms of threat to its neighbors and to the rest of the world, the name which stands at the top of this list is Iraq. For this very reason, U.S. President George W. Bush has vowed to eliminate Iraq's biological and other weapons of mass destruction and topple the dictator Saddam, by invasion if necessary.

What could Saddam Hussein have been thinking when, on August 2, 1990, he unleashed his military forces on the tiny kingdom of Kuwait? The Iraqis had always considered Kuwait a southern extension of their own country. Perhaps Saddam figured that was as good a reason as any to try and get it back. He must have believed the Western powers would do nothing about it; must have believed they had no stomach for a real shooting war so far from home, a war in which there could be many American boys sent back in body bags. Or perhaps he thought his arsenal of biological and chemical weapons would scare off any potential invaders. Then again, he might have deluded himself into believing his front-line troops would actually stand and fight when the shooting began.

Whatever the reasons for the invasion, the Iraqis quickly overwhelmed, occupied, then brutalized Kuwait, triggering the first U.S. cruise missile launch in retaliation on January 16, 1991. This marked the beginning of a massive allied air campaign. Iraqi forces retreated from Kuwait but were met by a 500,000-man ground invasion. The war ended with the Iraqi surrender on the last day of February, barely six weeks later.

Though plenty of SCUD missiles had been fired, Iraq used none of its weapons of mass destruction. This couldn't have been out of any moral compunction; Saddam had already gassed his own countrymen — the Kurds — in the late 1980s. And during the war with Iran (1980-1986) he had used both chemical and biological weapons; traces of anthrax were found in Iranian casualties during the conflict.

Why didn't he use them against the allies during the Gulf War? It wasn't because they didn't exist. Saddam's BW locker turned out to be even fuller than the allies had calculated before the war started. The only thing which might have kept the dictator from using them was fear of even greater retaliation, perhaps even with nuclear weapons launched from Israel.

Seeds

One of the remarkable oddities about international biological warfare programs during the 1970s and 1980s is their interconnectedness. The similarities between the Soviet and U.S. programs before the BWC treaty has already been mentioned. Both countries, in turn, probably gained much of their knowledge from WWII Japanese experiments on human subjects. Iraq, too, found a place in this calculus. It obtained seed cultures from the U.S. in 1986 and 1988 and used many of the same large-scale culture techniques, equipment and testing schemes that the Soviets and Americans had tried in their own programs.

The American Type Culture Collection (ATCC) is a biological supply company in the Maryland suburbs of Washington, D.C. It billed itself as the world's largest collection of bacterial strains, most of them developed during the Cold War years of the 1950s. It sold these germs principally to hospitals and medical facilities, who used them to create and run new diagnostic tests. The Rajneesh Medical Corporation, a front for the Oregon cult, purchased its salmonella strains this way, then went on to poison all those salad bars with them.

This same germ supply house, ATCC, also sold bacterial cultures to foreign countries with an ease equal to the sale of loaves of bread or automobile parts. The prospective foreign purchaser needed only to obtain a certificate from the U.S. Department of Commerce, which required merely the submission of a written application. Little or no investigation of the purchaser was undertaken, especially if it carried the name of a hospital, medical corporation, or university medical center. Once rubber-stamped by Commerce, the cultures were soon on their way across the ocean.

This was how, in May 1986, three different strains of anthrax, five botulinum variants, and three strains of brucella were sent to the University of Baghdad. At that time, the Iran-Iraq War was raging, and the U.S. considered Iraq an ally. Then, in 1988, four more strains of anthrax were sent to Baghdad, one of which was known as Vollum 1B. It had originally been developed as an offensive BW agent at Fort Detrick in 1951. Finally, in 1989, the Commerce Department woke up and prohibited the sale of any more pathogens to Iraq, Iran, Libya or Syria. But it was too late. The Iraqi industrialized production of BW agents was already going full throttle.

It began as early as 1973 — the year after Iraq signed the BWC treaty — under a civilian agency known as the State Organization for Trade and Industry. This was soon replaced by a Military Industrial Commission, which continued the work in deep secret. Evidence uncovered during the United Nations Special Commission (UNSCOM) missions, however, shows that from 1973-1979 early work on botulinum toxin and anthrax was carried out at the Al Hazan Institute near Baghdad. This facility was closed in 1979 because of allegations of fraud. But early BW work continued at Salman Pak, a facility on the Tigris River south of Baghdad. Little is known about the Iraqi program for the next half-dozen years. But in 1984 work began in earnest at both Salman Pak and at Al Hakam, a new facility built a few years later on the Tigris. Al Hakam operated under the cover of a chicken feed processing plant. Animal testing facilities were constructed and anthrax and botulinum were studied. In addition, experiments with the anti-crop agent wheat smut were started at Al Salman, a facility 25 miles south of Salman Pak.

By 1985, biological weapons research and production had also begun at the Al Muthanna chemical weapons plant north of Baghdad; storage of anthrax spores, gas gangrene spores and botulinum toxin was accelerated. These initial anthrax strains were mostly ones indigenous to Iraqi livestock. But when they obtained the American cultures in 1986 and again in 1988 — as well as a strain from France — the possibility for truly lethal BW agents became real. This initiated a period of Iraqi BW industrial production. It happened at about the same time the Soviets were revving up their own program.

Saddam's Arsenal of BW agents

The source material for information on Iraq's biological weapons program is principally the documents, photographs and visual inspection reports by the UNSCOM team which moved around the country in 1991 after the Gulf War. But this information was also confirmed by two Iraqi defectors. The first was General Wafiq al-Samarra'i, who fled in November 1994 and gave British and American intelligence officers much useful information. But the real catch came a year later: General Hussein al-Kamal, Saddam's own son-in-law. General Kamal was a very creditable witness and proved eager to assist the West during his debriefings.

The principal Iraqi lethal biological agents produced in quantity were:

- anthrax
- aflatoxin
- botulinum toxin
- gas gangrene (*clostridium perfringens*)
- ricin (derived from the castor bean plant)
- wheat smut

The production of aflatoxin, which is made from the fungus *aspergillum*, is intriguing. It has no immediate effect on the body and would, therefore, be of little value on the battlefield or as a weapon of terror. Over time, however, it causes liver damage, which leads to bleeding, jaundice, liver cancer and death. The suspicion is that Saddam was planning to use aflatoxins for slow ethnic cleansing of the Kurds, who, despite brutalization by him in the late 1980s, continue to clamor for a separate Kurdish state within Iraq.

Wheat smut causes a growth on wheat and millet, which can destroy the entire crop. Saddam grew it in an area around Mosul in the north but claimed he never harvested it for actual deployment. He could be planning to use it as a form of economic warfare against his neighbors.

Other agents in Saddam's BW arsenal were intended as incapacitants, capable of rendering an enemy unfit to fight but only lethal to the very young, the old and the infirm. These were:

- cholera
- shigella
- viruses: infectious hemorrhagic conjunctivitis
  rotavirus
  camelpox
  enteroviruses

Cholera, shigella, enteroviruses and rotavirus all cause intestinal infection, profuse diarrhea and dehydration. Infectious hemorrhagic conjunctivitis, as the name implies, causes painful, watery and red eyes and sometimes temporary or even permanent blindness. All five agents act quickly — within hours to days — and could be easily dispersed on the battlefield or in an enemy's food and water supplies.

Camelpox is an interesting choice. It is a viral illness unique to the Middle East. It is rarely infectious to humans living there. But westerners have had no exposure to it and are, therefore, completely susceptible, as susceptible as the American Indians were to smallpox during the French and Indian War. This may have been Saddam's thinking: camelpox could be devastating to any westerners who dared invade his domain. The camelpox virus is also very similar to smallpox. It might have been used as a research model for smallpox since both require the same cultivation techniques.

One agent not on the list is mycotoxins. This is because the Iraqis never provided UNSCOM with documentation of their interest in it.

Made from wheat mold, mytoxins can be ingested, inhaled or absorbed through a break in the skin. They are moderately lethal. During the 1970s, the U.S. accused the Soviet Union of supplying communist-led governments of Southeast Asia with mycotoxins. These were used against dissident groups like the Hmong tribesman, who called it "yellow rain" and complained that it burned their skin fiercely.

In their testing programs, the Iraqis, like the Russians and the Americans before them, used *b. thuringiensis* as a simulant for studying aerosol dispersion. They may also have used *b. subtilis*, a relative of anthrax only harmful to animals.

Much of the Iraqi hardware — fermenters, culturing vials, etc. — for the industrial production of BW agents came from Europe, where it was readily available for legitimate biological and medical research. The nutrient media on which the bacteria grew came from Great Britain. And of course, many of the seed cultures came from America. It was a truly international effort.

During the run-up to the Gulf War, the Iraqis built a number of plants to develop, produce, and store their BW arsenal. The largest of these was Al Hakam, constructed in 1988. It produced anthrax and botulinum toxin on an industrial scale and loaded them into munitions. Two 1450 liter fermenters were dedicated to the production of botulinum alone. By 1990, when Saddam invaded Kuwait, all these BW-filled weapons were deployed to secret sites around the country.

Salman Pak, a major research center, developed four weaponized strains of anthrax. It also developed botulinum toxin. Al Manal, otherwise known as the Daura Foot and Mouth Disease Vaccine Center, was situated in the desert east of Baghdad. It may once have worked on a vaccine for foot and mouth disease, an illness of cattle. But its principal mission in the late 1980s was to develop four viral BW agents: camelpox, infectious hemorrhagic conjunctivitis, rotavirus and enteroviruses. It may also have researched smallpox.

The Muthanna State Establishment, located north of Baghdad, was responsible for loading the BW agents into various munitions and missiles. The site at Al Salman continued its work on anti-crop agents.

In 1990, Iraq's BW program reached its peak. It was not as massive as the Soviet Union's Biopreparat, but it was big. To begin with, 8350 liters of anthrax had been produced and stored. That's 8,350,000 milliliters, each milliliter containing about a billion spores. Six thousand liters of this were used for weapon payloads. Fortunately, most of it was wet, in slurry form, the least favorable for aerosol dissemination. If it had been used in conventional munitions during the Gulf War, much of it would probably have been destroyed in the weapon's explosion. Still, the amount dispersed would have been so massive that enough of it could have survived to cause many casualties among allied troops.

In addition to anthrax, almost 20,000 liters of botulinum were produced, 12,000 liters of which were loaded into weapons. And 2000 liters of gas gangrene spores were deployed. Almost all of it came from a reference strain supplied by the U.S. in 1985. Twenty two hundred liters of aflatoxin and 10 liters of ricin rounded out the Iraqi arsenal.

Munitions

When the UNSCOM team conducted its first Iraq inspection in 1991, it found a panorama of weapons with biological payloads. These included bombs, missiles, artillery shells and sprayers.

About 200 bombs intended for use with BW agents were produced and deployed. One hundred of these were filled with botulinum toxin, 50 or more with anthrax, and 16 with aflatoxin. They were mostly modified versions of standard Iraqi 250 lb. (R250) and 400 lb. (R400) aerial bombs, capable of carrying 65 liters and 85 liters of biological agent respectively. The inside walls of the payload chamber were painted with epoxy to prevent the biological agent from coming into contact with the metal casing. The explosion chamber was in the center of the BW payload. When detonated, it would rupture the metal wall and disperse the germs. Some bombs were designed to float to earth by parachute. Bombs with biological payloads were painted with black stripes to differentiate them from regular munitions.

Iraq had also purchased 800 SCUD missiles from the Soviet Union. Some, known as Al Husseins, were designed for extended flight, though most had a standard range of 300 kilometers. Fifteen Al Husseins were loaded with botulinum toxin, 10 with anthrax, and 2 with aflatoxin, each with about 145 liters of biological agent. After the Gulf War, 10 of these SCUDS were found in an abandoned railway tunnel, the other

15 hidden in pits near the Tigris River, ready for rapid launch.

A few 155 millimeter artillery shells were filled with ricin, and some 122 millimeter rockets were packed with botulinum toxin, anthrax or aflatoxin. But none of these weapons caused much concern to the allies. What worried them most were the Iraqi sprayers.

Saddam had purchased forty 2000 liter, top-of-the-line Italian agricultural sprayers in 1990, then had their nozzles adapted to dispense anthrax and botulinum. Each sprayer could disperse 800 gals./hr. of lethal agent and could be mounted in the back of a pickup truck, on a small boat, or in a single-engine aircraft. In addition, aerial drop tanks were modified, mounted under jet aircraft, and filled with 2200 liters of anthrax spores or botulinum toxin, intended for aerial release over allied troops or neighboring population centers. There was even equipment — known as the "Zupaidy" device — which allowed BW agents to be sprayed from helicopters.

The most innovative Iraqi dispersal system was a Soviet MIG-21 jet fighter adapted to be remotely piloted. Belly tanks from a French Mirage F-1 aircraft and one of the Italian sprayers were fitted to the MIG and topped off with an aerosol simulant, probably *b. thuringiensis*. The weapon was apparently tested at least once, but the results are unknown.

The Iraqis probably also knew about the effects of weather on aerosol dispersion, may even have used simulants to test this. The allies estimated that 90% of their front-line troops could have been exposed to anthrax spores if the Iraqis used their sprayer systems during a weather inversion layer.

UNSCOM

In April 1991, barely two months after the Iraqi Gulf War surrender, the United Nations Security Council adopted Resolution 687. This offered to lift the economic sanctions on the sale of Iraqi oil when all of its weapons of mass destruction had been destroyed. By August, the first UNSCOM team had been deployed to Iraq. It consisted of a mix of scientists and diplomats from the U.S., Britain and Russia. The head of mission was Rolf Ekeus, a Swedish diplomat.

Within a month of its arrival, the UNSCOM team had discovered — mostly through documentary evidence — that Iraq had 8 sites where biological weapons had been developed and produced. Though

several had been hit in the allied bombing campaign which had preceded the ground invasion, only one, Salman Pak, had actually been
destroyed.

The first Iraqi site the UNSCOM team investigated, the one they
wanted to see most, was Al Hakam, Iraq's biggest and best BW plant.
They were met and escorted around the facility by Dr. Rihab Taha, a
senior Iraqi biochemist who had been educated in Great Britain and
who was soon nicknamed "Dr. Germ" by the investigators.

The Iraqis at first stalled, dissimulated and outright refused the
UNSCOM team what it wanted to see. For example, when the investigators asked to look into a locked warehouse at Al Hakam, they were
told that nothing important was stored there. When the investigators
persisted, they were flatly refused admission.

The Iraqis further maintained they had destroyed all their biological weapons in early 1991 to prevent their dispersal across the country from allied bomb and missile attacks. When UNSCOM inspectors
visited Al Hakam and asked what the huge 1450 liter fermenters were
being used for, "chicken feed manufacturing," they were told; the entire plant was supposedly a chicken feed company. At Al Walld, an
Iraqi airbase, the team found some bombs painted with black stripes.
The Iraqis said it didn't mean anything in particular. The investigators
were pretty certain it meant that those were weapons with biological
payloads.

Ultimately, in the face of overwhelming evidence, the Iraqis admitted that Al Hakam and the other facilities had produced and stored
biological weapons; and that some munitions had been loaded with
these payloads, some, in the case of bombs, designated with a black
painted stripe.

All BW stores at Al Hakam and wherever else they were found
were destroyed in a two-step process under the eyes of the UNSCOM
investigators.

- first, the biological agent was treated with solutions of
  formaldehyde and concentrated potassium permangenate;
- then the residue was scattered on the ground around
  the perimeter of the plant.

But UNSCOM could never certify that *all* BW stores had been destroyed. The Iraqis may simply have moved some to other secret sites

before the inspectors arrived.

All BW *munitions* were supposedly destroyed at the same time. The warheads were opened and the payloads chemically treated. Then the weapons were crushed under bulldozer tracks and burned in pits. But, once again, the inspectors could not guarantee that they had found and burned all munitions.

In 1996, the Al Hakam plant was blown up under the eyes of UNSCOM inspectors. During the same visit, the team found additional documents which raised suspicion there were still more BW stores to be discovered. But when it tried to go back and find them in 1998, Saddam Hussein put his foot down and refused permission. The team departed the country, and the UN did not press the matter. The Iraqis were left alone.

Has Iraq re-stocked its BW arsenal?

The short answer to that question is that no one really knows; there have been no UNSCOM inspections for over four years. But if you want a glimpse of the future, the old aphorism goes, just take a quick look at the past. Not only does Iraq's prior embrace of BW agents raise suspicions that it's at it again, but some recent information positively suggests it is back in the BW business.

For example, in July 1995, Russia was discovered to be negotiating with Iraq for the sale of large fermenters and other associated equipment used to make anthrax. These fermenters were nearly identical to the ones used at Stepnogorsk. Though the Iraqis professed they were only planning to use the equipment to grow protein for cattle feed, the Russians were pressured to cancel the sale. The suspicion is that Saddam went looking for the equipment elsewhere.

In 1998, the year UNSCOM was kicked out, the Iraqis claimed they had only manufactured 8,000 liters of anthrax spores. But that didn't tally with the amount of growth media ordered from Britain, an amount which could have yielded 3-4 times that much. Where had the rest of it gone? The Iraqis couldn't — or wouldn't — account for it.

Again in 1998, Iraq tried to export its BW technology and expertise. It sent scientists to Libya to teach them how to develop their own program. The Libyans converted a medical building in Tripoli into a BW laboratory and are probably busy at it right now.

Other tidbits of intelligence about Iraq's recrudescent BW

program have surfaced recently. They include the following:

- "Dr. Germ" has confirmed that Iraq had been working on an antibiotic-resistant strain of anthrax;
- Iraq may be working on a freeze-dried version of smallpox, similar to the one the Soviets were developing at Biopreparat;
- Prior to the Gulf War, most of Iraq's anthrax was in slurry form. In 1998, they learned how — by drying the slurry in aluminum-based clays and silicas — to make weapons-grade *powdered* anthrax, a considerably more aerosolizeable form of it.
- A *Time* article of September 30, 2002, reports that "defectors have told Western officials that Saddam loads bioweapons into sealed wells drilled 60 feet deep across the rural landscape." The report further speculates that "even if all of Saddam's germ factories. . . were eradicated, he would still possess the knowledge needed to rehabilitate."

Addendum: As of this writing, "Operation Iraqi Freedom" is under way. Launched in March 2003, a coalition led by the United States has made considerable progress toward its stated goal of ejecting the regime of Saddam Hussein and uncovering and destroying its Weapons of Mass Destruction. Suspicious chemicals have been found in a warehouse in southern Iraq. No biological weapons have been discovered so far.

CHAPTER 18

ARE WE PREPARED
FOR THE NEXT ONE?

O ur story has come full circle. From those 24 anthrax-by-mail cases in 2001, we've returned, after a 3250 year journey, to our point of origin. Now we must ask ourselves, when the next bioterrorist attack occurs, will we be ready for it? Will we be ready at all levels: national, state, local, and personal?

Preparedness at the National Level

The CDC is the lead agency for biopreparedness at the federal level. Its plan consists of five components:

1. Preparedness and Prevention
2. Detection and Surveillance
3. Laboratory Response
4. Communication
5. Training and Research

Preparedness and Prevention

CDC's Epidemic Response Center claims it is prepared to coordinate and distribute antibiotics, vaccines, IV supplies and other emergency equipment within 12 hours when state and local agencies are overwhelmed by an epidemic. CDC would also help, through its Epidemic Intelligence Service, in tracing and identifying case contacts and administering vaccinations to persons exposed to biological weapons. In the case of smallpox, this could extend to second, third and fourth generation cases.

To provide these emergency supplies to local health agencies rapidly, CDC will draw from the National Pharmaceutical Stockpile (NPS), created by Congress in 1999 and managed directly by CDC itself. This system, warehoused in various secret locations around the country, holds enough antibiotics for a 6-week course of treatment for 10 million people.

The NPS system is made up of 2 parts. The first consists of eight 12-hour Push Packets for immediate use. Each packet contains 50 tons of antibiotics, vaccines, medical equipment, and diagnostic tests for general field use. These packets are supposed to reach any affected U.S. area within 12 hours of their release. The second component, which should arrive on site 24-36 hours later, contains vaccines, antibiotics and equipment tailored to specific agents, such as anthrax, tularemia or plague.

Detection and Surveillance

Initial detection of bioterrorism cases will come from the local level, by primary care providers, other first responders (police, fire, etc.), and county health departments. Federal agencies like CDC can assist these local agencies in differentiating epidemics caused by Acts of God — floods, tornadoes, earthquakes, and hurricanes, which may themselves lead to outbreaks of disease from poor sanitation and unsafe water supplies — from man-made ones. This will be especially true if clusters of suspicious cases occur at two or more widely separated locations. But even this will require timely and accurate reporting by the locals. CDC has provided funding to improve such surveillance and reporting.

A spate of environmental anthrax detectors has recently been brought to market. One of these is known as the "Smart Ticket." It is not intended for the detection of invisible, airborne anthrax spores. Rather, its function is to test suspicious powders and other substances thought to be anthrax. The powder is dissolved in a reagent then fed into the device. Since false positives are frequent because of cross reactivity with other bacterial species, the device should not be used to decide whether a patient has been exposed and needs to be started on prophylactic antibiotics.

Another environmental detector being developed is the Hand Held Advanced Nucleic Acid Analyzer (HANAA). Battery powered and weighing only two pounds, this device IS designed to detect invisible airborne biological agents. If a sought-for germ is trapped in its chamber, it will bind to the DNA of the test material. This causes a reaction with a fluorescent dye, which then glows visibly. Its proponents claim that HANAA can detect a foreign germ within seven minutes.

All field detectors have serious flaws. CDC's most recent finding is that they all give rapid but unreliable results. This has led to buildings being shut down when they need not be, persons quarantined unnecessarily, and antibiotics dispensed when they are not required. In May 2000, for example, anthrax was detected by one of these field units in the mailroom of the World Bank. The ventilation system was shut down and 1200 workers sent home. In a similar case, 100 workers at the International Monetary Fund were given antibiotics when anthrax was detected. Both cases turned out to be false alarms.

In summary, both the FBI and the CDC advise against the use of any of these commercially available environmental anthrax detectors. Both false positives (a positive test when the germ is *not* really present) and false negatives (missing small amounts of the germ when it *is* present) are common to all of them. If firefighters, police or other local agencies are worried about a suspicious powder, they should send a sample to a CDC-approved lab, where they will get an answer within 12 hours.

One more CDC detection and surveillance program deserves mention; it's called Pulse Net. It is a national foodborne surveillance network. Its purpose is to detect foodborne illness due to common exposures occurring at the same time but at separate locations. Identification of *E. coli 0157:N7* outbreaks from contaminated meat, and salmonella disease from chicken, are two such examples. A similar program to detect bioterror agents in our food and water systems is being developed.

Laboratory Response

The same year, 1999, that Congress created the National Pharmaceutical Stockpile, it appropriated $121 million in emergency funding to CDC to enhance the nation's epidemiology laboratory capability. One of the biggest projects was the Laboratory Response Network (LRN), created in collaboration with the Association of Public Health Laboratories and the FBI. This network consists of 81 clinical labs in the U.S.

with the ability to diagnose BW agents in both clinical and environmental samples. Some labs, known as reference labs, can perform highly specialized tests beyond the standard cultures, gram stains, and PCRs.

The LRN is based on a 4-tiered concept of specialization. Local hospital labs with suspicious cultures send samples to county or state labs for confirmation (CDC even provides some of these labs with diagnostic aids and test reagants). The next level is the state lab, where ELISAs and immunological tests may be carried out. The final reference point is one of the CDC labs or USAMRIID.

Communications

If there was an obvious failure in preventing the terrorist attacks of September 11, 2001, it was the lack of communications between the White House, the FBI and the CIA; specifically, it was a failure to share the intelligence information each agency had gathered separately. The same problem could occur in a large-scale attack with a biological weapon. It's simple on paper: information must get up the chain of command and control from local providers and first responders to state and national health agencies, then to federal commanders and policy makers. These senior officials must then formulate plans and issue orders which flow back down the chain to those on the front lines of the attack.

To test how well senior policy makers would react in a biological attack, a "table top" exercise was held at Andrews Air Force Base on June 22-23, 2001. Called Dark Winter, it was a fictional scenario of a covert attack on the U.S. with smallpox. Twelve participants, each of whom already held a high-level government or military position, played the parts of National Security Council members. Five journalists played themselves during a mock press conference.

The exercise was divided into three segments, all of which took place over a make-believe time period of two weeks. In the first segment, 3,000 people were infected during attacks at shopping malls in Oklahoma City, Philadelphia and Atlanta. The initial diagnosis was delayed because very few doctors had ever seen a case of smallpox and because there is no rapid diagnostic test for it; initial diagnosis must be made by clinical observation alone. When the diagnosis finally was made and the patient isolated, it was already too late. Many others had already been infected. Since there is no known treatment for smallpox, and since routine vaccinations were discontinued years ago, the entire U.S. population is considered to be susceptible. Using a 30% death rate — the historical figure for smallpox epidemics — 1000 of the initial cases died.

The transmission rate of smallpox in the past has been 1 new case per 10 susceptibles, and 13 secondary cases are assumed to result from each initial case. This presumed ratio led to 300,000 secondary cases in Dark Winter, with 100,000 deaths. In the third generation of cases, 3,000,000 people were stricken with the disease, with 1,000,000 of them dying. The calculations were stopped here. But in a real epidemic, 4th, 5th, 6th and further generations of cases could be expected.

Many lessons emerged from Dark Winter. First, national leaders were completely unfamiliar with how an attack with a biological weapon would play out. They were equally unsure of existing resources for dealing with it. Another lesson learned was that the U.S. health care system lacks the surge capacity for mass casualties in the quantity envisioned by Dark Winter. Hospital beds were soon filled. When doctors and nurses became casualties themselves, health care was reduced further. Limited supplies of vaccines led to panic and violence in the streets as frantic people fought for them.

Finally, constitutional issues quickly surfaced over which agency had ultimate authority: local, state or federal. The problem was not helped by turf battles between agencies.

To improve some of the communication problems uncovered in Dark Winter and other bioterrorist exercises, CDC is working on a Health Alert Network (HAN). Its purpose is to provide high speed, secure internet connections among local agencies, and between them and CDC. Through HAN, disease surveillance reports will be available to other local agencies, and recommendations for prevention, treatment, lab tests, etc, can be transmitted by CDC or specialty centers back down to local health departments.

Currently, all 50 state health departments, three public health centers, and one specialty academic center have received funding from CDC to implement HAN.

Training and Research

To enhance long-distance learning, CDC has created the Public Health Training Network, a web site where individuals or agencies can upgrade their knowledge about infectious diseases and the technologies available for diagnosis and treatment.

Since terrorists with access to recombinant DNA technology may have designed BW agents with resistance to currently available antibiotics, second line drugs must be researched, developed, tested and stocked by the National Pharmaceutical Stockpile as well. And since PCR studies of the Sverdlovsk disaster demonstrated that the Soviets had been experimenting with at least four different strains of anthrax, the current vaccine probably would not be effective against all four, even if it was available. Furthermore, natural biological mutations of anthrax bacteria into vaccine-resistant strains are always a possibility. New vaccines, therefore — especially in forms more easily and rapidly administered — should be developed, tested and stockpiled.

State and Local Preparedness

Thomas P. "Tip" O'Neil, former Speaker of the U.S. House of Representatives, once remarked that all politics are local. The same is true for health care; it is all local. Primary care providers, clinics, hospitals, and county health departments are the points of contact for diagnosis and treatment and the prevention of routine illness now. The same will be true in a bioterrorist attack. Even the country's largest hospital chain, HCA — Hospital Corporation of America — views its corporate role in bioterrorist planning as one of setting a minimal level of requirements for its facilities. It expects each of its hospitals to then work within its community, county and state to prepare and drill for biological disasters.

From May 20-23, 2000, an exercise was carried out in Denver, Colorado to see how prepared local health departments, primary care providers and other first responders were. The scenario, called Operation TOPOFF — for "Top Officials" — envisioned an outbreak of pneumonic plague. The germs were pretended to be introduced as an aerosol into the ventilation ducts of Denver's Center for the Performing Arts during a performance. By the end of day 1, 783 make-believe cases had been reported, with 123 deaths. At the end of day 3, there were 3700 cases with 950 deaths. Hundreds of secondary mock cases appeared as the disease spread. Make believe cases even appeared in states outside Colorado and as far away as England and Japan.

Within five days, Denver's health care system was overwhelmed.

Most of the city's hospitals had no contingency plans for treating mass casualty incidents like this; they quickly ran out of antibiotics, vaccines, other medications and life saving equipment. Much of the overload came from the "worried well," people who didn't have the disease but wanted to be checked out anyhow. (Cases of epidemic hysteria and outright hoaxes would have added even more to the burden in a real outbreak.)

Communications between hospitals and local, state and federal agencies quickly failed. No one person was in charge; there was no central chain of command and control. Most health care providers are unaccustomed to working with public health departments to begin with. And hospitals are equally unfamiliar on how to work with federal and state agencies; this further degraded communications. These communications failures caused delays in reporting cases to public health agencies on the one hand, and in getting important information back from federal agencies on the other, information such as who should receive prophylactic antibiotics, i.e., just immediate contacts or a wider ring of people.

The arrival and distribution of medications from the National Pharmaceutical Stockpile, though good-looking on paper, failed miserably in practice. Antibiotics sat at the airport for hours before getting delivered to their designated distribution points. And when the medicine finally got there, these distribution centers were only able to serve 140 people per hour; this in a city of 2 million souls.

The principal lesson learned from TOPOFF was that unless controlling the spread of the epidemic was given an equal effort to the treatment of patients, the health care system had no chance of keeping up with the demands placed on it.

There are other criticisms of bioterrorism preparedness at state and local levels. Delay in diagnosis would be the rule due to the unfamiliarity of most physicians with the agents of bioterrorism. In 1970, as an example, a German citizen developed smallpox; nineteen others were infected before the diagnosis was made and the person quarantined. Physicians must become better trained in diagnosing these bioterrorist diseases and how to report them promptly.

Hospitals must also play more active roles. They must train their medical and nursing staffs on how to report suspicious cases. Resource sharing agreements should be developed between hospitals in the event one facility is overwhelmed. Disaster drills, using realistic bioterrorist scenarios, should be run frequently to test emergency staff call-up plans, the availability of supplies, and communications with state and federal public health care agencies.

Local public health departments have received a fair amount of criticism as well. They are "poorly staffed, poorly equipped, poorly trained," claimed a report in *USA Today*, October 29, 2001. Closed at nights and on weekends, some have no fax machines or email capability. These agencies must be certain their disease surveillance programs are adequate to detect clusters of suspicious cases. And they must be prepared to accept — and respond to — case reports at all times of the day or night, not just during regular business hours. Contact investigators must be available for rapid recall anytime. Response times should be tested through exercise scenarios.

Since Operation TOPOFF, considerable federal effort has gone into improving bioterrorist preparedness at the state and local levels, much of it from CDC's various programs. In addition, a $1 billion grant program managed by the Department of Health and Human Services is available to improve preparedness at these levels. As of August 2002, 24 states and two cities (Los Angeles and Washington, D.C.) have received approval for their plans and federal dollars have been released to them. All fifty states are expected to comply eventually. This money is intended to improve laboratory capability, recruit and train public health department staff, and develop education programs for primary care providers and local health department staff.

In April 2002, another large bioterrorism drill was held, this time in Oklahoma. Four cities were involved in three different but simultaneous scenarios. The exercise was called "Sooner Spring."

Oklahoma City: The State's Capitol served as the delivery point for training packages from the National Pharmaceutical Stockpile. The packages were then moved to the other communities for distribution.

Tulsa: Tulsa practiced a mock outbreak of smallpox. Participants included local hospitals, the state and county health departments, and CDC. Case tracing, contact interviews, hospital surveillance, and vaccine administration were practiced and evaluated. Nine confirmed mock cases were diagnosed, with 269 other persons exposed; 215 people received mock smallpox vaccinations (the others had contraindications for the vaccine).

Lawton: This city carried out a table top exercise involving an outbreak of botulism in a bottled water supply company. City officials, local hospital staff and county public health staff participated.

McAlester: This city practiced a scenario of a pneumonic plague outbreak. Once diagnosed, 8,000 imitation antibiotics were dispensed to first responders and other specialized groups (e.g., nursing home residents, penal colony inmates). Four distribution centers were set up to pass out the medicine to other citizens in the community. The city's goal was to distribute 10,000 packets of the mock antibiotics. When the exercise finally ended, 13,362 had been given out.

The results of Sooner Spring were gratifying. It appears some of the lessons from Operation TOPOFF had been well learned in the Sooner state. Other states should take a page from the Oklahoma example and run similar exercises.

Individual Preparedness

The individual citizen has both a personal role and a civic one in preparing for a bioterrorist attack. The civic responsibility is, first, to become informed about the agents of bioterrorism, how they are spread, and what their symptoms are. The citizen also has a duty to report suspicious behavior of others but not to accuse anyone without justification. Citizens also have a duty to follow civic and public health instructions and to seek medical care when appropriate, but *not* to seek unwarranted care. Such worried well behavior only overloads the health care system and deprives access to those truly in need of it.

If you think you've been exposed to a bioterrorist agent — such as airborne anthrax — there are simple, important steps to take. If the powder is in an envelope, place a cover over it and leave the area. Do not show the item to others or handle it. Wash your hands and exposed body parts with water. Call your local health department or designated emergency response network to initiate evaluation and, if necessary, immediate, specific testing of the material. Public Health

Laboratories are equipped to expedite necessary testing for rapid, reliable agent identification. If antibiotics are recommended, take as prescribed.

Other recommendations for handling suspicious powders, letters and packages, and how to prepare a family disaster kit, are discussed in detail in several recent books. Senator Bill Frist, M.D., has written a helpful one: *When Every Moment Counts*, Rowman and Littlefield, 2002. Another is *Anthrax: A Practical Guide for Citizens*, by the Parents' Committee for Public Awareness, Harvard Perspective Press, 2002.

The terrorist attacks of September 11, 2001, were a wake-up call to America. We have come to the painful realization that we cannot take our safety for granted. Much has been accomplished since then to secure our air travel system, eliminate terrorists, and sanction countries which harbor and finance them.

The anthrax-by-mail cases which followed on the heels of September 11, though only 24 in total number, were also attention getters. Considerable improvement in our country's preparedness for future biological terrorism, at all levels, has taken place since then. More needs to be done. But even then, as the final chapter points out, it may never be enough.

Addendum: As of this date, all 50 states and many large cities have received federal approval and funds for their biopreparedness plans. State and local drills are carried out regularly to test the effectiveness of the plans. They seem to be working.

FINAL THOUGHTS

O brave new world,
That has such people in't.

— **William Shakespeare,** ***The Tempest***

Generals, the saying goes, are always fighting the last war. The French and German fortifications built after WWI were easily defeated by the new WWII weapons of mobility, symbolized by the tank. Our germ warfare "generals" also appear to be planning for a new era of biological war and terrorism with yesterday's weapons. Stockpiling millions of doses of vaccines and antibiotics against germs already designed to defeat them is equivalent to building the Maginot and Siegfried Lines; like Guderian's Panzers and Patton's armor columns, our current biodefenses will be easily skirted by the new germs.

Consider the following scenario:

In his laboratory deep inside Iraq, Dr. Mohammed Ali Ossman — missing two fingers and a bride from allied air attacks during the Gulf War — felt his heart turn over with excitement. He looked at his watch: they are finally on their way! His six plague carriers were right now winging to six American cities, their missions not just to kill, but to sow panic and terror as well. His holy warriors didn't know it, but they themselves were the weapons. For they had been infected with the Medusa Strain, *a germ with the contagiousness of the common cold and the killing power of anthrax.*

Mohammed swivelled in his chair, his lip curled in a cruel smile. He thought about his diabolical plan to start the epidemic through infected air travelers. Airplanes are closed environments, he had reasoned; cabin air is recirculated and along with it Medusa. *Not only will passengers in seats next to Mohammed's plague carriers be exposed to millions of anthrax spores when they sneezed, coughed, snorted and hacked, but passengers many seats away will also become infected through the planes' ventilation systems. Mohammed permitted himself a chuckle. Not suicide bombers. Suicide coughers and sneezers! And in a few hours, when the planes landed, six separate epidemics of anthrax will start when the passengers head down the jetways and start for their homes.*

The Medusa Strain is my novel about the ultimate bioterrorist night-mare: an epidemic caused by a genetically-engineered, contagious strain of anthrax. While it is about a fictional bacteria, the technology of cutting and splicing genes is not fiction. Growing bacteria, dissolving their cell walls, and harvesting their DNA is now routine. Enzymes known as restriction endonucleases — sometimes referred to as "nuclear scissors"— are used to cut the DNA into discrete fragments. These, in turn, are separated and identified by a process known as gel electro-phoresis, which makes use of the different weights, sizes and electrical charges of the fragments. The PCR technique (Polymerase Chain Re-action) is a tool for amplifying the quantity of selected fragments, which can then be recombined with other fragments by enzymes known as DNA ligases.

Non-chromosomal loops of DNA found in bacterial cells — known as plasmids — have been discussed before. They can also be harvested, identified by monoclonal antibodies, and amplified by the PCR tech-nique. Plasmids are fascinating. They contain, for example, the char-acteristics which make a bacteria pathologic: its virulence, resistance to antibiotics, production of toxins, and the like.

Bacteriophages are another tool for the recombinant DNA engi-neer. They are viruses that infect bacteria instead of humans. They can be used to carry foreign DNA — designer genes — into bacterial cells. And the efficiency of this process is awesome. If a DNA fragment — a plasmid, for example — is inserted into a bacteriophage, when the phage infects the bacteria, it forces them to reproduce this plasmid along with its own DNA. Furthermore, all the bacteria's offspring will carry the phage *and* the plasmid, driving the progeny's bacterial metabolism to produce even more of it. And while the phage infection, if left unchecked, will ultimately kill the bacterium, even that can be prevented by a repressor plasmid, which is harvested from another bacterium and introduced by another bacteriophage.

There are other ways to insert bits of DNA from one cell into another, and along with them new characteristics for the host germ. One technique uses an electric current to force the foreign DNA across the host cell wall. Another — the so-called "DNA gun" — coats DNA onto microscopic pellets and fires them into the target cells.

It may seem like science fiction, but recombinant DNA technology is all too real, as are the possibilities for new biological weapons. Though anthrax is as old as Exodus, the new technology promises to give it a brand new look.

SELECTED BIBLIOGRAPHY

Chapter 1: An Act of Terror

Barakat, L; Quentzel, H; Jernigan, J: "Fatal inhalational anthrax in a 94-year old Connecticut Woman," *JAMA*, 287:863-868m 2002.

Bush, L; Abrams, B; Beall, A: "Brief report: index case of fatal inhalational anthrax due to bioterrorism in the United States," *NEJM*, 345(22), Nov. 29, 2001.

CDC update: CDC confirmed case of anthrax," CDC office of communication, November 7, 2001.

"CDC update: Case of cutaneous anthrax in a laboratory worker," CDC, office of communication, March 13, 2002.

"Human anthrax associated with an epizootic among livestock — North Dakota, 2000," *MMWR*, 50(32), Aug. 17, 2001.

Jernigan, J; Stephens, D; Ashford, D; et.al.: "Bioterrorism-related anthrax: the first 10 cases reported in the United States," *Journal of Emerging Infectious Diseases*, 7(6), Nov-Dec, 2001.

Mina, B; Dyan, J; Kuepper, F; et.al.: "Fatal inhalational anthrax with unknown source of exposure in a 61-year old woman in New York City," *JAMA* 287:858-862, 2002.

"Update investigation of bioterrorism-related inhalation anthrax — Connecticut, 2001," *JAMA*, 286(23), Dec. 19, 2001.

Chapter 2: Spores, Hoaxes and the Hunt for the Terrorist

Cole, L: "Risks of publicity about bioterrorism: anthrax hoaxes and hype," *AJIC*, 27(6), Dec. 1999.

Lemonick, M: "Profile of a killer," *Time.com*, Nov. 19, 2001

Recer, P: "New analysis may advance anthrax attack investigation," *Associated Press,* May 10, 2002.

Roche, K; Chang, M; Lazarus, H: "Cutaneous anthrax infection," *NEJM*, 345(22), Nov. 29, 2001.

"Update: adverse events associated with anthrax prophylaxis among postal employees — New Jersey, New York City and the District of Columbia Metropolitan Area, 2001," *JAMA* 286(23), Dec. 19, 2001.

Vastag, B: "Anthrax genomes analyzed," *JAMA,* 287(23), June 19, 2002.

Watson, T: "More federal sites struck by bacteria," *USA Today,* October 30, 2001.

Chapter 3: The View from the Petri Dish

"Investigation of bioterrorism-related anthrax and interim guidelines for clinical evaluation of persons with possible anthrax," *JAMA* 286(19), Nov. 21, 2001.

"Additional options for preventive treatment for persons exposed to inhalational anthrax," *JAMA* 287(5), Feb. 6, 2002.

Mitke, M: "Early anthrax identification," *JAMA* 287(4), Jan. 23/30, 2002.

Inglesby, T; O'Toole, T; Henderson, D; et.al.: "Anthrax as a biological weapon, 2002: Updated recommendations for management," *JAMA*, 287(17), May 2002.

U.S. Department of Agriculture, "Anthrax," *Veterinary Services Publication*, Nov. 2001.

Pitt, M; Little; S, Ivins, B: "In vitro correlate of immunity in an animal model of inhalational anthrax," *J. Applied Micro.* 88(2), Mar-Apr., 1994.

George, S; Mathai, D; Balraj, V; et.al.: "An outbreak of anthrax meningoencephalitis," *Trans. Royal Soc. of Trop. Med. & Hyg.* 88(2), Mar-Apr., 1994.

Okolo, M: "Studies on anthrax in food animals and persons occupationally exposed to zoonoses in eastern Nigeria," *Int. J. of Zoonoses,* 12(4), Dec. 1985.

Franz, D; Jahrling, P; Friedlander, A; et.al.: "Clinical Recognition and Management of patients exposed to biological warfare agents," *JAMA,* 278(5), August 6, 1997.

Shafazand, S; Doyle, R; Ruoss, S; et.al.: "Inhalational anthrax: epidemiology, diagnosis and management," *Chest,* 116(5), Nov. 1999.

Chapter 4: Moses and the Ten Plagues of Egypt

Exodus, *9:6.*

Exodus, 9:8-11.

Herodotus: *The Histories,* trans. Aubrey De Selincourt, Penguin Books, London, 1996.

Martin, T: *Ancient Greece,* Yale University Press, 1996.

Hopper, R: *The Early Greeks,* Harper and Row, 1976.

Longrigg, J: *Greek Medicine: From the Heroic to the Hellenistic Age,* Routledge, New York, 1998.

Margotta, R: *The History of Medicine,* Smithmark, London, 1996.

Chapter 5: The Plague of Athens, 430 B.C.

Cartwright, F: *Disease and History,* Dorset Press, New York, 1991.

Thucydides, *History of the Peloponnesian War,* trans. Rex Warner, Penguin Books, London, 1972.

Langmuir, A; Worthen, T; Solomon, J; et.al.: "The Thucydides Syndrome," *NEJM,* Oct. 17, 1985:1027-1030.

Poole, J; Holladay, A: "Thucydides and the Plague of Athens," *Classics Quarterly,* 29:282-300, 1979.

Langmuir, A: "The Thucydides Syndrome," *JAMA* 257(22), June 12, 1987.

Holladay, A: "The Thucydides Syndrome," *NEJM*, Oct. 1986.

Morens, D; Littman, R: "'Thucydides Syndrome' reconsidered: new thoughts on the 'Plague of Athens,'" *Am. J. of Epi.* 140(7), 1994.

Olson, P; Hames, C; Benenson, M; et.al.: "The Thucydides Syndrome: Ebola Deja Vu," *J. Emerging Infectious Dis.* 2(2), April-Jun., 1996.

Chapter 6: The Death of Alexander the Great, 323 B.C.

Fox, R: *Alexander The Great,* Penguin Books, 1973.

Savill, A: *Alexander the Great and His Time,* Barnes & Noble, 1993.

Dirckx, J: "Virgil on Anthrax," *Am. J. Dermatopathology,* 3(2), Summer, 1981.

Breimer, L: "Alexander the Great may have died of acute pancreatitis," *BMJ,* 316(7149), June 27, 1998.

Cirocco, W: "Alexander the Great may have died of postemetic esophageal perforation," *J. Clin. Gastro.,* 26(1), Jan. 1998.

Ruffin, J: "The efficacy of medicine during the campaigns of Alexander the Great," *Military Medicine,* 157(9), Sept. 1992.

Arrian, F: *The Campaigns of Alexander,* Dorset Press, 1958.

White, N: "Malaria," in *Manson's Tropical Diseases,* ed. by Gordon C. Cook, 20th ed., Saunders, 1996, pp. 1087-1164.

Molyneux, M; Fox, R: "Diagnosis and Treatment of malaria in Britain," *BMJ,* 306(6886), May 1, 1993.

Sbarounis, C: "Did Alexander the Great die of acute pancreatitis?" *J. Clin. Gastro,* 24(4):244-96, 1997.

Chapter 7: The Black Death, 1346-1350

Inglesby, T; Dennis, D; Henderson, D: "Plague as a biological weapon," JAMA 283(17), May 3, 2000.

Twigg, G: *The Black Death: A Biological Reappraisal,* Batsford Academic and Educational Press, London, 1981.

Zinsser, H: *Rats, Lice and History,* Little, Brown & Co., New York, 1936.

"Plague," CDC information site.

Gratz, N: "Rodent reservoirs and flea vectors of natural foci of plague," *Plague Manual,* WHO, 1999.

Boccaccio, G: *The Decameron,* trans. G.H. McWilliam, Penguin Books, London, 1972.

Horax, R: *The Black Death,* Manchester University Press, 1994.

Herlihy, D: *The Black Plague and the Transformation of the West,* Harvard Univ. Press, 1997.

Derbes, V: "De Mussis and the great plague of 1348," *JAMA* 196(1), Apr. 4, 1960.

Cantor, N: *In the Wake of the Plague,* Perennial Press, 2001.

Chapter 8: The Industrial Revolution, Public Health, and Woolsorter's Disease: Part I

Rosen, G: *A History of Public Health,* MD Publications, New York, 1958.

Frederick, G: *A History of England,* MacMillan, New York, 1950.

Hobsbawn, E: *Industry and Empire,* The New Press, New York, 1999.

Palmer, R; Cotton, J: *A History of the Modern World, 5th ed.,* Alfred Knopf, New York, 1978.

Hennekens, C; Buring, J; Mayrent, S: *Epidemiology in Medicine,* Little, Brown & Co., Jan. 1987.

Snow, J: *Cholera and the water supply in the south Districts of London, 1854,* Wellcome Institute for the History of Medicine, London.

Snow, J: *The Broad Street Pump,* Wellcome Institute for the History of Medicine, London.

Chapter 9: Woolsorter's Disease: Part II

Dalldorf, F; Kaufman, A; Brachman, P: "Woolsorter's Disease, an Experimental Model," *Arch. Path,* V. 92, Dec. 1971.

Cunningham, W: "The Control of Woolsorter's Disease," *Pharmaceutical Historian,* 5(1), 1975.

Cunningham, W: "The work of two Scottish medical graduates in the control of Woolsorter's Disease," *Medical History*, V. 20, pp. 169-173.

Spear, J: "The Woolsorter's Disease or Anthrax Fever," *Trans. Epi. Soc. of London,* V. IV, 1875-1881, pp. 610-630.

Eurich, F: "Anthrax in the woolen industry, with special emphasis to Bradford," *Proc. Royal Soc. of Med.,* V.6, 1912-1913, pp. 219-235.

Bell, J: "On Woolsorter's Disease," *The Lancet,* V.1, June, 1880.

Guidelines for the Surveillance and Control of Anthrax in Humans and Animals, WHO.

Laforce, F: "Woolsorter's Disease in England," *Bull. New York Acad. of Med.,* 54(10), Nov. 1978.

Chapter 10: Koch

Brock, T: *Robert Koch: A Life in Medicine and Bacteriology,* ASM Press, Washington, D.C., 1999.

Joklik, J; Willett, H; Amos, D; et.al.: *Zinsser Microbiology, 20th ed.,* Appleton and Lange, 1992.

Edelman, E: "On causes: Hippocrates, Aristotle, Robert Koch, and the Dread Pirate Roberts," *Circulation,* 104(21), Nov. 20, 2001.

Ogawa, M: "Uneasy bedfellows: Science and politics in the refutation of Koch's bacterial theory of cholera," *Bull. Hist. Med.,* 74(2):2000.

Carter, K (trans.): *Essays of Robert Koch,* Greenwood Publishing Group, 1987.

Chapter 11: Pasteur

Robbins, L: *Louis Pasteur,* Oxford University Press, Oxford, 2001.

Debre, P: *Louis Pasteur,* trans. Elborg Forster, Johns Hopkins Univ. Press, 1998.

Reynolds, M: *How Pasteur Changed History,* McGuinn & McGuire, 1994.

Smith, L: *Louis Pasteur: Disease Fighter,* Enslow Publishers, 2001.

Parker, S: *Louis Pasteur and Germs,* Chelsea House, 1995.

Chapter 12: The Dawn of Biological Weapons

Pile, J; Malone, J; Eitzen, E; et.al.: "Anthrax as a Potential Biological Warfare Agent," *Arch. Intern. Med.,* V. 158, Mar. 9, 1998.

Fox, L: "Bacterial Warfare: The use of Biologic Agents in Warfare," *Military Surgeon,* 72(3), 1932.

Christopher, G; Cieslak, T; Pavlin, J; et.al.: "Biological Warfare: A Historical Perspective," *JAMA,* 278(5), Aug. 6, 1997.

Boss, L: "Epidemic Hysteria: A Review of the Published Literature," *Epidemiology Reviews,* Johns Hopkins University Press, 1997.

Inglesby, T; Henderson, D; Bartlett, J; et.al.; "Anthrax as a Biological Weapon: Medical and Public Health Management," *JAMA,* 281(18), May 12, 1999.

DiGiovanni, C: "Domestic Terrorism with Chemical or Biological Agents: Psychiatric Aspects," *Am. J. Psychiat.,* 156(10), Oct., 1999.

Medical Management of Biological Casualties Handbook, 4th ed., USAMRIID, Feb. 2001.

Torok, T; Tauxe, R; Wise, R; et.al.: "A Large Community Outbreak of Salmonellosis Caused by Intentional Contamination of Restaurant Salad Bars," *JAMA,* V. 278, 1997.

Chapter 13: WWII and The Japanese Unit at Ping Fan

Christopher, G; Cieslak, T; Pavlin, J; et.al.: "Biological Warfare: A Historical Perspective," *JAMA,* 278(5), Aug. 6, 1997.

Williams, W: *Unit 731: Japan's Secret Biological Warfare in World War II,* Free Press, New York, 1989.

Harris, S: *Factories of Death,* Routledge, New York, 2002.

Rosebury, T: "Medical Ethics and Biological Warfare," *Perspectives in Biology and Medicine 6,* Summer, 1963.

Harris, S: "Japanese biological warfare research on humans: a case study of microbiology and ethics," *Ann. N.Y. Acad. Sci.,* V. 666, 1992.

Chapter 14: America's Biological Weapons Program

Friedlander, A; Pittman, P; Parker, G: "Anthrax Vaccine: Evidence for safety and Efficacy against Inhalational Anthrax," *JAMA*, V. 282, 1999.

Endicott, S; Hagerman, E; Furmanski, M; et.al.: "Biological warfare in the 1940s and 1950s" (letters), *JAMA*, V. 284, 2000.

Jelinek, P: "Military will end policy mandating anthrax vaccine," *Associated Press*, May 18, 2002.

"Anthrax: Virulance and Vaccines," (editorial), *Ann. Int. Med.*, 121(5), Sept. 1, 1994.

Miller, J; Engleberg, S; Broad, W: "U.S. Germ Warfare Research pushes treaty limits," *New York Times*, Sept. 4, 2001.

Moon, V: "The Korean War Case," *Ann. N.Y. Acad. Sci.*, V. 666, 1992.

Bernstein, B: "The birth of the U.S. biological warfare program," *Sci. Am.*, V. 256, 1987.

Cole, L: *Clouds of Secrecy: The Army's Germ Warfare Tests over Populated Areas*, Rowman and Littlefield, 1988.

U.S. Army activity in the U.S. Biological Warfare Programs, U.S. Dept. of the Army, Feb. 24, 1977.

Yu, V: "Serratia marcescens: historical perspective and clinical review," *NEJM*, V. 300, 1979.

Farmer III, J; Davis, B; Grimont, P; et.al.: "Source of American Serratia," *Lancet*, V2, 1977.

Chapter 15: Biopreparat

Miller, J; Engleberg, S; Broad, W: *Germs*, Simon and Schuster, 2001.

Davis, C: "Nuclear blindness: An overview of the biological weapons programs of the former Soviet Union and Iraq," *Emerging Infectious Diseases*, 5(4), July-Aug., 1999.

Alibek, K: *Biohazard*, Delta Books, New York, 1999.

Kortepeter, M; Parker, G: "Potential Biological weapons threats," *Emerging Infectious Diseases,* 5(4), July-Aug., 1999.

"Former Soviet biological weapons in Kazakhstan: Past, present and future," *Monterey Institute of International Studies,* Oct. 24, 1998.

"Biological Weapons: effort to reduce former Soviet threat offers benefits, poses new risks," (letter report), *U.S. General Accounting Office,* Apr. 28, 2000.

Chapter 16: Accident at Sverdlovsk, April, 1979

Rich, V: "Russia: Anthrax in the Urals," *Lancet,* V. 339, 1992.

Abramova, F; Grinberg, L; Yampolskaya, O; et.al.: "Pathology of inhalation anthrax in 42 cases from the Sverdlovsk outbreak of 1979," *Proc. Natl. Acad. Sci. (U.S.),* V. 90, 1993.

Meselson, M; Guillemin, J; Hugh-Jones, M; et.al.: "The Sverdlovsk Anthrax outbreak of 1979," *Science,* 266(5188), Nov. 18, 1994.

Alibek, K: *Biohazard,* Delta Books, New York, 1999.

Inglesby, T; O'Toole, T; Henderson, D; et.al.: "Anthrax as a biological weapon 2002: updated recommendations for management," *JAMA,* 287(17), May, 2002.

Wampler, R; Blanton, T (eds.): "Anthrax at Sverdlovsk, 1979," *National Security Archive Electronic Briefing Book 61,* Nov. 15, 2001.

Jackson, P; Hugh-Jones, M; Adair, D; et.al.: "PCR analysis of tissue samples from the 1979 Sverdlovsk anthrax victims: the presence of multiple Bacillus anthracis strains in different victims," *Proc. Natl. Acad. Sci (U.S.),* 95(3), Feb 3, 1998.

Guillemin, J: *Anthrax: The Investigation of a deadly outbreak,* University of Calif. Press, 1999.

Chapter 17: Saddam

Zilinskas, R: "Iraq's biological weapons," *JAMA,* 278(5), Aug. 6, 1997.

Mangold, T; Goldberg, J: *Plague Wars,* MacMillan, 1999.

Davis, C: "Nuclear blindness: An overview of the biological weapons programs of the former Soviet Union and Iraq," *Emerging Infectious Diseases,* 5(4), July-Aug., 2000.

Bellamy, R; Friedman, A: "Bioterrorism," *QJM,* 94(4), Apr. 2001.

Lumpkin, J: "U.S. worries Iraq's weapons would target troops," *Associated Press,* July 14, 2002.

Miller, J; Engleberg, S; Broad, W: *Germs,* Simon and Shuster, 2001.

Chapter 18: Are We Prepared for the Next One?

Davis, R: "Local health agencies unprepared for bioterrorism," *USA Today,* Oct. 29, 2001.

Appleby, J: "Bioterrorism changes how health care works," *USA Today,* Oct. 31, 2001.

Frist, W: *When Every Moment Counts,* Rowman & Littlefield, New York, 2002.

The Parents Committee for Public Awareness: *Anthrax: A Practical Guide for Citizens,* Harvard Perspective Press, Oct. 2001.

"Sooner Spring Bioterrorism Drills," *OSDH* information site, April, 2002.

"Recommended actions for medicine and public health in the aftermath of Anthrax attacks of 2001," *Center for Civilian Biodefense Studies,* The Johns Hopkins University, Aug. 14, 2002.

"Bioterrorism plans OK'd for 24 states," *Associated Press,* June 7, 2002.

Inglesby, T: "The state of public health preparedness for terrorism involving weapons of mass destruction: A six month report card," *Congressional Testimony,* April 18, 2002.

Brown, J: "Oklahoma bioterrorism drill simulates deadly aerial attack," *Associated Press,* April 13, 2002.

Khan, A; Morse, S; Lillibridge, S: "Public-health preparedness for biological terrorism in the USA," *The Lancet,* 356(9236), Sept. 30, 2000.

Lane, H; Fauci, A: "Bioterror on the home front: A new challenge for American medicine" (editorial), *JAMA,* 286(20), Nov. 28, 2001.

"Interim guidelines for investigation of and response to *Bacillus anthracis* exposures," CDC recommendations, *JAMA*, 286(20), Nov. 28, 2001.

Hoffman, R; Norton, J: "Lessons learned from a full-scale bioterrorism exercise," *Emerging Infectious Diseases*, 6(6), Nov Dec., 2000.

O'Toole, T; Mair, M; Inglesby, T: "Shining light on 'Dark Winter,'" *Clin. Infect. Disease*, V. 34, 2002.

Final Thoughts

Holmes, C: *The Medusa Strain*, Durban House, May, 2002.

Kreuzer, H; Massey, A: *Recombinant DNA and Biotechnology, 2nd Edition*, ASM Press, 2001.

Harrison, J: Sampson, J: "Enhancing Understanding of recombinant DNA technology," *J. Biological Educ.*, 26(4), Winter, 1992.

Check out these other fine titles by Durban House
online or at your local book store.

EXCEPTIONAL BOOKS
BY
EXCEPTIONAL WRITERS

NONFICTION

BEHIND THE MOUNTAIN   Nick Williams

FISH HEADS, RICE, RICE WINE   Lt. Col. Thomas G. Smith, Ret.
& WAR: A VIETNAM PARADOX

JIMMY CARTER AND THE RISE   Philip Pilevsky
OF MILITANT ISLAM

MIDDLE ESSENCE—   Landy Reed
WOMEN OF WONDER YEARS

WHITE WITCH DOCTOR   Dr. John A. Hunt

PROTOCOL   Mary Jane McCaffree, Pauline Innis,
                                    and Richard Sand.

For 25 years, the bible for public relations firms, corporations, embassies, foreign governments, and individuals seeking to do business with the Federal Government.

DURBAN HOUSE FICTION

A DREAM ACROSS TIME   Annie Rogers

Jamie Elliott arrives from New York onto the lush Caribbean island of St. Lucia, and finds herself caught up in Island forces, powerful across the centuries, which find deep echoes in her recurring dreams.

AFTER LIFE LIFE   Don Goldman

A hilarious murder mystery taking place in the afterlife. Andrew Law, Chief Justice of the Texas Supreme Court, is the Picture of robust health when he suddenly dies. Upon arriving in The afterlife, Andy discovers he was murdered, and his untimely has some unexpected, and far-reaching consequences—a worldwide depression, among others. Many diabolical plots are woven in this funny, fast-paced whodunit, with a surprising double-cross ending.

an-eye-for-an-eye.com   Dennis Powell

Jed Warren, Vietnam Peacenik, and Jeff Porter, ex-Airborne, were close friends and executives at Megafirst Bank. So when CEO McAlister crashes the company, creams off millions in bonuses, and wipes out Jed and Jeff, things began to happen.

If you wonder about corporate greed recorded in today's newspapers, read what one man did about it in this intricate, devious, and surprise-ending thriller.

BASHA   John Hamilton Lewis

LA reviewer, Jeff Krieder's pick as "Easily my best read of the year." Set in the world of elite professional tennis, and rooted in ancient Middle East hatreds of identity and blood loyalties, Basha is charged with the fiercely competitive nature of professional sports, and the dangers of terrorism. An already simmering Middle East begins to boil, and CIA Station Chief Grant Corbet must track down the highly successful terrorist, Basha, In a deadly race against time Grant hunts the illusive killer only to see his worst nightmare realized.

THE CORMORANT DOCUMENTS   Robert Middlemiss

Who is Cormorant, and why is his coded letter on Hitler's stationary found on a WWII Nazi bomber preserved in the Arctic? And why is the plane loaded with Goering's plundered are treasures? Mallory must find out or die. On the run from the British Secret Service and CIA, he finds himself caught in a secret that dates back to 1945.

CRISIS PENDING   Stephen Cornell

When U.S. oil refineries blow up, the White House and the Feds move fast, but not fast enough. Sherman Nassar Ramsey, terrorist for hire, a loner, brilliant, multilingual, and skilled with knives, pistols, and bare hands, moves around the country with contempt, ease and cunning.

As America's fuel system starts grinding to a halt, rioting breaks out for gasoline, and food becomes scarce, events draw Lee Hamilton's wife, Mary, into the crisis. And when Ramsey kidnaps her, the battle becomes very personal.

DANGER WITHIN   Mark Danielson

Over 100 feet down in cold ocean waters lies the wreck of pilot Kevin Hamilton's DC-10. In it are secrets which someone is desperate to keep. When the Navy sends a team of divers from the Explosives Ordinance Division, a mysterious explosion from the wreck almost destroys the salvage ship. The FBI steps in with Special Agent Mike Pentaglia. Track the life and death of Global Express Flight 3217 inside the gritty world of aviation, and discover the shocking cargo that was hidden on its last flight.

DEADLY ILLUMINATION   Serena Stier

It's summer 1890 in New York City. A ebullient young woman, Florence Tod, must challenge financier, John Pierpont Morgan, to solve a possible murder. J.P.'s librarian has ingested poison embedded in an illumination of a unique Hildegard van Bingen manuscript. Florence and her cousin, Isabella Stewart Gardner, discover the corpse. When Isabella secretly removes a gold tablet from the scene of the crime, she sets off a chain of events that will involve Florence and her in a dangerous conspiracy.

HANDS OF VENGEANCE   Richard Sand

Private detective Lucas Rook returns still haunted by the murder of his twin brother. What seems like an easy case involving workplace violations, the former homicide detective finds himself locked in a life and death struggle with the deadly domestic terrorist group, The Brothers of the Half Moon. A must-read for lovers of dark mysteries.

HOUR OF THE WOLVES

Stephane Daimlen-Völs

After more than three centuries, the *Poisons Affair* remains one of history's great, unsolved mysteries. The worst impulses of human nature—sordid sexual perversion, murderous intrigues, witchcraft, Satanic cults—thrive within the shadows of the Sun King's absolutism and will culminate in the darkest secret of his reign; the infamous *Poisons Affair*, a remarkably complex web of horror, masked by Baroque splendor, luxury and refinement.

A HOUSTON WEEKEND

Orville Palmer

Professor Edward Randall, not-yet-forty, divorced and separated from his daughters, is leading a solitary, cheerless existence in a university town. At a conference in Houston, he runs into his childhood sweetheart. Then she was poverty-stricken, American Indian. Now she's elegantly attired, driving an expensive Italian car and lives in a millionaires' enclave. Will their fortuitous encounter grow into anything meaningful?

JOHNNIE RAY AND MISS KILGALLEN

Bonnie Hearn Hill
and Larry Hill

Based on the real-life love affair between 1950's singer Johnnie Ray and columnist Dorothy Kilgallen. They had everything—wealth, fame, celebrity. The last thing they needed was love. *Johnnie Ray and Miss Kilgallen* is a love story that travels at a dangerous, roaring speed. Driven close to death from their excesses, both try to regain their lives and careers in a novel that goes beyond the bounds of mere biography.

THE LATERAL LINE

Robert Middlemiss

Kelly Travert was ready. She had the Israeli assassination pistol, she had coated the bullets with garlic, and tonight she would kill the woman agent who tortured and killed her father. When a negotiator for the CIA warns her, suddenly her father's death is not so simple anymore.

LEGACY OF A STAR

Peter Longley

Greed and murder run rampant—the prize: desert commerce of untold wealth, and the saving of the Jews. From the high temples to Roman barracks; from bat filled caves to magnificent villas on a sun-drenched sea; to the chamber of Salome, and the barren brothels where Esther rules, the Star moves across the heavens and men die—while a child is born.

LETHAL CURE

Kurt Popke

Dr. Jake Prescott is a resident on duty in the emergency room when medics rush in with a double trauma involving patients sustaining injuries during a home invasion. Jake learns that one patient is the intruder, the other, his wife, Sara. He also learns that his four-year-old daughter, Kelly, is missing, and his patient may hold the key to her recovery.

THE MEDUSA STRAIN   Chris Holmes
Finalist for *ForeWord Magazine's* 'Book of the Year'. A gripping tale of bio-terrorism that stunningly portrays the dangers of chemical warfare. Mohammed Ali Ossman, a bitter Iraqi scientist who hates America, breeds a deadly form of anthrax, and develops a diabolical means to initiate an epidemic. It is a story of personal courage in the face of terror, and of lost love found.

MR. IRRELEVANT   Jerry Marshall
Booklist Star Review. Chesty Hake, the last man chosen in the NFL draft, has been dubbed Mr. Irrelevant. By every yardstick, he should not be playing pro football, but because of his heart and high threshold for pain, he endures. Then during his eighth and final season, he slides into paranoia, and football will never be the same.

OPAL EYE DEVIL   John Hamilton Lewis
"Best historical thriller in decades." *Good Books.* In the age of the Robber Baron, *Opal Eye Devil* weaves an extraordinary tale about the brave men and women who risk everything as the discovery of oil rocks the world. The richness and pageantry of two great cultures, Great Britain and China, are brought together in a thrilling tale of adventure and human relationships.

PRIVATE JUSTICE   Richard Sand
Ben Franklin Award 'Best Mystery of the Year'. After taking brutal revenge for the murder of his twin brother, Lucas Rooks leaves the NYPD to become a private eye. A father turns to Rook to investigate the murder of his daughter. Rook's dark journey finds him racing to find the killer, who kills again and again as *Private Justice* careens toward a startling end.

ROADHOUSE BLUES   Baron R. Birtcher
From the sun-drenched sands of Santa Catalina Island to the smoky night clubs and back alleys of West Hollywood, Roadhouse Blues is a taut noir thriller. Newly retired Homicide detective Mike Travis is torn from the comfort of his chartered yacht business into the dark, bizarre underbelly of Los Angeles's music scene by a grisly string of murders.

RUBY TUESDAY   Baron R. Birtcher
When Mike Travis sails into the tropical harbor of Kona, Hawaii, he expects to put LA Homicide behind him. Instead, he finds the sometimes seamy back streets and dark underbelly of a tropical paradise and the world of music and high finance, where wealth and greed are steeped in sex, vengeance, and murder.

SAMSARA   John Hamilton Lewis

A thrilling tale of love and violence set in post-World War II Hong Kong. Nick Ridley, a captain in the RAF, is captured and sent to the infamous Japanese prisoner-of-war camp, Changi, in Singapore. He survives brutal treatment at the hands of the camp commandant, Colonel Tetsuro Matashima. Nick moves to Hong Kong, where he reunites with the love of his life, Courtney, and builds a world-class airline. On the eve of having his company recognized at the Crown Colony's official carrier, Courtney is kidnapped, and people begin to die. Nick is pulled into the quagmire, and must once again face the demon of Changi.

SECRET OF THE SCROLL   Chester D. Campbell

Finalist 'Deadly Dagger' award, and ForeWord Magazine's 'Book of the Year' award. Deadly groups of Palestinians and Israelis struggle to gain possession of an ancient parchment that was unknowingly smuggled from Israel to the U.S. by a retired Air Force investigator. Col. Greg McKenzie finds himself mired in the duplicitous world of Middle East politics when his wife is taken hostage in an effort to force the return of the first-century Hebrew scroll.

SECRETS ARE ANONYMOUS   Frederick L. Cullen

A comic mystery with a cast of characters who weave multiple plots, puzzles, twists, and turns. A remarkable series of events unfold in the lives of a dozen residents of Bexley, Ohio. The journalism career of the principle character is derailed when her father shows up for her college graduation with his boyfriend on his way to a new life in California.

THE SEESAW SYNDROME   Michael Madden

A terrifying medical thriller that slices with a scalpel, exposing the greed and corruption that can happen when drug executives and medical researchers position themselves for huge profits. Biosense Pharmaceeuticals has produced a drug named Floragen, and now they need to test it on patients to gain FDA approval. But there's a problem with the new drug. One of the side effects included death.

THE SERIAL KILLER'S DIET BOOK   Kevin Postupack

Finalist ForeWord Magazine's Book of the Year' award. Fred Orbis is fat, but he dreams of being Frederico Orbisini, internationally known novelist, existential philosopher, raconteur, and lover of women. Both a satire and a reflection on morals, God and the Devil, beauty, literature, and the best-seller-list, The Serial Killer's Diet Book is a delightful look at the universal human longing to become someone else.

THE STREET OF FOUR WINDS   Andrew Lazarus

Paris, just after World War II. A time for love, but also a time of political ferment. In the Left Bank section of the city, Tom Cortell, a tough, intellectual journalist, finally learns the meaning of love. Along with him is a gallery of fascinating characters who lead a merry and sometimes desperate chase between Paris, Switzerland, and Spain in search of themselves.

TUNNEL RUNNER   Richard Sand
A fast, deadly espionage thriller peopled with quirky and sometimes vicious characters, *Tunnel Runner* tells of a dark world where murder is committed and no one is brought to account, where loyalties exist side by side with lies and extreme violence.

WHAT GOES AROUND   Don Goldman
Finalist *ForeWord Magazine's* 'Book of the Year' award. Ray Banno, a medical researcher, was wrongfully incarcerated for bank fraud. *What Goes Around* is a dazzling tale of deception, treachery, revenge, and nonstop action that resolves around money, sex, and power. The book's sharp insight and hard-hitting style builds a high level of suspense as Banno strives for redemption.

DURBAN HOUSE NONFICTION

BEHIND THE MOUNTAIN: Nick Williams
A CORPORATE SURVIVAL BOOK
A harrowing true story of courage and survival. Nick Williams is alone, and cut off in a blizzard behind the mountain. In order to survive, Nick called upon his training and experience that made him a highly-successful business executive. In *Behind the Mountain: A Corporate Survival Book*, you will fine d the finest practical advice on how to handle yourself in tough spots, be they life threatening to you, or threatening to your job performance or the company itself. Read and learn.

FISH HEADS, RICE, RICE WINE & WAR   LTC. Thomas G. Smith (Ret.)
A human, yet humorous, look at the strangest and most misunderstood war ever, in which American soldiers were committed. Readers are offered an insiders view of American life in the midst of highly deplorable conditions, which often lead to laughter.

JIMMY CARTER AND THE RISE   Philip Pilevsky
OF MILITANT ISLAM
One of America's foremost authorities on the Middle East, Philip Pilevsky argues that President Jimmy Carter's failure to support the Shah of Iran led to the 1979 revolution. That revolution legitimized and provided a base of operations for militant Islamists across the Middle East. A most thought provoking book.

MIDDLE ESSENCE...   Landy Reed
WOMEN OF WONDER YEARS
A wonderful book by renowned speaker, Landy Reed that shows how real women

in real circumstances have confronted and conquered the obstacles of midlife. This is a must have guide and companion to what can be the most significant and richest years of a woman's life.

PROTOCOL   Mary Jane McCaffree,
(25th Anniversary Edition)   Pauline Innis, and
                                                  Richard Sand

    Protocol is a comprehensive guide to proper diplomatic, official and social usage. The Bible for foreign governments, embassies, corporations, public relations firms, and individuals wishing to do business with the Federal Government. "A wealth of detail on every conceivable question, from titles and forms of address to ceremonies and flag etiquette." Department of State Newsletter.

WHITE WITCH DOCTOR   John A. Hunt
    A true story of life and death, hope and despair in apartheid-ruled South Africa. White Witch Doctor details, white surgeon, John Hunt's fight to save his beloved country in a time of social unrest and political upheaval, drawing readers into the world of South African culture, mores and folkways, superstitions, and race relations.

Chris & marilyn
751 - 9660
Hidden meadows
Sunnedoak